Mike Wallace

A Life

Mike Wallace

A Life

PETER RADER

Thomas Dunne Books

St. Martin's Press ⚏ New York

THOMAS DUNNE BOOKS.
An imprint of St. Martin's Press.

MIKE WALLACE. Copyright © 2012 by Peter Rader. All rights reserved.
Printed in the United States of America. For information,
address St. Martin's Press, 175 Fifth Avenue, New York, N.Y. 10010.

www.thomasdunnebooks.com
www.stmartins.com

Book design by Claire Naylon Vaccaro

Library of Congress Cataloging-in-Publication Data

Rader, Peter.
    Mike Wallace : a life / Peter Rader.—1st ed.
        p. cm.
    Includes bibliographical references and index.
    ISBN 978-0-312-54339-6 (hardcover)
    ISBN 978-1-4668-0225-4 (e-book)
    1. Wallace, Mike, 1918–. Television journalists—United States—
Biography.   3. Radio journalists—United States—Biography.
4. Investigative reporting—United States.   I. Title.
    PN4874.W283R33 2012
    070.92—dc23
    [B]   2012004395

First Edition: April 2012

3   5   7   9   2   4   6   8   10

For Paola, Matteo & Luca

Contents

Mike Wallace

A Life

Introduction

The Two Faces of Mike Wallace

When Wallace gets that look on his face, when his dimples dimp, you know that the bad guy is about to get zapped. There's no warmer moment in all of Television Land.

—RICHARD COHEN,
THE WASHINGTON POST

The phone call came on a chilly day in February 1980. "Bill," said Jimmy Carter, "I really hate to bother you."

"That's perfectly all right, Mr. President," responded CBS News chief William Leonard.[1]

"Bill," continued the president, "*60 Minutes* is a very important show, and this is a critical time in the history of our country. We think it's very important for the country that you all don't run that program, or at the very least postpone it until this hostage thing is resolved."

Carter was referring to "The Iran File," an explosive Mike Wallace news story scheduled to air in two days' time. The Shah of Iran had been deposed the previous year in an Islamic revolution that brought about the rise of a fundamentalist regime. After the Carter administration granted the exiled Shah's request to enter the United States in October 1979 for medical treatment, livid Iranian students seized the U.S. embassy in Tehran, taking sixty-six Americans hostage.

If the so-called "War on Terror" has a beginning, it was here—the moment that America first experienced a broad display of Islamic fervor in its chilling potential to capture global headlines and endanger significant numbers of American lives. Mike Wallace's upcoming report suggested that we had only ourselves to blame for this aggression; the piece was a scathing indictment of the U.S.'s three decades–long role in propping up the Shah and funding SAVAK, his brutal secret police. Indeed, the hostage crisis was to last 444 days and become an international humiliation that would doom Carter's presidency.

Iran was the biggest news story of the day and Mike Wallace, the biggest newsman on the biggest news show in history, was all over it. He had already landed the ultimate scoop by getting the first-ever television interview with Iran's new Supreme Leader, militant Islamist Ayatollah Khomeini, who had been largely responsible for fomenting the Iranian Revolution from his base in exile. And now Mike had exclusive insider accounts of how the CIA had trained SAVAK in brutal interrogation and torture techniques. No wonder the White House was pulling out all the stops to kill the segment. But to have the Commander-in-Chief *himself* make the call—a sitting president personally begging a newsroom not to run a story spoke volumes about the power of Mike Wallace, the man who changed the face of TV journalism.

"I hope you'll give it every consideration," repeated the beleaguered president.

"You can be assured that I will, Mr. President," responded an astonished Bill Leonard.

"Well, I very much appreciate it," Carter signed off.

Shaking his head in disbelief, Leonard summoned Mike into his office to solicit his thoughts on the matter. Wallace, a reporter who took pride in staring down terrorists, mass murderers, divas and dictators, had never been one to pull punches. Standing up to a U.S. president was just business as usual for him. He insisted that his piece should air. And so it did, just one of the thirty blistering segments that he would file in 1980, a prolific year that vaulted *60 Minutes* to the number one spot in the Nielson television ratings—a triumph the show would repeat five times.

The dazzling popularity of *60 Minutes*, which ranked in the top ten TV shows for twenty-three seasons in a row, is unique in the history of broadcasting and will likely never be matched. By the measures of ratings and profitability, it is the most successful program of all time,[2] a monumental feat due in large measure to the journalist we know as Mike Wallace.

And, in the winter of 1980 when Mike added a U.S. president to the roster of those who had begged for his mercy, he seemed to be at the top of his game. Wallace commanded a movie-star salary as well as the accompanying fame and mystique. "The four most dreaded words in the English language," boasted a banner ad that appeared in newspapers coast-to-coast: "*Mike Wallace is here.*"

In a few short years, however, Wallace would hit rock bottom in an abyss of suicidal despair. He would find himself wading through netherworlds of melancholy, where moment-to-moment survival required monumental effort. The darkness would be everywhere; the choices few. One bleak evening, he would have his stomach pumped in an emergency room after taking enough pills to make him sleep forever.

It came as a shock to all who knew him, for he had gone to great lengths to conceal his dark side, even from himself. The public saw him as a barracuda, the man who raised intimidation to an art form. Yet his bravura was a carefully crafted front to conceal the deep troubles that had tormented him since his youth.

"I was not a happy kid," he admitted. "Back in those days, I remember the sick, gray days were better. Because when it was sunny, I'd feel worse."[3]

His early melancholy stemmed in part from his overbearing and chronically depressed mother, Zina, who clung to Mike (the youngest of four children) after the others had left home. Mike's adolescence, moreover, was marked by a case of acne so severe that it left both emotional and physical scars that persisted well into adulthood. "Being fifteen, sixteen years old in high school and not wanting to even look at yourself in the mirror is very hard," lamented Mike.

For decades, Mike remained deeply insecure about his physical appearance, ironic for a man whose outer image bordered on the omnipotent. Critics would remark that his "pockmarked, prizefighter's face" served to enhance the abrasive tone of his interviews.

Mike Wallace was indeed a master pugilist, but he's a fighter with a past that haunts him. While many regard him as the most formidable newsman of his time, for the better part of his career he harbored gnawing insecurities about his journalistic credentials. That's because it took years—decades, really—for Wallace to command even a modicum of respect in the newsroom. Journalists would snigger behind his back and even to his face: You're no reporter. You're a fraud. An actor, reading lines. And they were right.

Mike Wallace, before age fifty, was what many would call a "television personality." A breezy raconteur who hosted chat shows, quiz shows and the like, he was the pitchman for Parliament Cigarettes and Fluffo shortening from Procter & Gamble. His baritone voice announced the arrival of *The Green Hornet.* He emceed third-rate beauty pageants and daytime game shows. He even did a stint on Broadway as a hustling art dealer in a mediocre comedy, *Reclining Figure,* which ran for an unremarkable one hundred performances. In short, he dabbled here and there, earning decent paychecks across the entertainment world. Author Gary Paul Gates, who collaborated with Mike on both of his memoirs, puts it bluntly: "Wallace practically wallowed in schlock."[4]

In his gut, Wallace knew he had something unique to offer, but he had yet to find his niche in television news. It was depressing, certainly, and it took the form of a mild but steady malaise that Mike felt most of his adult life. As always, he camouflaged his innermost feelings in ever-increasing drive and ambition. But his workaholic tendencies took their toll in four marriages and several estranged children. More than one of Mike's family members committed suicide, and there were other tragedies as well.

One such calamity proved a turning point. It occurred almost exactly at the midpoint of his life—the devastating loss of a child upon whom

Mike had pinned all of his hopes and dreams. But unlike lesser men who might have withered in the face of such a tragedy, he embraced it as an opportunity to catalyze a complete makeover of his public persona.

What makes his journey truly inspiring is how he managed to transform the brooding melancholy of the "inner" Mike Wallace into a journalistic phenomenon. In his forty-year career as a journalist, he has entered the ring well over a thousand times in face-to-face interviews with the likes of Malcolm X, Richard Nixon, Mickey Cohen, Yasser Arafat, Nelson Mandela, Deng Xiaoping, Menachem Begin, Anwar Sadat, Manuel Noriega, General William Westmoreland, Vladimir Putin and Iranian president Mahmoud Ahmadinejad, just to name a few.

Mike's journalistic career, moreover, spanned one of the most tumultuous periods of American history, with twin wars that wreaked havoc on the American psyche. No sooner had we learned the lessons of Vietnam than we repeated them in Iraq, another war with shifting objectives, no exit strategy and an underground enemy. His reporting, in both cases, was riveting and helped to transform public opinion.

Likewise, the influence that Wallace has had on his journalistic colleagues cannot be overstated. He was at the forefront of nearly every change in the way that news is transmitted—from the early days of radio to the first TV broadcasts, the advent of color television, morning news, specials, newsmagazines, 24-hour news and the Internet.

Mike was decades ahead of his peers in realizing that in order to sell the news, you have to sex it up. He pioneered and perfected the no-holds-barred interrogation, undercover reporting, the "ambush" interview and the hidden-camera exposé, all of which became television fixtures, widely imitated by every newsmagazine that followed *60 Minutes*, from *20/20* to *Taxicab Confessions*. These innovations made stories more exciting, visually dynamic and ultimately more telling. But they also risked being labeled as sensationalistic—an issue that dogged Wallace his entire career, particularly since he got his start as a TV "showman." The truth is that Mike is both a journalist and an entertainer and he has walked this tightrope with brilliance and finesse.

It was his training and experience as an actor that allowed him to empathize and listen to his interviewees—to go off script into an entirely spontaneous line of questioning, to raise an eyebrow, to grimace, to mock with a barely noticeable facial tick that ultimately provoked the most extraordinary and revealing response of the interview. Barry Lando, one of his longtime producers, said that Mike's strongest question was often wordless, a pregnant pause that the increasingly uncomfortable interviewee was forced to fill. Or sometimes equally electric results were produced by the single word: "And?"

The fourth estate has been greatly empowered by the contributions of Mike Wallace. He has earned the distinction of being one of the most aggressive, self-assured and unflinching journalists in the business. But when we peel back the layers what do we find? A depressed loner. A "would-be" reporter who remains insecure about who he is. A guilt-ridden absentee father still grieving the loss of a child. A man who is hurting. And hiding.

Yet it is precisely this emotional split within Mike Wallace, the chasm between his outer persona and his inner self, that has made him into the probing journalist that he is—for Mike's life work has been a dogged, almost feverish mission to uncover the inner truth of those in his crosshairs. By doing so, he has quelled the sorrow within his own heart, a grief that nearly swept him to suicide.

Mike Wallace is both a tragic figure and a true hero. His charisma and determination helped him triumph over major obstacles to become the most recognizable journalist of his time. But it's been a restless journey punctuated by bouts of hopelessness, tribulation, and rife with Shakespearian plotlines.

The pages that follow will reveal the two faces of Mike Wallace—on the one hand, the most formidable reporter of his era; on the other, a profoundly scarred man for whom the most dramatic confrontation is the one within himself.

Chapter One

A Boy Named Chinky

I *hate mirrors*, thought the boy. Especially this one. The full-length looking glass in the bank lobby was unforgiving. It revealed all. And, sadly, there was little about his appearance that this little boy liked.[1]

Those skinny bowed legs. Ugh. Later in life, having become intensely competitive, he would force those skinny legs to run the half-mile on his college track team. His time would be respectable, but he would nonetheless give up in disgust when he realized half the team ran faster. Even at age eight, Myron Wallace wanted to be the best—which brings us to the face that stared back at him in that mirror. What to do with that face? Complexions that surrounded him in Brookline, Massachusetts, were snow white and freckled. This was Kennedy country.

"One of my claims to fame is the fact that Jack Kennedy was born five doors away from me, about a year before me," says Mike. "We went to grammar school together for a very short time."[2]

Mike's coloring was darker than the other kids in the neighborhood. His skin was olive, like a gypsy's. And those eyes, squinty and slanted. That's why the other kids called him "Chinky." Everyone had a nickname in those days, and little Myron Wallace was as close to Oriental as the

Irish neighborhood lads had seen. He didn't particularly mind the moniker. It had an edge.

"Vanity!" teased his father, Frank, cuffing him gently on the neck, as
he retrieved "Chinky" from the lobby of the bank, where he remained gazing at his own reflection.[3] The doorman opened the door for them with a
friendly nod. Everyone loved Mr. Wallace. A man of his word. A man of
integrity.

As Mike puts it: "My dad was the gentlest, sweetest, really most honorable fellow that a son can imagine."[4]

The elder Wallace succeeded in America from the most humble of
circumstances. As a fifteen-year-old immigrant from Kiev at the end of the
nineteenth century, Friedan Wallick (whose name was changed at Ellis
Island) began selling groceries from a pushcart on the streets of Boston.
With a keen mind and a strong will, he soon landed a job at the Standard
Grocery Company, where he met his future wife, Zina Scharfman, a bookkeeper, also from Kiev. Zina was tiny, no taller than 4'5", but powerful—a
force to be reckoned with. She came from a family of ten, one of numerous
middle children who needed to establish a high-relief personality in order
to stand out.

Gentle Frank was impressed by the sheer strength that came in such
a small package. They wed and had four children in quick succession—
two girls and two boys. Mike (born Myron) was the youngest and by far
the most temperamental.

He came into the world on May 9, 1918, near the close of World War I.
Frank had established his own wholesale grocery company at this point,
Frank Wallace & Sons—though neither of his two boys would follow in
his footsteps, despite the fact that the business was booming. Frank was
one of the pioneers in establishing grocery stores in a unified chain. With
several million soldiers still deployed in Europe, the demand for transat-
lantic food supplies had become staggering. Sensing opportunity, Frank
teamed with several partners and invested in a boatload of Jamaican ginger bound for Europe, but the ship never made it. A sudden storm swallowed

the vessel whole, sinking it without a trace. The cargo was uninsured—and Frank lost everything.

He left the grocery business in dejection, and in a nod to his own recklessness, became an insurance salesman. Too proud and too principled to declare bankruptcy, Frank Wallace ended up rebuilding himself and paying off every penny he owed. That's why at the bank and elsewhere Frank Wallace was considered an honorable man.

Throughout his career, Mike would pride himself on the kind of integrity he learned from his father. Despite the gun-slinging bravado of his *60 Minutes* persona, he held himself to a high standard when it came to the rules of journalism—so much so, that when this value came under fire later in life in a series of very public and humiliating lawsuits, it nearly destroyed him.

Mike uses few words to describe his mother, Zina: "upwardly mobile" . . . "moody" . . . "humorless." She was the family disciplinarian. Where Frank's nature was sweet and forgiving, Zina came off as strict and uncompromising. Her demand for obedience was at odds with Mike's antiauthoritarian nature and the two locked horns with regularity. Says his co-biographer Gary Paul Gates: "He was absolutely the mischievous one. Basically he had the kind of personality as a kid that he did as an adult.

"One of the things about understanding Wallace is that he is an expert and compulsive and unrelenting needler and ragger . . . I mean, this is his whole persona. If you can't take his needling, then you're not going to have a relationship with him. And I think he was that way as a kid."[5]

Older brother Irving had wisely chosen the path of conflict avoidance, becoming the "good boy" of the family, a stance mimicked by his sisters, Helen and Ruth, as well. That left Mike with only one option: hell-raiser, a role he took on with gusto. The willful boy was particularly hard to discipline.

"My father would start to give him hell and Mike would have him laughing," says Irving. "My father was never able to punish Mike. My mother could, though. My mother was a tough dame."[6]

She needed to be tough with a son like Mike, who was stormy, willful and above all curious, always looking to do something exciting, out of the ordinary and often dangerous. So rambunctious was he that his exasperated mother actually summoned the police to their home to threaten her own son with arrest, hoping to terrify him into submission. It happened more than once.

On the first such occasion Mike was eight. Sitting on the stoop one day with a friend and armed with his keen powers of observation, Mike noticed the mailman delivering an identical piece of mail to every mailbox on the block. Further investigation revealed that the item in question happened to be free samples of chewing gum. Seizing the moment, the boys proceeded to help themselves to armfuls of free gum, until a neighbor spotted Mike's hand in her mailbox. She blew the whistle on the boys, summoning Mike's mother, Zina, who read her son the riot act but soon realized her maternal dictums would only go so far, given Mike's rebellious nature. It was not the first time that he had been caught stealing.

"I was picked up for shoplifting at the five and ten cent store only a half a dozen times," grins Mike.[7]

But Zina had had quite enough of it. So, to Mike's shock, she flagged down the local cop. "Stealing is a crime," deadpanned Zina. "You're going to jail."

Mike blanched in a sudden panic as the brawny beat cop entered the Wallace home and looked him in the eye. A long lecture ensued about the perils of embarking on a life of crime and the demeaning nature of jail time. Zina let Mike sweat it out for nearly ten minutes before dismissing the policeman, having extracted a firm promise from her wayward son never to steal again.

To both their credits, Mike remained true to his word. He crossed that particular misdemeanor off his list—but that left plenty of other ways in which to get into trouble. Two years later, at age ten, he found himself back in the hot seat.

In an attempt to clean up his image, Mike had joined the Boy Scouts. One day, he and a fellow scout assembled a pile of twigs and crumpled newspapers to practice lighting fires. They wisely took the precaution of having a bucket of water standing by to extinguish the flames. There was only one problem. The location Mike had chosen for his pyrotechnic practice was *indoors*—the basement of his apartment building, where paints and combustible solvents were stored.

Excitedly, Chinky struck a match and lit the pyre, which burst nicely into flames. The scouts shared a look of delight, oblivious to the impending disaster on their hands.

It was another neighbor, fortunately, who saved the day, galloping down the steps with a shriek. He pushed past the boys and grabbed some old carpets to smother Mike's campfire. Then he took the young troublemaker by the ear and delivered him to his fuming mother. Again, Zina summoned the police. It happened to be the same cop.

The expected lecture ensued (fire safety and arson), but Mike was on to the routine by now and two years more mature. He argued back that he and his friend had taken proper precautions—the bucket of water and so on. The ten-year-old felt strangely empowered as he stood up to an authority figure more than four times his age. He realized that he had a gift. He had a voice. Though his preadolescent intonation was somewhat higher than the mellifluous baritone that later became his signature, Mike's voice was already powerful.

As described by a childhood friend: "When we played baseball on the vacant lot near his apartment, we always got Myron to go up to the door and talk to people after we broke their windows. One time someone hit a ball through the window of the meanest man in town. We were sure he'd call the cops, so we sent skinny little Chinky to face this guy who was yelling and screaming. But old Chinky talked rings around him. He didn't even ask us to pay for the broken window."[8]

But while the young Mike had found a voice, the triumph was almost derailed by the physical transformation brought on a few years later when Mike hit puberty. He awoke one morning to the shock of what appeared to be an attack of chicken pox. It was, in fact, the worst case of teenage acne imaginable, a condition that haunted Mike throughout adolescence and precipitated the onset of a childhood depression so severe that he preferred overcast days to sunshine, for the sunlight made his facial pockmarks even more pronounced. "If the sun were there, I suddenly was exposed in all of my painful ugliness." He takes a breath. "That was not a happy time."[9]

Many adolescents faced with this level of torment simply would have withdrawn. And part of Mike did, eschewing team sports for the more solitary pursuits of tennis and studying the violin.

One afternoon, an elderly teacher, Louise Hannan, invited little Myron to her home for a special "private tutoring session." He remembers feeling some trepidation as he climbed the steps of the Longwood Towers, and followed her inside the musty apartment. She was a graying woman with a puffy wig. Staring compassionately at the pimply boy, Miss Hannan asked for his hands. She guided them gently to touch her belly and the small of her back. Miss Hannan then proceeded to close her eyes and deepen her breathing, a series of long heaving sighs. It suddenly occurred to the boy what was happening.

"She was showing me how to breathe," says Mike. "She taught me how to produce a voice."[10]

With newfound control over his diaphragm, Mike's voice became richer and deeper, and he soon became enamored of it, using it at every occasion that presented itself. He'd read directions for his teachers in class or do things on stage at school assemblies. He joined the Dramatist Society and got the lead in the school play.

Thus, Mike forced himself to become an extrovert, which marked the beginning of an emotional sleight of hand that he performed his whole life—being outwardly aggressive in an attempt to mask what he felt within.

Mike became intensely competitive, too, battling for better grades than the other students, and often succeeding. "It used to burn him up if someone did better than he did," said a high school friend.[11]

Despite this drive, however, Mike's classroom performance, unlike that of his siblings, proved inconsistent. Unable to produce more than a B-average, he turned his attention to extracurricular activities, becoming captain of the tennis team, concert master of the orchestra and sports editor of the high school paper.

One time, he got into an argument over a sports story with the editor-in-chief, a smart no-nonsense girl. Mike wanted his story to run on the front page—and she didn't. So he rushed over and said, "You obviously don't know a thing about journalism. You have no news judgment. You wouldn't know a good story if it jumped out and bit you."[12]

He harangued the poor girl like the browbeater he'd one day become on *60 Minutes*. The editor just stood there flabbergasted, unable to get a word in edgewise. And finally she agreed to run the story.

Mike found that he relished the art of altercation. He argued at every chance he got. "Every week, he'd come in and give me 15 reasons why he didn't have time to practice," recalls violin teacher Harry Dickson, who later became conductor of the Boston Pops and the father-in-law of future governor Michael Dukakis.[13]

On the rare occasions when he *did* practice, Mike would open all the windows, so the whole neighborhood could hear him. Even at this young age, he liked being the center of attention.

In addition to all his other activities, Mike became Brookline High School correspondent for the *Brookline Chronicle*—$2 a column, or $4 a column if you made the front page. And Mike did his best to ensure that his stories received the prominence he felt was their due. His persistence paid off.

By senior year, Mike's Brookline High classmates voted Myron Wallace "Most Prominent Boy." Known by now for his personal voice, Mike chose to start the graduation Class Oration with the words of another:

Classmates:—

Seven years ago tonight, in 1928, the Class Orator of that year began his speech in this manner:

"Classmates, the gates are open! This vast, confusing, 20th century world stretches before us, and with little fear, but great self-confidence we venture forth into this world of vexing problems. We see an era of unheard of prosperity, of

new standards of living . . . a time of free thinking and free expression . . . Fate has placed us in this ultra-modern age."

Would that we, in this, our last formal assemblage before our graduation, might be able sincerely to repeat those words!

The world is just as bewildering: free thinking and expression have become even a little more free. But the gates, once flung wide, have been blown almost shut by the winds of Adversity, and their steel riveted hinges, once diligently oiled, have been rusted into disuse by the storms of Depression.

And through those gates, indeed, in the words of Edmund Gosse: "The future comes like an unwelcome guest."[14]

Chapter Two

False Starts

W hen the letter arrived in 1935 from the University of Michigan, Mike found himself uncharacteristically queasy. He snatched the envelope from the mailbox and darted up to his room to open it in seclusion. This was his last chance. Every other college he wanted to attend had turned him down.

Mike was the black sheep of the family when it came to academics. Brother Irving had been admitted to Harvard, just across the Charles River, on a full scholarship. Mike both envied and pitied him for it; what a fool Irving was to have opted for geographic proximity to their mother and her many moods.

As if on cue, Zina burst into the bedroom unannounced and plucked the envelope from her son's hands. Mike felt a surge of indignation before his face dropped, reading the cold expression in his mother's eyes. Zina shook her head and glared at him: "Once again, you've humiliated us."

She tossed the letter into the trash and paced brooding to the window. "Not a word to anyone," she decided. "If Leo hears of this. . . ."

Her voice trailed off, unwilling to ponder the mess they faced. Zina's brilliant brother, Leo Scharfman, was an esteemed Professor of Economics at the University of Michigan—head of the department, in fact. Numerous nieces and nephews of the Scharfman clan had attended the university, and though Zina would have preferred Myron to be closer to home, she was counting on Leo's ability to keep an eye on her unruly son. Michigan was certainly respectable, the "Harvard of the Midwest." But even this compromise was not an option anymore. Zina sighed heavily, staring vacantly at the gray wintry sky.

"I'm going to Chicago," declared Mike. The University of Chicago was the one school that had admitted him. Zina frowned as expected. "*Chicago?* We don't know a soul in Chicago!" Exactly, thought Mike. And it was even *farther* from home than Ann Arbor.

But Zina was hardly done with the matter. Despite her embarrassment, it wasn't long before Zina exposed the family secret in a deliberate "slip" during a casual phone call to her brother.

"Chicago?" barked Leo. "Why in the world is Myron going to Chicago? We've got to get this young man to the University of Michigan."

And Leo quickly intervened, just as Zina had hoped. "He put a little grease on Dean Joseph Bursley, and presto!" recalls Mike. "I was promptly tattooed maize and blue."[1]

Despite some wounded pride at his mother's intervention, Mike was secretly pleased. He had never been west of the Massachusetts border and welcomed the idea of having family nearby in his first foray from the nest. As he describes it: "Uncle Leo and Aunt Min ran a kind of youth hostel for refugees from our ancestral home in Boston."[2] Cousins, in-laws, and variegated Scharfmans all descended upon Leo and Min for an occasional home cooked meal and pep talk.

Father Frank found himself welling up as he bid farewell to his youngest child at South Station. Zina held her tears in check. With a nervous final wave, Mike carried his bags onto the Wolverine, an overnight train from Boston to Michigan, and set off for his future.

"Debarking at the Ann Arbor station qualified as genuine adventure," Mike recalls. "I remember some trepidation as I lugged my bags up the hill, on State Street."[3] It was the beginning of a young man's voyage of discovery.

During his orientation week, Mike got a note from Dean Joe Bursley, asking him to report without delay to his office. Terrified, the freshman complied at once. The dean sat Mike down, explaining in no uncertain terms: "We made an exception for you, Myron . . . it's only because of your uncle's intervention that you have a place on this campus. Don't let him down."[4]

Renegade Mike couldn't help himself, however. Though Uncle Leo fully expected Mike to major in economics, as most of the other Scharfman cousins had, Mike has never been one to comply with expectations. He found his coursework dreadfully boring—and his grades suffered accordingly. Mike thought he might become an English teacher or a lawyer, perhaps. But it was extracurricular pursuits that really got his juices flowing.

"One of the happiest moments of my freshman year," recalls Mike, "was when I made my freshman numerals for running the half-mile in 2:04.5 . . . not bad for a skinny bowlegged fellow from Boston."[5] He soon realized, however, that truly impressive times were five or six seconds faster. Never one to settle for second best, Mike quickly abandoned track and looked elsewhere for accolades. He ran for class treasurer and lost, then did some acting on the Lydia Mendelssohn Stage. But Mike's epiphany came when he wandered into a building known as Morris Hall, "where Professor Walter Abbot held forth with some courses on the exotic art of broadcasting, aided and abetted by a pipe-smoking graduate student [Jerry Wiesner], later to become the President of MIT."[6]

Mike's infatuation with the newfangled medium was instantaneous. "I had gotten hooked, that was what I wanted to do, that was where I wanted to spend my time, not in the squat, ugly, musty economics building, but in the mysterious and glamorous [broadcast center] called Morris Hall."[7]

But how was he going to break the news to Uncle Leo? An occasion soon presented itself. "It was Easter vacation in my freshman year," recalls Mike. "I didn't have the cash for the train fare home. . . . Aunt Min took pity on me and invited me to dinner."[8]

When Mike showed up at the Scharfman house at 1108 Baldwin Avenue, he was surprised—and somewhat relieved—to discover that his uncle was out of town. Min could tell that something was troubling her nephew, so she offered him a drink—his first cocktail.

"Whiskey, Old Fashioned, I remember," Mike muses ruefully. Several of them. "I passed out cold after getting sick all over their living room. But that small disaster established a special secret bond between Min and me."[9]

He soon confided in her that he had no stomach for economics. "Min said she'd work it out for me, she'd take care of Leo. All I had to do was get through one full year of economics with at least a C, preferably a B, and she'd drop the bomb on him that his nephew was going to major in speech and broadcasting. I remember that, even to me, it smacked then of majoring in vaudeville."[10]

But young Mike had clearly found his element and was soon thriving. He spent all his waking hours at Michigan's college radio station, where he became a rising star. But Mike's debut on the national airwaves turned out to be nothing short of a catastrophe.

There was a popular NBC radio program at the time called *Information Please*, broadcast coast to coast out of New York, with Clifton Fadiman moderating a panel of erudite and witty pundits. From time to time, the show invited college students to be guest panelists, and Mike was asked to represent the University of Michigan, an honor that made him almost feverish with excitement.

Mike had never been to New York City, so Aunt Min accompanied him on the train. Feeling even cockier than usual, Mike began to hatch a plot as the train rattled into Penn Station. He recalled his send-off in Ann Arbor a few days back, when he and several buddies were celebrating his good fortunes. One friend, Steven Filipiak, had told a joke. A very bad joke.

"You're going to have tough sledding next week," prompted Steve.

"Why?" Mike took the bait.

"No snow," responded Filipiak, grinning from ear to ear.

The boys groaned, agreeing that it was perhaps the worst joke they had ever heard. But Mike, feeling full of hubris, announced that he was going to tell that very joke on the air. With Filipiak particularly incredulous,

Mike sealed the deal by betting him five dollars, a small fortune for these starving students.

Several days later, Mike found himself sitting in the NBC broadcast studio of *Information Please* with a notable panel of urbane intellectuals, including Franklin P. Adams and John Kieran. The guest chair where Mike sat was typically occupied by such luminaries as Clare Boothe Luce, Fred Allen, Dorothy Parker and Orson Welles. And here was Myron Wallace, sophomore from the University of Michigan, staring perversely at the moderator, waiting for a moment of dead air to jump in with: "Mr. Kieran is going to have tough sledding."

Host Clifton Fadiman glanced from panelist John Kieran to Mike and queried: "Why is Mr. Kieran going to have tough sledding?" And Mike blurted out: "No snow."

Sure enough, it fell completely flat.

Recalls Mike: "There was a gasp from the studio audience. It was my Aunt Min. The crowd began to titter. The panelists looked stricken. I was suddenly bathed in flop sweat. Somehow the show continued. The panelists ignored me, no doubt thinking: 'Is this the best guy they can come up with from the University of Michigan?'

"On the train back to Ann Arbor, my Aunt Min said: 'Myron, don't worry about it. Your fellow students will understand.'

"My fellow students will understand, hah! They greeted me at the radio station with a unison cry of: 'You screwed up.' The professor said: 'You were a disgrace to your school.' I never lived it down. But at least Steve Filipiak paid me the five bucks. He also said: 'You weren't funny.' And I'm still not funny."[11]

To this day, Mike claims not to be able to tell a joke. Yet there's a prankster streak in him that turns up on occasion, often at the most inopportune moments. It gets him attention however. Indeed, by the end of his sophomore year, Mike had caught the eye of a young freshman named Norma Kaphan, who hailed from a well-to-do Jewish family. She was bright and athletic and Mike enjoyed her company. They dated for the remainder of his tenure in Ann Arbor.

Upon his graduation in 1939, Norma could tell that Mike was yearning to spread his wings. Determined not to lose him, she skillfully pressured him into getting engaged, even though Mike was far from ready. He had exactly $50 to his name (a gift from his father). No job waiting, no prospects. Mike had tried to get work as a radio announcer, without luck. Mike's father tactfully suggested that he come home. But Mike would not hear of it: "I was scared to death to go back to Boston. I was afraid if I went back I would probably go into the department store business or something."[12]

Then came a break. University of Michigan music professor Joe Maddy happened to be running the National Music Camp up in Interlochen, and he needed an assistant for the radio classes taught by Jerry Wiesner, who'd go on to be the science advisor to Jack Kennedy. It only paid $25 for the summer, plus room and board, but Mike jumped at it. He taught several classes in radio broadcasting to young campers who wanted a break from their viola lessons and orchestra rehearsals. His classes were popular, but Mike was yearning for a "real" job.

As luck would have it, just a month later, his other professor, Waldo Abbott, gave him a call: "Myron, I think I have an interesting audition for you. Get yourself down to WOOD in Grand Rapids."

"Actually it was one [radio] station with two sets of call letters," corrects Mike. "WASH until noon because a laundry company owned half of it, and WOOD in the afternoon because a furniture company owned the other half."[13]

WOOD/WASH was looking for a versatile on-air announcer and Mike got the job—$20 a week for a split shift, 9 A.M. to 1 P.M. and 4 to 8 P.M. Even with that modest salary, Mike managed to save money. His room cost a mere $4 per week. Every night he'd eat a $1.19 steak dinner at Thompson's Restaurant, which was located on the ground floor of the bank building that housed the radio station.

"So I saved money out of the twenty dollars and I decided that this was a big force with me. I wanted to make money," admits Mike. "I confess to that shameful ambition."[14]

But, much like the debacle on *Information Please*, Mike would soon humiliate himself in his first ad lib interview on the air—and nearly lose his job. It involved a local promotion modeled on NBC's *Pot o' Gold*, which featured a substantial cash giveaway to listeners of bandleader Horace Heidt's wildly popular national radio program. By spinning a "Wheel of Fortune," Heidt zeroed in on a phonebook page, then another spin would identify a particular name on the page, which would be that night's prizewinner.

"We at WOOD put together a marked-down nightly carbon copy of it called 'The Sack o' Silver,' " recounts Mike. "Horace Heidt's prize was $1000. Ours was $20."[15]

"Well, on the night in question, I spun the wheel, came up with a lady on the phone and hyperventilated that 'This was Myron Wallace' and wasn't she thrilled to death to hear that she'd just won the WOOD 'Sack o' Silver' . . ."

"Oh no, oh no, oh no," she sobbed. "Oh no!"

Mike quickly realized that the lady was really in distress. "What's the matter?" he asked.

"My husband, he just died! Just now, he just died!"

"Oh no! Oh no!" cried Mike in turn. Then he blurted: "Jesus Christ, what a shame!"[16]

No sooner were the words out of his mouth than Mike realized what a monumental gaffe he had committed. His fiancée Norma, who was listening to the show with some friends in her senior dorm room, gasped and covered her mouth in shock.

In Grand Rapids, a Dutch Reform stronghold, they take their religion very seriously. Uttering the Lord's name on the air was profane, and certainly grounds for dismissal.

Says Mike sheepishly: "Obviously, you don't hire a novice to do ad lib shows."[17] Both Norma and Mike were convinced that he had blown his first broadcasting job.

The next day Mike was scheduled to go down to Detroit for an audition for WXYZ, a more prestigious station in the Michigan Broadcast Network—so he missed that night's *Sack o' Silver.* The switchboard at WOOD was flooded with irate calls from listeners who assumed that Mike had been fired for his indiscretion, and were insisting that he be reinstated.

"The poor fellow, he was distraught . . . he didn't know what he was doing . . . it was just human error, everyone's entitled to one mistake."[18]

So Mike hung onto his job by a thread, but it wasn't the last time he would put his foot in his professional mouth. The following year he found himself in Detroit. His audition had been successful and WXYZ, a much larger operation, owned and syndicated a number of popular shows, including *The Lone Ranger, The Green Hornet* and *Ned Jordan: Secret Agent*.

Mike, in his distinctive baritone, would intone the famous opening: *"With his faithful valet Kato, Britt Reid, daring young publisher, matches wits with the Underworld, risking his life so that criminals and racketeers within the law may feel its weight by the sting of the Green Hornet!"*

"I remember all those dramatic potboilers came out of one fetid 12' by 20' radio studio at the top of the Maccabees building in Detroit," says Mike.[19]

Since this was the era before you could reliably prerecord segments on wax platters, the technology of the day, each episode was repeated three times, one for each time zone. The first live broadcast began at 6:30 P.M. for the East Coast, followed by a repeat performance at 7:30 P.M. for the Midwest. Then the cast and crew would go out for a leisurely dinner before returning to the studio at 10:30 P.M. for the West Coast broadcast. That last broadcast, says Wallace, could be quite unpredictable, "if the cast had indulged too freely at dinner."[20]

According to Wallace, the fee for all three shows under the 1940–41 American Federation of Television and Radio Artists contract was $38— big money for a twenty-two-year-old rookie. WXYZ was also the place where Mike cut his teeth on the news. Though he had announced headlines at WOOD/WASH, it was strictly a "rip and read" operation—meaning the news copy was ripped from the wire service printer and read on the air, unchanged and unpolished. At WXYZ they had a pair of writers to spiff up the copy for their news program, which was sponsored by the Cunningham drugstore chain. It began with the buzzing sound of a P-38 prop plane and accompanying fanfare: *"The Cunningham News Aces... on the air!"* Mike was one of the "aces."

His career on the ascendancy, Mike returned to Ann Arbor, ring in hand, and proposed to Norma, who was overjoyed. Mike had some lingering doubts about the whole question of betrothal, however. His first love remained the airwaves and he was reticent about any commitment that would interfere with it. But marriage seemed to be the thing that a working man was expected to do in the 1940s and Mike followed suit. The whole thing unnerved him, however, and it wasn't long before Mike committed another professional gaffe that nearly upended his career.

"This time it was the night before I was leaving for New York to get married and they were throwing a farewell party for me in the orchestra studio across the hall," remembers Mike.[21]

So Mike put on a wax platter, knowing full well they were considered unreliable. Nonetheless, cocky as always, Mike abandoned his post to play a prerecorded segment—in this case, a speech by Roosevelt's Interior Secretary, Harold Ickes. Platter spinning, the bridegroom-to-be slipped across the hall to have a few drinks.

Ickes was on a tirade against the notorious Moses Annenberg, a Philadelphia publisher who had recently been jailed for tax evasion. As Mike sipped his martini, he heard the broadcast through the monitor speaker in the hall.

"Moe Annenberg is one of the most corrupt . . . one of the most corrupt . . . one of the most corrupt . . . one of the most corrupt . . . one of the most corrupt."

Mike, aghast and pulse racing, dashed next door into the studio. "It repeated twenty-one times before I could get to the turntable and get the needle onto the next groove," he confesses in embarrassment.

Mortified, Mike snuck out the back door of WXYZ and darted off to his impending nuptials, convinced he had once again lost his job. Too embarrassed to admit the affair to his wife-to-be, Mike went through the ceremony in a daze. Norma tried to read her husband's mood as they drove in silence to their honeymoon on Cape Cod. But as much as Mike hoped the disaster would disappear, it was unrelenting. No sooner had they landed in Provincetown, than he picked up a copy of *Time* magazine; to Mike's utter horror, there was the story in black and white:

When Harold Ickes aired his speech ... baffling was the result to many a Detroit listener. Cried the recording: "Moe Annenberg, one of the most corrupt—one of the most corrupt—one of the most corrupt—one of the most corrupt—one of the..." Horrified, a studio employee grabbed the phonograph arm. Although WXYZ immediately aired an explanation, some people in Detroit were convinced that Secretary Ickes stuttered.[22]

"What's the matter, Myron?" asked Norma, seeing the color drain from her husband's face.

"I lost my job," he wailed. "I lost my job!"

Sure enough, upon the Wallaces' return to Detroit, Mike found a message from his boss waiting in his box: *Mr. Trendle would like to see you at your earliest convenience.*

"I went downtown to his office, cooled my heels, was bidden to come in, stood there for a full five minutes, it seemed, while he finished what he was doing. He looked up, pushed a copy of *Time* in front of me and asked if the story was accurate. I stammered that it was."[23]

George Trendle, president of King-Trendle Broadcasting, took a deep breath, staring intently at the young man who stood before him, bathed in perspiration.

"Well, Wallace," said Trendle, "my wedding gift to you is your job. You've still got it, but barely. Go back to work."

But it wasn't long before restless Mike decided to make a move to an even bigger pond: Chicago, the city where he had nearly gone to college.

Says Mike: "Chicago was addictive. It was the center of the soap opera and radio. It was the center of some evening drama. It was the center of a lot of activity and there was money. And I, for whatever reason ... that is what really drove me. Because I could do announcing and news and a little acting and ... films and whatever. I did them all."[24]

Indeed, the 1941 move to Chicago began a period where Mike became relentless about advancing his career, chasing any job he could get his hands on. Perhaps it was his determination to shake the false starts that had plagued him in Michigan. Perhaps he was sobered by the global unease of a world at war, with Hitler now firmly entrenched in much of Europe.

To complicate matters, Norma was now pregnant and Mike decided the best thing he could do for his family was to work as much as he could. He landed a job on *The Road of Life*, a Chicago-based soap opera, for $150 a week. He worked on such serial dramas as *Ma Perkins* and *The Guiding Light*, and played Detective Flamond on *The Crime Files of Flamond*.

"It was the first of the psychological detective thrillers; and I must admit, I had trouble reading the script," admits Mike. "I didn't understand detective stories."[25]

But that didn't stop him. At WEBM, he became a cast member on *The Whistler* ("When he whistles, someone dies!"). Later, he read introductions and closes on ABC's *Sky King Show*, an action-adventure series. He dabbled in news, as well, earning an additional $55 a week at the *Chicago Sun Radio*, a broadcast version of the newspaper. On WLS, he was also tapped to announce the first-ever Peabody Awards—the highest accolade in broadcasting, which Mike would go on to win three times himself, in the decades to come.

Mike describes this jack-of-all-trades Chicago period as "the start of a versatility kick born of necessity."[26] Beyond versatility, however, there was something almost obsessive about his inability to turn down job offers. In perhaps the most curious example of the many hats he wore, once a week Mike would don a dinner jacket to emcee *Tavern Pale Beauty Contest* on WGN-TV, a pageant show sponsored by local pubs in industrial neighborhoods such as South Chicago and Belmont-Cragin. The contest featured gum-smacking blue-collar "beauties" traipsing around in swimsuits. "It was the greatest unintentional comedy show I've ever seen," recalls Mike.[27] But it was hardly the worst indignity Mike would suffer. One particular day on the set of *Super Circus* proved far more humiliating.

Super Circus was a one-hour program that aired on Sunday afternoon, bringing an actual live circus to children across America. Mike's role on the show was that of a straw hat–wearing barker for Peter Pan peanut butter.

"They had an elephant act," recalls Mike. "And [before] the dress rehearsal, they had forgotten to 'rout' the elephants,"[28]—that is, to encourage the animals to relieve themselves before the show.

So, on this particular Sunday, the "unrouted" elephants lumbered into the ring for the final rehearsal before airtime. Sure enough, like clockwork, they proceeded to produce pile upon pile of dung, creating an overpowering stench and sudden panic on the set. "Nonetheless, the music was going on and [drum majorette] Mary Hartline was dancing around the stage, getting elephant debris all over her bare beautiful legs," remembers Mike.[29]

With less than twenty minutes to airtime, director Greg Garrison ordered the stagehands to clean up the mess, but they refused, pointing instead to the animal handlers. There was a jurisdictional dispute as to who was responsible for clearing the set. With no time to lose, Garrison rolled up his sleeves and grabbed a shovel. He ordered his associate director to do likewise, then he turned to Mike.

"Me?" gasped Mike. Garrison nodded. Garrison was the director who had cast Mike in his first Chicago soap opera, *The Road of Life,* and he figured that Mike owed him. Mike reluctantly picked up a spade and started shoveling. In ten minutes of feverish work, the unlikely trio managed to clear the stage—but not the smell. When the live audience of children filed in, many were reluctant to take their seats. But the show went on.

Then came time for the first commercial break—in this era before videotape, all commercials were live. Mike dutifully took his spot at the announcer's microphone, while a child actor stood before the camera holding a jar of peanut butter and a fresh slice of Wonder bread.

"See little Johnnie?" voiced Mike. "See how he spreads his bread with Peter Pan Chunky? Now watch little Johnnie as he takes a bite."

But the poor kid was so overwhelmed by the enveloping stench of manure, he took one look at the gooey peanut butter and burst into tears. Needless to say, it was the last time Peter Pan sponsored *Super Circus,* or, for that matter, any other show featuring live elephants.

That night, Mike spent an especially long time in the shower. Though as busy as ever, he felt he was getting nowhere. Mike knew that some changes were in order—so he started with his name.

"People began to call me Mike a lot earlier on," said Wallace, "but I did a show in Chicago and somehow *For the Love of Myron* didn't sound as good as *For the Love of Mike*."[30]

But, by 1943, an even bigger change was in the works. After narrating the dramatic series *First Line*, part of a recruiting program for the U.S. Navy, Mike's conscience got the better of him and he decided to enlist.

Norma must have had mixed feelings about it. She had just given birth to a son, Peter, and here was Mike doing his disappearing act. The man seemed incapable of settling down. In fact, patriotism was only part of Mike's motivation for enlisting—he needed time to reassess himself. Joining the navy offered a way to put on the brakes and, in his own words, "give Mike Wallace a real overhaul."[31]

Thus, Ensign Wallace became a communications officer on the U.S.S. *Anthedon*, serving first in Honolulu, then in Perth, Australia. The *Anthedon* was a support ship that never saw combat; so, gazing across Pacific waters, Mike had plenty of time to think. His first conclusion: "I had made one serious mistake. The goal I chose was success and big money, instead of finding myself as a real person."[32]

He developed some lifelong relationships on board the ship, including one with fellow officer and attorney Jerry Johnson, who would later become Mike's financial advisor. Also, according to author Gary Paul Gates, Mike fell in love.

Like many U.S. servicemen stationed abroad, Mike found himself spending time with a local girl in Perth, but it became far more than a casual affair. Says Gates: "Mike has always been a kind of romantic. He's the type of guy who got smitten very fast, and it would be consistent with other aspects of his personality—why screw around here, I mean, I know what I want. Let's do it."[33]

Mike fell head over heels for the Australian lass. As a way to assuage his guilt, he began to dissect all of Norma's apparent flaws. He became convinced he had married too early, and had settled for someone far too similar to his own mother. He began to toy with a radical idea: settling down in Perth, after the war.

But then Mike received word that Peter, now age three, had contracted tuberculosis, and Norma was suffering from nervous exhaustion. Sensing from his dispassionate letters that Mike was adrift, Norma became intent on securing her husband an early discharge. She had her physician draft the following letter to the Navy:

> *Mrs. Wallace consulted me because of chronic fatigue, headaches and backaches. Her symptoms can be explained on a functional basis: the absence of her husband who is in the United States Navy is working a real hardship on her. Mrs. Wallace's health would probably improve greatly if her husband were discharged from the service.*[34]

Ironically, Mike had just petitioned his own commanding officer for an early discharge in Perth, Australia, but the commander wisely insisted that Wallace return to Chicago, to give his marriage another chance.

On December 26, 1945, Mike was transferred to the Great Lakes Training Facility as a radio officer, and discharged with the rank of lieutenant junior grade the following March, having served just over two years.

To Mike's credit, he worked sincerely to repair his marriage, trying to form a bond with little Peter, who hardly knew him. And he toiled even harder to relaunch his career. By 1947, Norma was pregnant again. But it wouldn't be long before Mike vanished for good.

Chapter Three

Life Imitates Art

One year after Mike's discharge from the navy, his life was hit by a torpedo. Her name: Buff Cobb. Blond and buxom, Buff had grown up rubbing elbows with Hollywood celebrities. When she met Mike at age eighteen, she had already been married twice, both times causing minor scandals. After Buff was done with Mike, his life would be in shambles.

It began on a midsummer morning in 1947. Mike straightened his jacket as Norma rummaged through the hall closet of their Chicago apartment for his hat. He thanked her with a detached peck on the cheek, which disappointed Norma, though she was loath to show it. She was trying hard. They both were.

It had taken a while, but Mike seemed finally to be settling back into the routine of married life. Daydreams of his wartime romance in Perth had faded. He was grateful that his commanding officer had forced him to come home to Norma, who was now pregnant with their second child.

Mike's career was likewise back on track, though his current radio gig, an afternoon chat show called *Famous Names* on WGN, was hardly groundbreaking. "A frivolous enterprise," he would later remark, "a puff-and-patter exchange with show-business celebrities who were in Chicago to plug their latest play or movie."[1]

Mike enjoyed the assignment, however. It was his debut as an interviewer, the place where he first discovered how much he thrived on "the parry and riposte of interviewing."[2] But these lightweight duels hardly produced the adrenaline that Mike needed in order to thrive. "It was all so sweet and gay, and, as I look back, pretty damn deadening."

Occasionally, he'd ask a tough question of a celebrated guest and people would look at him as if he had just committed an indecent act. " 'Tut-tut, Wallace,' the radio vice presidents would say. 'These people are our guests, not our enemies.' "[3]

Even defanged, however, Mike made a habit of boning up on the person he was about to interview. He didn't have the resources to hire a researcher in those early days, so his wife stepped in—and Norma enjoyed perusing the papers and gossip rags for tidbits on her husband's upcoming celebrity guests. She must have had a field day doing the research on Buff Cobb.

B uff was Hollywood royalty. Her grandfather, cigar-chomping, triple-chinned author, actor and humorist Irvin S. Cobb, was among America's top celebrities, more famous in his day than Johnny Carson or Jay Leno. Author of more than sixty books, Irvin Cobb had been compared favorably to Mark Twain. While working for Joseph Pulitzer, he became the nation's highest paid journalist.

Irvin fathered a single child, Elisabeth, who later became Buff's mother. Elisabeth had aspirations as a writer, and though she struggled under the formidable paternal shadow, she ultimately produced two books. One of them, *My Wayward Parent*, was all about Irwin.

With his prodigious girth, her father was literally larger than life. A star of radio and motion pictures, Cobb had hosted the 1935 Academy Awards. He received the French Legion of Honor and two honorary doctorates. A bridge over the Ohio River, parks, a major hotel and a brand of cigars were named after him. In short, Irvin Cobb was a force to be reckoned with.

In the fall of 1928, Elisabeth found herself abroad and pregnant in Italy, where her husband, Frank Chapman, a singer, was performing in a Florence opera house. They rented a villa just outside the city, and Elisabeth spent her days writing about her father and preparing to give birth. It was there, however, that Frank encountered the mesmerizing actress and singer Gladys Swarthout, who possessed, according to one critic, "the most blandishing voice of our age." Gladys would go on to perform sixteen seasons at the Met, sing several duets with Bing Crosby and appear in half a dozen musicals. Frank Chapman was instantly smitten and would soon leave his wife for her. Buff, who was born several weeks after Frank and Gladys met, learned from an early age that men had the potential to walk all over you.

Elisabeth and her daughter moved back to Hollywood, where Buff came of age and promptly abandoned her birth name, Patricia Chapman— inherited from her absentee father—for the more alluring Buff Cobb (a nickname of her mother's). Though not classically beautiful, Buff was a head-turner and certainly knew how to work a room. She began her acting career, fittingly, as a harem queen in *Anna and the King of Siam*, after which Fox Studios signed her as a contract player.

Buff soon set her sights on the man who would become husband number one: power attorney Greg Bautzer. To say that Bautzer was a player is putting it mildly. His list of conquests reads like a *Who's Who* of Hollywood starlets: Dorothy Lamour, Ginger Rogers, Barbara Payton and Jane Wyman, first wife of Ronald Reagan. He also had a tryst with Lana Turner, who subsequently revealed that Bautzer had taken her virginity. Bautzer would later represent Turner in multiple divorce proceedings, after becoming the divorce lawyer to the stars and representing such notable clients as Howard Hughes and Joan Crawford—with whom, naturally, he had a passionate affair.

Bautzer, big and handsome, had been a dockworker in San Pedro harbor, before going to law school at night and beginning his determined climb to the top. Actor George Hamilton described him as "a great dancer and a nasty drunk."[4]

Buff was only sixteen when she met Bautzer in 1944 and the relationship horrified her granddad. "You aren't going to let that baby get married," sputtered Irvin to daughter Elisabeth. "Why, she ought to be playing with dolls!"[5] But Buff had a talent for getting her way—and the following year she and Bautzer were married. It lasted all of six months. Buff didn't lose much sleep over it, for another opportunity soon appeared.

Fox Studios had a scandal on their hands at the time involving their in-house matinee idol, William Eythe, who was battling rumors about his sexual orientation. They needed an ambitious ingénue to enter into an arranged marriage. Buff agreed, but the nuptials were, of course, doomed. On January 19, 1948, *Time* reported:

Actress Buff Cobb, granddaughter of the late Humorist Irvin S. Cobb, sued her second husband for divorce after seven months of marriage. She said that the husband, Actor William Eythe, had hit her a couple of times last fall. Two days later, in a seesawing mood, she called the whole thing off.

The fact was that being the spouse of a celebrity had its advantages. In the spring of 1947, Eythe introduced Buff to Tallulah Bankhead, with whom he had starred in *A Royal Scandal*. Tallulah took a liking to the young actress and offered her the part of Sybil in a revival of Noel Coward's *Private Lives* that Bankhead was taking on tour. The run began in Westport, Connecticut, where the final dress rehearsal started at 8:00 P.M. and lasted until dawn, because of tantrums by Tallulah. Cobb, both riveted and terrified, recalls: "It was absolutely outrageous. She just went bananas. Screaming and yelling: she wouldn't work in that set, she couldn't do this, she couldn't do that."[6]

After a rocky week in Westport, the show opened in Chicago on July 22, 1947—and that was where Buff Cobb met Mike Wallace, in a curious case of life imitating art. The plot of *Private Lives* concerns a divorced couple, Elliot and Amanda, who re-meet on their respective honeymoons to second spouses. Realizing that they are still in love, the two abandon their new spouses and run off together, though they are soon caught up in the same violent arguments that originally plagued their passionate but stormy marriage, an inescapable cycle of love and hate.

What happened between Mike and Buff was precisely that: passionate, stormy and mired in love and hate. When they met in 1947, both were stuck in marriages where they didn't belong, with spouses who fundamentally failed to understand them. Mike's relationship with Norma lacked the fire and excitement that he was seeking at that point in his life. Besides, Norma was both moody and needy—not unlike Mike's mother, a comparison that filled him with dread. She wanted him at home; he yearned for his place in the limelight.

In Buff, he had found a mate who would support his media aspirations. She understood well the importance of seizing center stage—it was in her blood. Grandfather Irvin had dabbled in acting and had this to say about it: "I began by demanding the center of the picture. I believe this is customary among the veterans of the profession. I insisted that all the other performers so favored as to be permitted to appear in the same film with me should take the background and make themselves as unobtrusive and inconspicuous as possible."[7]

Like Irvin, Buff was also a natural storyteller. Leading man Victor Mature, whom Buff dated briefly between husbands one and two, described her this way: "She has a flair for relating commonplace incidents, embellishing them and making them amusing. Most gals start to tell a story, go off on tangents, finally wind up telling you what a divine hat they saw in a window. Buff tells a wonderful story. Inherited the talent, no doubt, from her Grandpa."[8]

Aside from sexual magnetism, Buff possessed a broad range of talents, too. Though still in her teens, she was hard at work on her first book, *Memoirs of a Subdeb in Hollywood*. The manuscript would eventually be shelved, but Buff had already published several articles in film magazines, as well as in *Vogue*. She was an artist, too, and designed her own clothes. An impressive athlete once described as an "expert at tennis, golf, swimming and horsemanship," she had made the Women's Polo team at Pebble Beach.[9] In short, Buff Cobb, like Grandpa Irvin, was a force to be reckoned with. Mike couldn't help himself.

"She was ... a glamorous figure to me at that time," Mike said in a recent understated interview. "So I succumbed."[10]

Naturally, Mike is somewhat abashed about how quickly it all happened. To promote her play, Buff agreed to appear on Mike's radio show, *Famous Names,* which was broadcast live from the Balinese Room of the Blackstone Hotel. Mike had already interviewed the show's star, Tallulah Bankhead, in an earlier show. Though Buff was a second-tier celebrity, she certainly had a colorful past. Writes Gary Paul Gates in Mike's 1984 memoir *Close Encounters*: "In preparing for the interview, he read that Miss Cobb had married Hollywood attorney Greg Bautzer when she was seventeen ... and had divorced him to marry an actor, William Eythe. Mike couldn't wait to ask her about all *that*."[11]

But Mike's killer instincts were entirely disarmed that afternoon. Though the incident is largely glossed over in *Close Encounters*, Gates described it more graphically in a subsequent interview: "When Buff walked into the studio, he was absolutely knocked on his ass ... it went from 'Hi, pleased to meet you' to an intimate relationship very quickly."[12]

Though Mike was twenty-nine at the time, he was clearly on an upward trajectory. He had made a solid name for himself in Chicago radio, and Buff could sense that he was destined for greatness. Thus began their secret tryst.

After performances at the Harris Theater on Dearborn Street, Mike would pick Buff up to drive her home to the Ambassador Hotel, but they'd park somewhere on Michigan Avenue. "It speaks volumes that she was reluctant to take him upstairs," muses Gates. "I think that at some point that happened, but I always found it very entertaining to picture Mike Wallace and Buff Cobb acting like a couple of teenagers in a car on one of the busiest boulevards in the country."[13]

The relationship ran through the summer and into the fall of 1947 and it was becoming far more than a casual affair. Mike found himself in turmoil, drawn inexorably into Buff's web. On October 12, 1947, Mike's second son, Chris, was born. Exactly one week later, Buff celebrated her nineteenth birthday. Mike faced a choice. He chose Buff.

Norma could not contain her fury when Mike moved out to shack up with a twice-married Hollywood starlet, leaving her with a toddler and a newborn. Buff, for her part, felt somewhat guilty about the circumstances, but not overwhelmingly so—her father, after all, had left *her* in infancy.

The fact is that Mike and Buff were good for one another—not just personally but professionally, too. With Buff, Mike saw a solution to the constant battle of balancing his home life with his feverish dedication to work—she, in effect, could enable his workaholism.

"Shortly after we were married in 1949," recalls Mike, "Buff decided she wanted to keep on working and I suggested we do it together."[14]

Both in radio and the just-emerging medium of television, husband-and-wife teams were all the rage in the 1940s and '50s. Tex McCrary and Jinx Falkenburg were making a big splash with their *Tex & Jinx Show*, a sensation in talk radio. William Safire, who worked for them in his teens as a researcher, dubbed McCrary "a handsome and daring warrior news-man."[15] As an Army Air Corps colonel, Tex had led the first journalists into the ruins of Hiroshima. Jinx was a knockout cover girl and tennis star.

Tex taught Jinx how to coax out human-interest stories from guests. Says Safire: "Tex and I cooked up a list of 'couch questions' to help Jinx elicit anecdotes . . . and with her appealing enthusiasm, she became a bet-ter interviewer than her monotonal husband."

Mike figured he could do the same with Buff, and the perfect oppor-tunity presented itself. WMAQ, the local NBC radio station, was looking for a new show to replace Dave Garroway, who had been a hugely popular late-night fixture, entrancing his Chicago audience with his offbeat but civilized chatter. But television duties on *Garroway at Large* led him to give up his radio show and WMAQ needed a replacement fast.

"When I suggested an interview show hosted by Buff and me," recounts

Mike, "no one at WMAQ seriously questioned what prior experience in radio she had. They simply said yes and they hired us to do a nightly hour and a half."[16]

The WMAQ brass had no notion that Buff had never asked a question in public of anyone in any medium. "What followed was a crash course in the art of the interview," remembers Mike. "A course that consisted mainly, as I remember it, of driving endlessly through Chicago streets. I have no idea why we decided that we had to be mobile while I talked, with me tormenting Buff with 'I'm Betty Grable, ask me ten questions' . . . 'I'm Martin & Lewis, ask me ten questions.' "

Mike's automobile had served them well in their courtship and it served them well again. Buff was a quick study and soon became a proficient interviewer. Their show went on the air in the spring of 1950, with an added twist—it was broadcast live from Chez Paree, one of Chicago's hottest nightclubs.

Jack Eigen had popularized this format several years earlier in *Meet Me at the Copa*, an enormously successful show that originated at New York's Copacabana. The program, which ran five nights a week, began at midnight with: "Good morning, ladies and gentlemen, this is your Broadway and Hollywood reporter, Jack Eigen, coming to you from the very beautiful and very glamorous lounge bar of the Copacabana at Ten East Sixtieth Street in New York City . . . the room is really jumpin', folks. I see Milton Berle, Frank Sinatra, Ida and Eddie Cantor, Judy Garland, Perry Como, Lucille Ball and Desi Arnaz, Jane Russell . . . I'll have a lot of these famous people up here at the microphone with me before the evening's over, so don't go away."

Needless to say, the program was wildly popular, allowing folks across America vicariously to rub elbows with showbiz celebrities. Then, in 1950, recalls Eigen: "I was doing my nightly chatter show from the Copa lounge . . . a note came to me which read: 'We are here to steal everything you do. We open in the Chez Paree in Chicago over NBC, next Friday night.'—Signed Mike and Buff."[17]

The Chez Show, as it was known, became an instant hit. "We developed a substantial following—not, incidentally, solely for our interviews," says Mike, "but equally for the candor and asperity with which we publicly discussed each other's assorted shortcomings. We bickered on the air and the audience enjoyed it hugely."[18]

The relationship between Mike and Buff was as volatile as it was passionate. She was bright, highly opinionated and no pushover, and so was he. It made for great entertainment. Viewers and critics noted approvingly that Mike and Buff avoided the usual "domestic cooing and idle chatter of most husband and wife programs."[19] More edgy and exciting than its competition, *The Chez Show* blossomed on WMAQ from May 1950 to June 1951.

With their notoriety on the rise, Mike and Buff got word that her former movie star husband, William Eythe, was coming to town to supervise a play he was producing. Buff gave Mike an earful about how Eythe had mistreated her, and Mike decided to take action. As reported in the *Chicago Tribune*:

William J. Eythe, movie actor and stage producer, was jailed yesterday, after a pursuit from California to New York to Chicago, as the result of a claim by his former wife, Buff Cobb, an actress, that he owes $2,500 on their divorce settlement. Eythe, who arrived secretly from New York Saturday, was taken into custody on a writ of ne exeat, a process used to prevent a person from leaving a state to avoid legal proceedings. Miss Cobb's present husband, Myron Wallace, a radio announcer, accompanied Deputy Sheriff Emil Rackly when the writ was served on Eythe in the Croydon Hotel at 616 Rush St.[20]

Eythe was stunned by the indignity of his seizure: "Miss Cobb and I have been good friends despite our divorce. I don't understand it. I suppose I do owe the money, but I'm a bum bookkeeper and a bum business man." Indeed, Eythe, who was down on his luck, had trouble posting bail. *The New York Times* coverage explained: "The actor's lawyer, Archie Berman, said he telephoned Hollywood, New York and other places in an attempt to raise the $5,000 bond but was unsuccessful."[21]

After several days in jail, Eythe managed to scrape together the money that he owed Buff and was ignominiously released. Buff felt vindicated and Mike realized she was not a woman to be crossed—something he would soon experience personally.

"Word eventually filtered East to CBS, who were looking for new talent wherever it lurked for their budding television network," says Mike.[22] They had already poached talent from the Chicago radio pool, bringing in Gary Moore and Ransom Sherman from Chicago's *Radio Club Matinee*. Now they came to look at Mike and Buff. A stream of program executives from CBS New York made the trek west.

"They sat in the Chez lounge and watched and listened and went back to New York . . . then came another covey of executives and finally the top man, Hubble Robinson," remembers Mike. He spent twenty-four hours with them, went back to New York and twenty-four hours later the offer came—a guarantee of $15,000 each.

"The money was hardly grand—about a quarter of our income from *The Chez Show* and my other chores." Mike was decidedly lukewarm about the prospect of uprooting and moving to New York, a city where, unlike Buff, he had no contacts. With a string of diverse and successful programs, Mike had established himself in Chicago as "Mr. Radio." He didn't want to start all over again in a new town. Equally daunting for Mike was the prospect of switching mediums from tried-and-true radio to the nascent and untested world of television. Buff was accustomed to cameras—she loved them and they loved her. Mike, however, still self-conscious about his appearance, decided to decline the offer. "I felt I would probably never make it in television because cosmetically, perhaps, I wasn't sufficiently interesting looking or pleasant looking."[23] He chose, therefore, to stay in Chicago, which was a "safe and lucrative happy ground."

Buff, however, had her heart set on New York and refused to take no for an answer. As Gary Paul Gates explains, "She didn't go off and do *Private Lives* in Chicago with the idea of spending the rest of her life in Chicago."[24] Telling Mike she was going on vacation, Buff snuck off to New York, where she met with the CBS brass on her own, secretly shaking hands on their offer.

"I guess it's the traditional role of a wife to give her husband a swift boot once in a while," Mike sighed philosophically in an interview at the time. "I just hope we're a cut above the average husband-and-wife routine in this business."[25]

When the young couple moved to New York, "there was, it is recorded, no brass band there to meet them at La Guardia airport," novelist Robert Crichton comments dryly.[26] Mike had established himself as a big fish in Chicago—but here, he had to begin anew.

"It was foreign territory to me . . . I felt like an outsider, almost a hick. CBS put me up at the Warwick Hotel, wined and dined me, but still I was apprehensive . . . this was the 'Big Time.' First night in town, there was dinner at 21, tickets to *South Pacific*, and in the days that followed, my first glimpses of the glitter of 5th and Madison. There were traffic jams from the Hudson to the East River, an infectious hum or urgency, vitality and somehow importance. But New York was brusque, too, impersonal, self-absorbed. I wasn't sure I liked it."[27]

It took some time for CBS to launch the show—and while Buff enjoyed the days off, workaholic Mike became extremely restless. "When Mike wasn't working, Mike was going nuts," said Buff. "We got an option from CBS, they paid us big money just to sit and wait for a call. Could we enjoy it? Could we take a vacation? The man was wild about it. Our whole life was work. We were locked in with it."[28]

CBS finally put them to work on several shows at once—first and foremost was a forty-five-minute daily grind, originally entitled *Two Sleepy People* until the programming executives opted for the more direct *Mike and Buff.* In a bid to improve ratings, it was one of the first shows to be broadcast in color, which, though exciting, was also unnerving to Mike, who remained self-conscious about his complexion.

Things got off to a rough start. On the first night, only one paper bothered to review the show, calling it "clumsy, inept, lumbering."[29] It was a brand-new medium for Mike; unsure before the camera, he became flummoxed, and quickly demoralized. Mike took it out on Buff, saying he should never have listened to her. They should have stayed in Chicago.

Buff, never one to back down in a fight, gave it right back to him, accusing Mike of losing his focus. Insults and objects were hurled back and forth across their hotel suite. Then Buff had an inspiration—it was heated on-air arguments like these that had made *The Chez Show* so entertaining. "Why not show the audience what we're really like?"[30]

So Mike and Buff pulled off the gloves and dove into spirited altercations about nearly every subject and guest on the show, whether Harry Belafonte, Mickey Spillane or the new Revised Standard Version of the Bible. Their constant differences of opinions sparked heated on-air arguments— and it worked like a charm. *Mike and Buff* soon became the talk of the town. As covered in *The New York Times*:

The age-old dramatic formula of boy meets girl, loses her and then gets her back is being used by a young husband-and-wife television team as the peg for—of all things—a chitchat show...Each afternoon's episode finds Mike meeting Buff, "losing" her in a heated discussion of a selected subject for the day and reconciling their differences after talking with guest experts.[31]

"We hope it's working out alright," Mike speculated nervously in a 1951 interview. "Buffie and I, like two normal people, have differences of opinion and that's the premise of the show."[32]

"This bickering on the air was a conceit by design," declares Gary Paul Gates.[33] "They would consciously set out to disagree about something and get into a quarrel knowing to a large extent that it was an act . . . it was kind of a ritual, clearly patterned on the Ameche thing."

There had been a very popular radio show a few years earlier called *The Bickersons* with Don Ameche and Frances Langford. "The name speaks for itself," continues Gates, "about a married couple who were horrible to each other but it was funny. It was amusing, I suppose in the way that *Who's Afraid of Virginia Woolf* is amusing, but not quite that severe."

Mike felt deeply uncomfortable with the format; he was desperate to sink his teeth into weightier fare. The broadcaster he most admired at the time was Clifton Utley, a Chicago-based newsman who had started his career at WMAQ, the same NBC radio station that had aired *The Chez Show*. Utley had then made a successful transition to television news—but unlike Mike, Utley was a respected journalist "long recognized as a master in news reporting."[34]

"Much of what I learned about news and interviewing," Mike said, "I got from Clifton Utley, a man with insatiable curiosity and a fine news sense."

What's more, Utley had married another bona fide journalist, Frayn Utley, who moderated her own daily foreign-affairs broadcast on CBS, and eventually took over her husband's show, after he suffered a stroke. Mike may have naively believed that he and Buff could follow in the Utleys' footsteps—Buff, however, was far more interested in ratings than journalistic integrity.

Mike found solace in the other show that CBS had given them—*All Around the Town*, which aired at 6 P.M. on Saturdays, a weekly program with greater depth. Mike and Buff would take their cameras and questions to places of cultural interest around New York City, such as the Statue of Liberty, Empire State Building, Rainbow Room, Chinatown, the Bowery, the George Washington Bridge, the Cloisters and to Radio City Music Hall, interviewing visitors and the people who worked there.

The critics loved it. When they went to examine the paintings of Matisse at the Museum of Modern Art, Jack Gould of *The New York Times* wrote: "Mike and Buff effectively refuted any notion that a visit to a museum must be a dry or dull experience . . . the presentation constituted an object lesson in how television can be eminently educational without being self-conscious about it."

Mike was thrilled. "I've been a hack for a long time in radio and television," he confessed in a 1951 interview, "but the Saturday show is the first one I've found really exciting."[35]

Yet even here, Mike and Buff had their differences. "I feel like a fifth wheel on the Saturday show," she complained. "It's not so enjoyable for me as the afternoon one."[36]

The audience agreed with her. *Mike and Buff* was the program that had everyone talking—and Buff relished their newfound fame in Manhattan social circles. The young couple would turn heads when they entered cocktail parties. They could walk into Sardi's or Lindy's unannounced and get the best table in the house. Their escapades would be covered in *Argosy*, America's first pulp magazine. Mike enjoyed the attention, too.

Says Gary Paul Gates: "Buff brought Mike into a world he'd never been. He met all kinds of people in the theater and in the arts, and in general, that he had only heard of."[37]

But Mike felt dissatisfied and was determined to tackle something of substance. He persuaded CBS to let them take *Mike and Buff* on the road to the 1952 Republican National Convention in Chicago, which ushered in Eisenhower and Nixon on their anticommunist platform. Mike was exhilarated to be back in Chicago and covering real news. Buff, on the other hand, couldn't wait to return to Manhattan.

Indeed, discord between the two was mushrooming, along with increased onscreen bickering and after-hours domestic quarrels of alarming intensity. Explains Gates: "As time went on the line between the act on the air and reality became more and more blurred . . . the quarreling would continue after they got off the air."[38]

Every night they'd be screaming about how the other had dropped the ball on the show, then launch into more fireworks about how to handle tomorrow's topic. At times, the altercations veered toward the absurd. The *New York Post* reported at one point that Buff had decided that the bridge of Mike's nose was rather too broad and suggested he have an operation to correct the problem.[39] Considering Mike's sensitivity about his face, it was a low blow, even for Buff.

With their marriage on the rocks, Mike resorted to his old pattern of burying himself in work to avoid friction at home. The only problem was that, this time, Buff was in both places. So Mike demanded that CBS offer him more shows—and they did, in the medium he had left behind. Mike found himself back on the radio, hosting *Stage Struck*, a one-hour program that covered Broadway behind the scenes. He crossed paths with many theater types, including Pulitzer Prize–winning director Abe Burrows. But

Mike was underwhelmed. "I must say that I was rather unimpressed—not with them as human beings, but with the whole enterprise of Broadway Theater, which seemed to me to be an overblown, slick *Liberty* magazine story."[40]

Nonetheless, Burrows, who was prepping a new production, goaded Mike into giving Broadway a shot. "You really don't know what you're talking about. Why don't you try out for this play and learn about the theater firsthand."

Mike, seldom inclined to demur when the gauntlet is thrown, auditioned and ended up landing the leading role in *Reclining Figure*, a new comedy by Harry Kurnitz.

Buff was speechless. The theater was *her* domain and here he was, upstaging her once again. But Mike was only getting started. Building on his momentum, he also signed on to emcee a game show, *I'll Buy That,* and a quiz show, *The Big Surprise.* He was tireless, and Buff got a clear view of his relentless competitiveness and obsession with work.

"It was that damn puritan business," Buff explained. "I like to work, but I don't have to nail myself to the cross each day to prove the point. I remember once we finally took a day off and went to the beach. I lay down in the sand and Mike looked at me with astonishment. 'What's the matter, girl?' he said. 'No moral fiber?' "[41]

It was the final straw. Buff decided she was through with Mike and moved out of the apartment. Though Mike knew their relationship had fizzled long ago, he was still taken by surprise. He, too, had been contemplating separation, but Buff had now upstaged *him* by taking the initiative. Matters were complicated by the fact that, contractually, they still had a show together on CBS. It was sheer torture. Says Mike bluntly, "It's very difficult to do a husband-and-wife show if you're not married."[42]

As Robert Crichton described it: "They would meet in the studio, mutually loathe and hate one another, go on the air and do their routine."[43]

The charade lasted only a few weeks before CBS pulled the plug, and Mike found himself busy on a string of shows that meant nothing to him.

"It was those words that began to bother me," says Mike, "Host, Emcee, Moderator, Panelist . . . all those TV jobs that don't lead anywhere, that don't grow."[44]

But his malaise was only just beginning. Mike had strayed too far from his true calling and it gnawed at his soul. In the evenings, he had begun rehearsals for *Reclining Figure,* in which he played Sam Ellis, a hustling art dealer trying to unload a forgery on an unsuspecting collector. It was another case of art imitating life, for Mike felt like a fake who had been selling himself in all the wrong ways.

Then events took an ironic turn. On the morning of June 18, 1954, he received an anonymous call. "You love your wife?" demanded a husky voice.

"Who is this?" snapped Mike.

"Shut up and listen," growled the man, who proceeded to threaten Buff's life unless Mike put $500 in an envelope and delivered it to St. Bartholomew's Episcopal Church on Park Avenue, opposite the Waldorf Astoria Hotel.

Hanging up the phone, Mike felt his mind racing. His separation from Buff had not been made public. The caller clearly assumed they were still together.

Numbly, Mike dialed the police. Plainclothes detectives shadowed him as he went to make the drop at St. Bartholomew's. Mike left the envelope in the last pew, as instructed. Police seized the extortionist as he went to collect it. An unemployed Bronx truck driver, Frank Talarito Jr. had targeted the TV couple to pay off his mounting debts. Mike shuddered as the man was cuffed and driven off by police. The misguided trucker thought he had an easy mark in Wallace. And indeed Mike may have wondered if that was precisely what had gone through Buff's mind when she walked through the oak doors of the Balinese Room to their first encounter in Chicago.

"Need a ride home, Mr. Wallace?" offered a detective.

Mike shook his head, mumbling that he was fine. But that was far from the truth. In fact, when the squad cars pulled away and Mike was left alone on the New York sidewalk, he looked around in a daze. No idea where to go. Ensign Wallace had lost his rudder.

Chapter Four

Enter the Muse

T he fall of 1954 was brutal. Mike loathed coming home to an empty apartment. He found himself going through the motions at work, then showing up halfheartedly for evening play rehearsals. He had the lead, but it was one of those roles that involves a lot of standing around.

In act 2 of the text, his young female costar, who has been trying to win him over, declares: "The right kind of wife can be a loyal helpmate by your side, struggling with you every step of the way and never leaving you even at the darkest moments." Mike's scripted response was: *"That really sounds ghastly."* It was a laugh-line, of course, and Mike delivered it with the appropriate punch. But the fact is that Mike was still a romantic at heart, a man who needed a loyal partner at his side. And he was beginning to get a taste of those "darkest moments"—the all-consuming depression that would later overwhelm him.

The Buff relationship may have been doomed from the start, but Mike had always abhorred failure—the word was simply not in his lexicon. And yet here it was—thirty-three years old with two marital strikes against him, he was treading water in a career without purpose and careening helplessly into a gloomy New York winter. Mike could not simply withdraw into a cave to lick his wounds. He was forced into the limelight, quite literally: center stage at Broadway's Lyceum Theater.

The play opened on October 7, 1954 to humdrum reviews. "A smooth and pleasant comedy," opined the *Daily News*. *New York Herald Tribune*'s Walter Kerr wrote "Wallace makes the transition from radio to Broadway with ingratiating ease."

But in truth, Mike had no idea what he was doing. One night, in the middle of the "loyal wife and helpmate" exchange, Mike leaned over and brushed his head across the cheek of his costar, Georgianne Johnson, a gesture they had never rehearsed and which came out of nowhere. At the first opportunity, she asked him why he had done it. "You had a smudge on your face," he exclaimed. Georgianne Johnson knew from that moment that Wallace was no actor. "He didn't realize that he was in over his head," she recalls.[1]

The 1954 holiday season was particularly dismal. On Christmas and New Year's Day only about seventy-five of the Lyceum's 950 seats were filled. The play closed shortly thereafter and Mike found himself directionless.

With the near-constant pressure of his alimony and child-support payments, Mike took on another commercial. Already the pitchman for Parliament Cigarettes, he now became national huckster for Fluffo Shortening by Proctor & Gamble. It was a new low. According to Gary Paul Gates, "His professional life had no focus, no coherence, no clear sense of purpose . . . He had been too willing to try his hand at any game in town, just to drift along from one free-lance job to the next."[2]

January of 1955 was not a particularly cold month by New York standards, but to Mike it was benumbing. Desperate for a change, he decided to drop all his frivolous jobs to create space for some self-examination. "Taking time out to think was not a new idea," he explains. "I had done it earlier when I was a communications officer in the Navy subtender in the Pacific."[3]

He spent time reading, "everything from philosophy to biography to religious tracts."[4] And his thoughts began to gel. He was able, for one, to get some perspective on his whirlwind relationship to Buff and put a positive spin on it: "I progressed from a yokel to a guy enchanted by the world of glamour in the big city, to a man who learned to appreciate the things that really mattered."[5]

He was able to pinpoint what caused the failure of his first marriage, too: "In those days . . . I was a taker, not a giver. I had no understanding of how much I was required to give. My first thoughts were of my job, money and success. I'm afraid that this was true even after my two sons were born."[6]

In fact, Mike was practically a stranger to these sons. Mike missed them. He missed the normalcy of family life.

"When you've lived the New York party life, the kind you read about in the columns for a number of years, you can get thoroughly sick of it," he said. "No matter where you go, the people are always the same. I [found] myself lunching with people I didn't care much about, dining with people I didn't especially like."[7]

"I wanted something other than that," he concluded. "Something more solid and peaceful."

Eager for a bit of warmth, he accepted an invitation to fly to San Juan, Puerto Rico to emcee a March of Dimes ball in February of 1955. It was here that Mike met a woman he would soon describe as the love of his life. She would also become his muse. At least, the *female* one.

Unlike women that Mike had known, Lorraine Perigord exuded sophistication. Dark and raven-eyed, she was refined, mysterious and elegant. An artist by profession, half French, half American, Lorraine lived a free-spirit lifestyle in Haiti, where she painted and owned an art gallery with a fellow Caribbean painter, Angel Botello. The pair opened a second gallery in San Juan, which is where she and Mike met in early 1955.

Too lonely to be holed up in his hotel room and lacking the will to go outside, Mike found himself wandering through the lobby of the Caribe Hilton after his duties at the charity ball. He came upon the recently opened Galerie des Antilles. There was Lorraine. Mike locked eyes with her and became entranced. He entered, pretending to examine one of the paintings.

"What do you think?" smiled Lorraine.

"Sold," Mike replied without hesitation.

It wasn't one of her paintings, however, but a canvas by her partner, Angel Botello, whom critics had dubbed "the Caribbean Gauguin" for his bold use of colors and depiction of island scenery. Purchasing the painting was simply a ruse to ask Lorraine out to dinner, a meal that sealed the deal for him.

Wallace, the rough-and-tumble street kid from Brookline, saw Lorraine as a woman of finesse, sophistication and a great deal of class. She was the princess to his frog.

"He had never met anyone of that social standing," explains Lorraine's brother, James.[8]

Lorraine's parents were artists and intellectuals. Her mother, Emily McBride, a painter, filled the house with art and inspired both of her children to follow her into that profession. Her father, Paul Perigord, a French professor and statesman, had been instrumental in helping to establish the League of Nations.

Yet, despite her worldliness, Lorraine was totally insulated from American popular culture and knew nothing of the media and celebrity scene. After Mike's years with Buff, who had elevated networking to an art form, he found Lorraine's ingenuousness refreshing and charming.

Ironically, Lorraine and Buff had some notable biographical details in common—both were raised in Los Angeles and had been twice married there, though Lorraine felt disdain for the Hollywood lifestyle. Like Buff, she was young when she embarked upon her first short-lived marriage, which produced one child. Then, in her mid twenties, she wed Miklos Dora, a suave Hungarian who worked as the U.S. wine representative for Baron Philippe de Rothschild, and had another child before that marriage fizzled, too. Lorraine took her kids, Anthony and Pauline, and fled to Haiti, where her father was in semiretirement, working as editor of *The Port-au-Prince Times*.

Having children from a former marriage gave Mike and Lorraine something in common. Secretly, Mike felt that a relationship with Lorraine could help mend the alienation he felt from his own children. Though she had no desire to become a media wife, Lorraine found herself strangely drawn in by Mike's charisma and dogged pursuit.

With no need for secrecy this time, Mike decided to be entirely transparent about his intentions in this courtship. Over Easter, he flew back to the Caribbean to ask for the blessing of Lorraine's father. It turned into a weeklong discussion of politics, philosophy and morality. As deeply as Mike felt about Lorraine, he became equally enamored of her intriguing father.

A decorated war hero, Professor Paul Perigord had multiple degrees in ethics and philosophy, as well as a PhD from Harvard, which he had attended around the same time as Mike's brother, Irving. But Paul gave up his studies in 1917 to enlist as a private in the French army during World War I. Rising quickly to the rank of captain, he saw firsthand the brutality of trench warfare and was twice wounded, receiving the Croix de Guerre and the Légion d'honneur for his valor.

After the war, Paul Perigord devoted considerable time to public service, becoming a vocal advocate for world peace. At the request of President Woodrow Wilson, he went on a nationwide tour to promote the formation of the League of Nations, speaking in all the major cities of the United States. Ultimately, he became an U.S. citizen in 1923 and settled in Los Angeles, where he worked as a professor of French civilization at UCLA. Professor Perigord found himself much in demand as a public speaker for his contagious enthusiasm, sparkling wit and great personal charm.

As described by a close friend, "Paul Perigord was profoundly a Christian and a gentleman in the traditional sense, in the fullest sense of the word. He was an extremely tolerant, kindly soul who took genuine interest in the problems of others and who gave those seeking it sound advice that reflected his thorough understanding of human nature."[9]

It's not difficult to see how Mike was utterly taken by this gentleman. He reminded Mike of his beloved father, Frank. Mike's fondness for Paul Perigord was one of the deciding factors for Lorraine, too, in her ultimate embrace of Mike's advances. Part of her was disillusioned with monogamous relationships, having failed miserably in two marriages. But seeing the warmth between her father and this pushy American suitor helped sway her over the edge of doubt.

After several days of being in Paul's company, Mike cleared his throat one evening and solemnly asked the Frenchman for his daughter's hand in marriage. Paul nodded his approval, but was inwardly saddened by the fact that he would lose Lorraine to an urban metropolis. Lorraine enjoyed nature and all things natural. She was a country girl who loved simplicity and island sunsets. And she was delicate. Far more delicate than she appeared. How would she survive in the chaos of Manhattan?

The fact is that she wouldn't. It would take decades, but a slow erosion of Lorraine's fragile spirit would contribute ultimately to a deeply tragic demise. In this breezy and bucolic Caribbean island spring of 1955, no one but Paul Perigord had the slightest foreboding about the outcome of his daughter's latest romance. Thus, in May of that year, Lorraine ventured up north to test the waters with Mike. With home court advantage, he pulled out all the stops. By July, they were wed.

What Mike adored about Lorraine was her rare combination of feminism and femininity. She was strong, independent and free-willed, yet she was also traditional in an old-world sense—i.e. willing to be subservient. As Mike characterized it in a 1975 interview with *Mother Jones*: "Lorraine, before we got married, supported her children with her galleries and paintings, liberated by no movement, liberated by herself, and in spite of it Lorraine is essentially feminine. So many feminists in our business lose that soft, round appealing quality. I don't know how else to define it."

Good Housekeeping, for its August 1957 issue, turned the tables on Mike, giving Lorraine the opportunity to interview *him*—and her final questions were:

> **LORRAINE:** *Do you think of me as an American woman or a European woman?*
>
> **MIKE:** As a European woman, of course. Your father's French, you were born and partly brought up in France—oh, you're definitely European. You have that certain deference to the male, which

I confess I like in European women. I'm not suggesting that a wife should walk one step behind her husband—but it helps! It's a "by-your-leave, my lord" attitude that you just don't find in American women—they're infinitely more self-absorbed. European women let the men run things and quite right they are, too.

LORRAINE: *So... That's just what I thought you thought. But what I'm trying to get at is where you ever picked up this total myth, this fond legend that you believe in so touchingly. I know European women very well indeed and I'm convinced that in their own very subtle, shrewd, sly, infinitely self-absorbed way, they make their men do exactly as they wish. I consider myself an American woman, an honest woman. So a question I'd love to have you answer, Mike, is this: Exactly how many European women have you known well?*

MIKE: Say, who do you think you are, Mike Wallace? This has gone far enough.

Though clearly a lightweight exchange, it hinted at some fundamental differences between Mike and Lorraine that would eventually snowball. There were, after all, enormous gaps to overcome. By moving in with Mike into his Manhattan town house, Lorraine and her kids would be hit with a profound case of culture shock.

Lorraine's two children, Anthony and Pauline, respectively fifteen and eight at the time, were yanked from their Caribbean beaches into a muggy New York summer. Pauline and Anthony found it difficult to adjust to life with elevators and doormen. Ironically, the children's well-being had been a factor in Lorraine's decision to say farewell to the Caribbean and give marriage another try. She had come to realize how desperately they needed a father figure, particularly fifteen-year-old Anthony. But the boy and Mike clashed. As tensions rose in the house, so did Mike's consumption of cigarettes, which concerned Lorraine, who was quite health-conscious decades before such concerns were common. Indeed, some of her health-related rituals perplexed Mike.

"Every day I see you go in the kitchen and put into a grinder two onions, two tomatoes and two carrots, a head of cabbage, three turnips, an eggplant and six other vegetables I wouldn't even care to name," he said to her in half-jest one day. "And then I see you drink the resulting brew. I'd like you to stop this utterly repulsive practice."[10]

She didn't. In fact, Lorraine got Mike to overhaul his eating habits. At Lorraine's insistence, Mike began a diet heavy on grains, yogurt and vitamins. His breakfast routine for years had been coffee and little else. Lorraine got Mike to add an orange, some whole-wheat toast and hot water with lemon.

Emboldened by her success in reshaping Mike's diet, Lorraine soon dropped an even bigger bombshell. "I can't live in Manhattan," she declared. "I miss birds and fresh air. I need the countryside."

Even though Mike had been an apartment-dweller for nearly forty years, he agreed. He could see that Lorraine was withering in the urban environment. He had begun to sense Lorraine's fragility and it didn't scare him—in fact, Mike felt a deep need to take care of her.

So they made a move to a rambling old house in Snedens Landing, a small community along the Hudson River about thirty minutes from midtown Manhattan. They acquired the requisite dog and cat to round out the household; and, most important, they invited Lorraine's father, Paul, to come live with them. That's when Lorraine finally exhaled and began to paint again.

Mike got busy with his work, as well, but unlike Lorraine, he remained unable to gain true satisfaction from it. His slate included a smorgasbord of jobs, as usual. He became an alternate panelist on *To Tell the Truth*, a CBS TV show. At NBC, he was hosting another game show, *The Big Surprise*. The network also handed him a daytime radio gig called *Weekday*, where they teamed him up with the daughter of a former president.

The only child of Harry S. Truman, Margaret Truman was attending college when her father assumed the presidency in 1945. The first presidential progeny to come of age in the era of mass media, Margaret was thrust into the limelight, which wasn't altogether bad, considering the profession she chose to pursue. Aspiring to be a singer, Margaret made her debut in

1947 with the Detroit Symphony. She later played the Hollywood Bowl, and, after her father was reelected in 1948, she landed an appearance on the stage to which all artists aspire—New York's famed Carnegie Hall.

Critics, however, were unimpressed with her vocal talent.[11] *The Washington Post*'s Paul Hume wrote that Truman possessed "a voice of little size and fair quality . . . [she] cannot sing very well . . . is flat a good deal of the time . . . has not improved in the years we have heard her . . . [and] still cannot sing with anything approaching professional finish."

Enraged, President Truman seized a piece of White House stationery and fired off the following letter:[12]

THE WHITE HOUSE
WASHINGTON

Dec. 6, 1950

Mr. Hume:

I've just read your lousy review of Margaret's concert. I've come to the conclusion that you are an "eight ulcer man on four ulcer pay."

It seems to me that you are a frustrated old man who wishes he could have been successful. When you write such poppy-cock as was in the back section of the paper you work for, it shows conclusively that you're off the beam and at least four of your ulcers are at work.

Some day I hope to meet you. When that happens you'll need a new nose, a lot of beefsteak for black eyes, and perhaps a supporter below!

It was such an odd case of executive impulse that copies of the letter were widely circulated and discussed in Washington. One such copy ended up hanging in the Clinton White House. Back in 1955, the note made page one news and, while not the sort of publicity an aspiring artist seeks, it certainly sold tickets. Margaret found herself in demand in the emerging world of broadcasting.

On May 27, 1955, she was brought in to substitute for Edward R. Murrow on his *Person to Person* TV show, where Margaret interviewed her parents in their Independence, Missouri home. Shortly thereafter she was tapped for the radio gig with Mike Wallace, who accepted the assignment halfheartedly, frustrated that, once again, he would be sharing the stage with an amateur, someone twenty years his junior. He took small comfort in the fact that, this time at least, they were not also married.

"We're going to do a little of just about everything," Margaret Truman explained excitedly to a reporter.[13] "We'll do interviewing, present news, spin some records. We may do some drama. I may even do some whistling. Of course I whistle. Nearly every girl learns to whistle."

Mike just rolled his eyes. At least she was not invited to sing. It went over his head, perhaps, that in her naive enthusiasm Margaret had just described what was essentially a thumbnail of Mike's career to date— jack-of-all-trades, master of none. Robert Sarnoff, then NBC's executive vice president, had high hopes for the show, saying that *Weekday* "will be both companion and counselor to women everywhere."[14]

In one of the earliest iterations of the Oprah phenomenon, program executives realized that they had a captive and potentially enormous audience in housewives and homemakers. And radio had an advantage over television, in this instance.

"Radio doesn't grab you like TV," said NBC president Pat Weaver. "It's more like a companion."[15] That is, it doesn't demand focused attention, making it easy to cook, clean and engage in other forms of domestic multitasking while listening. As *Time* put it: "[*Weekday*'s] appeal to housewives, mothers, matrons and maids is contained in the show's opening lines: 'Don't stop! Don't look! Listen!'" *Time* went on to quote Weaver's slightly misogynistic description of his scheme for wooing his target female audience as "Friendly penetration."[16]

But Mike was uninspired—it was yet another unremarkable job in his thus far medium-profile career. So Mike began doing what he always did when he got bored: needle, rag and play pranks on anyone and everyone within his sphere. Margaret Truman, not particularly fond of Mike's antics, left the show after less than a year. She was replaced by Virginia Graham, a more experienced and formidable co-host who would happily dish anything she got from Mike right back at him—which, of course, took the fun out of it.

At home, Lorraine, a sensitive soul, detected Mike's growing malaise. She knew that her husband had yet to find his true calling.

"What makes you happy?" she would ask him from time to time.

"What does that have to do with anything?" he'd bark in response.

"You should be doing what you love," she would respond sweetly.

"It's not that simple," he'd retort. "I have a family to support. *Two* of them."

And they would drop it. Until the next time.

To Mike's credit, he did make some attempts to figure out what might fulfill him. As much as he loathed his experience on Broadway, Mike actually undertook another theatrical production, this time not as an actor but as a producer, figuring he would explore the stage from another angle. In the summer of 1955, he partnered up with Andrew McCullough and Donald Wolin to present a comedy, *Debut*, by actress-turned-playwright Mary Drayton. The show opened at Theater By The Sea in Matunuck, Rhode Island, an out-of-town preview they hoped would lead to a run on Broadway. The play did eventually move on, first to Boston, then to New York in 1956. But Mike was long gone by then, having proved to himself what he already suspected: he would never be a theater man, neither on the boards nor in the wings.

The opportunity Mike had been waiting for came in the fall of 1955. The New York NBC station, where Mike reported to work once a week as host of *The Big Surprise*, had a manager by the name of Ted Cott. Young, bright and ambitious, Ted was lured away to a rival network, Dumont, which owned Channel 5, WAMD. Cott wanted to transform WAMD into a major player in the New York market by forming, among other things, a strong, independent news department—and he invited Mike to be a part of it.

So Mike began to anchor two newscasts on Channel 5, one at 7 P.M. and another at 11 P.M. It meant that, with his daytime duties at *Weekday*, Wallace would be working practically around the clock. His new bride stopped seeing him altogether, but Lorraine took it in stride. She had her father in the house, after all. And Mike's energy had shifted. He seemed happy.

In fact, Mike was thrilled. For the first time in his career, he was occupying an anchor chair, reading news and building an audience. But the exhaustion of rushing nonstop from one studio to another began to take its toll.

In fact, one morning on the set of *Weekday*, Mike thought he might be hallucinating. Virginia Graham, the gabby co-host who had replaced Margaret Truman, suddenly launched into an unscripted rant about subjects that were completely taboo on the airwaves—orgasms, premature ejaculation and more. This was live TV. Mike desperately tried to steer the conversation to more appropriate subjects, but Graham continued unabated.

"Everything will be alright, dear," muttered an increasingly anxious Mike, who suspected that his co-host might be in the throes of a nervous breakdown.[17] She glared at him with daggers. "Virginia, please," he pleaded. "We'll take good care of you."

Mike started signaling several stagehands that an immediate intervention was needed, at which point the entire studio burst into laughter.

Mike had been punked. It was not a live broadcast, after all, but an elaborate practical joke—they had been airing a prerecorded segment that hour, and everyone knew it but Mike. He looked around in speechless shock for a moment, then let loose a string of epithets at Virginia and her co-conspirators. Mike, the consummate prankster, had gotten a taste of his own medicine and he found it hard to swallow. But part of him was secretly impressed. It wasn't often that Mike met his match, but he had met it in Virginia Graham.

Over at WAMD, it would happen again, and then some. His name was Ted Yates, a gentleman cowboy from Wyoming. Young, talented and driven, Ted had been working at Channel 4, WNBC, when he was poached by the other Ted—Ted Cott—to run the nascent news department at WAMD. What the two Teds and Mike would achieve in the newsroom of Channel 5 was nothing short of a broadcast revolution. Ted Yates would become the most inspiring partner Mike had ever known. In fact, he was the one who put Mike Wallace on the map. In less than a year, Mike would be the most talked about TV newsman in America.

Chapter Five

The Inquisitor Finds His Beat

T ed Yates was born in Sheridan, Wyoming in 1930, and the values of the Wild West would follow him throughout his career as a news producer and correspondent—honor, justice, rugged individualism, bravery. When the danger increased, so did Yates's determination. Later in his career as a field reporter, Yates would be fired at by the North Vietnamese in Laos, stoned by communists in Sumatra, chased out of Cambodia, and, in Java, caught between rioting students and a charging palace guard, who bayoneted his driver in the mouth.[1]

Lanky, handsome, athletic, a man of few words, Yates had, according to one associate, "the social graces of a prince."[2] He could go anywhere, deal with anyone. Yates was self-made, self-taught. As one of his sons puts it: "For most of his life, he was in a hurry to do great things."[3]

Yates attended the University of Virginia for two semesters before concluding he was not made to sit in lecture halls. So he got on his bicycle and pedaled some 800 miles across four states to return to his family home in Florida.

That summer, he went back to the West. A superb horseman, big, tough and strong, Yates entered the Bronco Busting contest at the Cheyenne Frontier Days Rodeo. The first day of the competition, his horse threw him and he broke his back. He went home to Florida to recuperate and became a sports trainer, then a general beat reporter at various Florida newspapers. But the stakes weren't high enough for this young daredevil, and Yates soon enlisted in the Marines, serving in the Korean War as part of the press corps.

After his tour, he wound up with an honorable discharge in New York, where he began his career in radio and television. It was there that Yates met Mary, the woman who would become his wife. Mary Yates figures prominently in the story of Mike Wallace, too. Thirty years later, Mary would marry Mike, after quite literally saving his life.

Mary was an astonishing beauty. Al Ramrus, who worked with Mike and Ted as a writer and researcher, describes her this way: "If you had to explain it to a Martian, 'What is the ideal, American, beautiful, blond girl?' It was Mary. Lovely and warm and friendly . . . I never saw any sharp edges on her. She was like the perfect 1950s American wife."[4]

When Ted and Mary set eyes on one another in the spring of 1954 their attraction was so immediate and intense that they were married within a week. Mike met them in early 1956, just before he married Lorraine. He knew instantly that there was something extraordinary about this charismatic young couple.

"The first thing that struck me about [Ted] was his desperate determination to learn everything," recalls Mike. "He read and read and read—from philosophy to history to biography. His curiosity and his appetite to know were a delight to those who worked with him, and a goad as well. He was considerably younger than I, twelve years, and yet I felt that Ted Yates taught me a great deal about television and reporting in the five years that we were partners."[5]

One thing that Ted taught Mike was to think outside the box, to question conventional wisdom as to how news should be gathered and presented. Ted was both conservative and highly irreverent, an unusual combination in an era when there were precious few, if any, conservatives in the media. His politics had a libertarian bent and he didn't discuss them readily.

Yet Yates saw value in provoking other people to discuss their privately held views, particularly in the buttoned-down 1950s. The Korean War was still in the collective consciousness when Khrushchev took power in the Soviet Union and uttered his infamous declaration: "We will bury you." Meanwhile, at home, civil rights tension was on the rise, following the landmark 1954 *Brown v. Board of Education* Supreme Court ruling outlawing segregation in public schools.

By the fall of 1956, an election year in which Dwight Eisenhower and Richard Nixon were seeking a second term, Ted Yates thought the time was ripe for some broadcasting subterfuge. In a moment of prescient inspiration, he persuaded his boss, Ted Cott, to launch *Night Beat*, a new type of interview show with hard-hitting questions and a take-no-prisoners attitude.

WAMD had been broadcasting two nightly newscasts with Mike Wallace, one at 7 P.M. and a repeat at 11 P.M. Yates suggested that they replace the second broadcast with his provocative new program. Ted Cott was intrigued by the idea of *Night Beat* but quickly brought up practical considerations: an interview show requires a studio and fancy set, but there was no money to build one.

Yates took it in stride. Far from being dissuaded, he decided to turn the limitation into a virtue. We don't need a set, Yates declared, just some black drapes, a pair of stools and a spotlight. Why not give the show the look and feel of a police interrogation? That's when Mike lit up. *Bingo!*

It was revolutionary. Studio talk shows at the time typically featured floral arrangements, cozy divans and soft lighting. Guests were treated gingerly, with softball questions and cloying flattery. And Mike was as guilty as the rest of the field in that regard.

"I had served up my share of pablum on *Mike and Buff*," he admits. "What Yates persuaded me we should do on *Night Beat* was to hurl a thunderbolt into that smug and placid world."[6]

Mike had developed just enough anger and frustration at that point in his career to give his guests a good grilling. It was the role he had been waiting for. Armed with aggressive questions from writer Al Ramrus, Mike dove with gusto into the most hot-button and controversial subjects of the day. Sex, religion, politics, race, money—all were fair game on *Night Beat*.

When Sammy Davis Jr. came on the show with his blond Swedish wife, May Britt, Mike asked them: "What do you feel when you wake up in the morning and you see a black man or a white woman next to you?"[7]

"Nobody would dare do that," says Ramrus of Mike's competition in the world of television interviewers. Mike has never been shy about probing into what happens behind bedroom doors. Indeed, sexuality has always been something of an obsession with Mike. Ramrus recalls an incident after Mike interviewed actor Anthony Quinn.

"Quinn was a huge imposing guy with this glowering face and deep voice. And after the interview Mike came up to me and said, 'Can you imagine the kind of fuck that guy throws?'"[8]

Later, they did an interview with actress Anne Bancroft, and the task of preinterviewing her fell on the shoulders of an all-too-eager Ramrus. "She charmed the pants off of me," he remembers. "I don't how much of it was real. With Mike, she gave the same exact performance." But, after the interview, Mike came up to Ramrus and said, "I had my hand right up her pants."[9]

Ramrus puts all of this into perspective: "Before Mike Wallace and *Night Beat*, radio and TV interviewing was very sedate and proper—and bloodless and ball-less."[10]

The most popular interview program of the day was Edward R. Murrow's *Person to Person*, which involved a vicarious visit to the home of a celebrity. Murrow would ask questions from his desk in the studio, while a remote camera crew filmed the opulent celebrity home from various angles, which were fed "live" onto a screen in front of Murrow. Questions typically began with talk of the local weather, then moved on to household pets, furnishings and hobbies, all highly scripted, rehearsed, planned and vetted in advance by studio publicists.

Says Ramrus: "There was poor Ed sitting there in the studio and saying, 'So this is the living room, is that right?' 'Yes sir, this is our living room.' 'Well, that's a very interesting armoire; where did you get it?' 'Oh, I bought it in an antique auction.' 'Oh it's wonderful.'" And so on.

"Even if [Murrow] had politicians or distinguished authors, they were treated very gently with great respect," continues Ramrus. "[On *Night Beat*] we had no automatic respect for anybody. Anybody was fair game to be revealed, exposed, bloodletted."

And the media took notice. "Wallace is providing a happy relief from all the dull, superficial and saccharine question and answer sessions now cluttering the airwaves," wrote Larry Wolters in the *Chicago Tribune*.[11] "Mike is a sharp astringent in a sickeningly syrupy sea of TV interviewers."

Mike famously got Norman Mailer to declare that "President Eisenhower is a bit of a woman." He extracted an admission from New York high-society hostess Elsa Maxwell that she was still a virgin at seventy-three. He cajoled John Barrymore's troubled daughter, Diana, into discussing her multiple suicide attempts. He got a union boss to scream at him, brought cartoonist Al Capp to the edge of a breakdown. Night after night, Mike eviscerated them like a matador.

Mike's style of questioning—aggressive and rapid-fire—was driven in large measure by a single, often-overlooked factor: the show was *live*. Four days a week, two guests per show, Mike's top responsibility was to keep the viewer's attention. There was nothing to cut away to—no sidekick, no bandleader, no musical interlude, no commercial break. Just the conversation.

"If a guest began to veer off the subject or lapse into a long-winded response, Mike would not hesitate to chop him off—even in mid-sentence," explains Gary Paul Gates.[12] Thus, Mike became a crackerjack on-the-spot editor—thinking on his feet, interrupting an answer if it became dull or meandered, redirecting, provoking, jabbing, persuading. This unique quality of the Mike Wallace "interrogation," necessitated originally by the constraints of live TV, would later become his signature on *60 Minutes*.

And it wasn't just the questions on *Night Beat* that were probing. The show was equally assertive in the style of its cinematography. Instead of the stock-in-trade medium close-up, standard angle for all TV interviews, the cameramen hired by Ted Yates would zoom their lenses into extreme telephoto shots, revealing every bead of perspiration, every nervous tic, every tremor of the hapless guest. It made for riveting television. As described years later by commentator Eve Berliner:

For the first time in television, Wallace cast aside the usual pandering, simplistic, pot-boiler questions, and let loose with abrasive, bruising inquisitions of well-known guests. His researchers were in-depth and intrusive. His guests loved it and feared it. With only a black backdrop and smoke from his cigarette for atmosphere, the hunter asked the provocative question and the prey squirmed in tight close-up, sweaty shots.

The types of people chosen for interviews on *Night Beat*, likewise, sparked outrage. Mike and Ted, along with Marlene Sanders, the talent scout they had hired, went out of their way to book interviews with controversial figures such as strippers, mobsters, Klansmen, birth-control advocates, drug-addicts and homosexuals—people who had never been seen or heard on television. Episodes like these had the town buzzing, and *Night Beat* became the ultimate "water cooler" show, generating more next-day press than practically any other programming on the airwaves.

It was tantamount to broadcast anarchy in the placid cultural climate of the late 1950s. As Al Ramrus put it: "I think that culturally *Night Beat* was a very significant opening salvo of the '60s."[13]

Almost overnight, Mike had become a part of pop culture. Critics dubbed him "Mike Malice . . . the terrible Torquemada of the TV Inquisition." *The New Yorker* published a cartoon of a beleaguered man lying on a couch beside his shrink who declares, "As soon as we find out what you're trying to hide, we'll find out why you're running away from an interview with Mike Wallace."[14]

Lorraine had to adjust to the overnight celebrity of her husband. Mike had previously had a certain degree of notoriety, but this was of another order of magnitude. Now people would stop them in the street to say, "Go get 'em, Mike!" The sudden attention made Lorraine slightly uneasy. But she was certainly proud of her husband, and began a clipping file of newspaper articles in which Mike was mentioned. She would keep this up, obsessively, for the next three decades.

Newspaper clippings, in fact, were a significant factor in the success of *Night Beat*. As staffer Marlene Sanders explains it: "Shortly after we went on the air, we got a call from a guy named Bill Lang, who had been a radio announcer in upstate New York. He came in and said, 'I spent all this time sitting in an announcer booth and I was very bored and I started collecting newspaper clippings.' Turns out he had a garage full of clippings organized by subject and by name. I mean these things were voluminous."[15]

Bill Lang's trove filled nearly 400 square feet of space, fastidiously organized folder by folder. Al Ramrus, head writer of *Night Beat*, lit up when he saw it. Nearly a half-century before Google made access to biographical information a matter of a mouse click, Lang was offering them something no other news show had—comprehensive folders on every public figure in America. This level of organization surpassed most public libraries, which might have had periodicals on microfilm, but they would not have been indexed so meticulously by celebrity or by hot-button issue.

Having ready access to these files became a highly effective component of *Night Beat*. When a guest skirted an issue or tried to deny a matter already in the public record, Mike would reach decisively for the clipping file in front of him and declare smugly that he had documentation to prove his point—evincing squirms and sweat from the interviewee that were photographed, naturally, in excruciating close-up. This methodology would later be raised to an art form on *60 Minutes*.

Another *Night Beat* practice was to conduct a thorough pre-interview with the subject, which might uncover areas of potential controversy or vulnerability. This task fell to writer Ramrus, who would meet the guests several days in advance, then prepare a script for Mike based on his research and conversation with them. Ramrus typed the suggested questions in capital letters followed by expected answers in lowercase. Unlucky was the interviewee who dared to deviate from a prior position he or she had taken on a particular issue.

Yet eight guests a week proved a blistering pace, and the team soon realized Ramrus needed help. They tried, and failed, to bring in additional writers—one from Dartmouth, another from Princeton. But fancy alma maters meant nothing to college dropout Ted Yates or Al Ramrus, a self-described "street-fighter" from CCNY. As Yates put it, they went through writers "like shit through a goose."[16]

Another Ivy Leaguer, Burton Bernstein, lasted less than a month on the staff of *Night Beat* before being shown the door. Bernstein, a native of Brookline like Mike, and brother of famed conductor Leonard, would go on to a successful career at *The New Yorker* as a staff writer for more than three decades; but somehow he could not write two pages of satisfactory questions for Mike Wallace. So frustrated did Mike become with Bernstein that he would dress him down in front of everyone like a drill sergeant, often shouting a string of epithets at the top of his lungs.

Pressures on *Night Beat* were enormous and the working conditions, harsh. The staff was crammed into windowless cinder-block caverns, so small they had to climb over each other's desks to enter and exit. The intimate offices caused strain, to be sure, but also a sense of a shared mission. As Mike describes it: "We reveled in a spirit of camaraderie and self-righteous zest as we sat in our crowded cubicles plotting how we were going to nail this pompous ass or that fatuous blowhard who would be stepping into our lair."[17]

Interestingly, blowhards started lining up in droves to enter the ring with Mike Wallace. "People wanted to come on and wrestle with me," he explains, ". . . and wanted to be challenged with difficult, sometimes abrasive, sometimes skeptical questions."[18]

So they came—Hugh Hefner, Harry Belafonte, John Kenneth Galbraith, Salvador Dali, Frank Lloyd Wright, William F. Buckley Jr., Thurgood Marshall, just to name a few. Says Marlene Sanders, "When the show became the talk of New York, I either had to beat people off with a stick who wanted to be on; and then on the other side I was going crazy trying to get the people we wanted."[19]

One of the people they wanted *desperately* was a sponsor. Advertisers tended to shy away from controversial programs and *Night Beat*, despite its success, was no exception. It took months before they landed even a single sponsor and, as Mike puts it, "A less likely benefactor could not have been imagined."[20]

Hawthorne Books, a small publishing house, had purchased airtime on *Night Beat* to promote *The Heirloom*, a new edition of the Bible. Then, some weeks later, Chase Manhattan came on board. "A bank to go along with our Bible," laughs Mike. "Once we had God and Mammon in our corner, there was no resisting us."[21]

Though *Night Beat* was a local program broadcast only in the New York market, it received attention coast to coast and attracted its share of copycats. "Literally everyone is imitating what they heard are [Mike's] methods of questioning, most of them even without ever having seen him," wrote author-producer Al Morgan in 1957. "They have asked highly personal questions and used words that they mistakenly heard Wallace had used in some of his interviews. As a result, you have never heard so much irresponsible and dirty talk in all of your life."[22]

"The Mike Wallace program . . . threatens to set off a chain reaction that may prove unfortunate," concurred *New York Times* TV critic Jack Gould. "There are growing signs that certain elements in television may embark on a race to outdo each other in the realm of sensational journalism."[23]

So *Night Beat*, in addition to being one of the most bold and original shows on the airwaves, also gave birth to TV sensationalism—and it spread rapidly through the world of broadcasting. Mike's technique, in the view of AP journalist Charles Mercer, even influenced hosts Tex and Jinx McCrary, whose radio program years earlier had inspired the creation of *Mike and Buff*. But, despite all this replication, said Mercer, "None of Wallace's imitators has been as successful as he."

Mike Wallace was one of a kind. When the networks realized this in early 1957, they came pounding on his door, offers in hand. Within months, he would have his own countrywide show on ABC. But it was at this moment, with Mike poised on the brink of national stardom, that the whole thing blew up in his face.

Chapter Six

Two Lawsuits and a Nemesis

M ike was slightly unnerved by the whole thing. Certainly, it was flattering—*The Mike Wallace Interview*, a national show on ABC. But, just as he had had doubts about uprooting from Chicago to restart in New York a decade earlier, Mike harbored reservations about this latest career move. He knew there would be a price to pay. Back at Channel 5, Mike and Ted Yates ran their ship without interference—booking whoever they wanted and asking the questions they wanted to ask—and that's what gave the show its edge. Now, they'd be beholden to programming committees and ABC corporate lawyers, who were proving to be formidable adversaries in the contract negotiations. The two sides were at loggerheads over a final sticking point and Mike wondered if their deal would ever close. Mike's agent, Ted Ashley, was demanding a guaranteed primetime slot for one year, so that the program could find and build its audience. The ABC brass said it was out of the question, especially for a risky show like this one. The negotiations went on and on.

After a particularly grueling eight-hour session on a Saturday, an exasperated Ted Ashley took off his shoes, put his feet up on a chair and proposed that they take a break to watch some television. Sid Caesar's wildly popular *Caesar's Hour* was on—the nation's top-rated comedy show, which featured skits and parodies by Caesar, Carl Reiner and other collaborators. Ashley figured a few laughs would ease the tension in the room—but he got much more than that. It was, in fact, a gift from heaven.

As the attorneys turned their attention to the television screen, they beheld a terrified Caesar sitting in a stark, formidable studio across from Carl Reiner, who seemed to be interrogating him with an insolent sneer. With Caesar's lips trembling, Reiner took a long drag from his cigarette and blew a cloud of smoke into the face of his hapless victim, then launched into an absurdly aggressive line of questioning, which left Caesar practically babbling in a pool of perspiration.

The attorneys turned to one another in astonishment. By an extraordinary coincidence, on that particular show, Carl Reiner happened to be doing a hilarious parody of Mike Wallace on *Night Beat*, causing Sid Caesar, according to one critic, "to set a record for primetime sweating."[1]

It was remarkable. "A local program on a small independent station in New York was being parodied by the biggest comedy show on television," writes Gary Paul Gates.[2] Ted Ashley looked around the conference room at the ABC lawyers and grinned in satisfaction, knowing that Mike would soon have his guaranteed slot in primetime.

Thus, the Yates/Wallace team ensconced themselves in a spacious suite of offices at ABC and got to work on the new show, which would have some notable differences in format. While *Night Beat* ran four nights a week with two guests per show, *The Mike Wallace Interview* would air just once a week with a single guest. That put far more pressure on the team to deliver something truly memorable. ABC president Oliver Treyz along with his chief deputy, Leonard Goldenson, had high expectations for the show. Goldenson pulled Mike aside one day, declaring: "You will not succeed in the job unless you make this building shake."[3] And Mike took it to heart. Perhaps too much so. By the fourth interview, they had their first lawsuit. The interviewee: mobster Mickey Cohen.

"Neither Ted Yates nor I wanted our guest list to be confined to conventional celebrities," explains Mike.[4] "Mickey Cohen was described as a 'get.'"

Cohen, who fancied himself a West Coast Al Capone, counted some 200 tailored suits in his walk-in closet and an equal number of firearms. He got his start as a small-time bootlegger and sometime prizefighter in Chicago, then quickly rose through the ranks of the mob as a ruthless enforcer. He moved back to his birthplace, Los Angeles, to work for Bugsy Siegel, before seizing control of his operations following Siegel's murder in 1947. Cohen ran his Los Angeles operation out of "Michael's Exclusive Haberdashery," a sham façade on the Sunset Strip that fronted for a gambling operation.

On orders from Meyer Lansky, his boss in the Jewish Mafia, Cohen funneled $75,000 into the 1950 senatorial campaign of Richard Nixon, according to journalist Drew Pearson. There is evidence that Nixon and Lanksy were later involved in business dealings in pre-Castro Cuba. Interestingly, Nixon, who was by then vice president, refused to be interviewed by Wallace—but both Drew Pearson and Fidel Castro would be solicited to appear on the program in a deepening imbroglio that would soon cause *The Mike Wallace Interview* to implode.

Cohen arrived in New York for the scheduled interview accompanied by two beefy sidekicks named Itchy and Arlene. Al Ramrus conducted the pre-interview, as usual, and reported back to Mike and Yates, full of adrenaline.

"Al assured me that Cohen was 'ready to sing,'" said Mike gleefully. "All I had to do was push the right button."[5]

Cohen had supposedly given up his life of crime and gone "legit," but Mike soon had him reminiscing about the good old days. And it didn't take long for Mike to start prodding him, brazenly asking how many men Cohen had killed.

"Well . . ." Cohen hesitated.

Mike knew of one victim, Maxie Shaman. That was in the public record—purportedly a self-defense killing by Cohen over a gambling debt.

"How many more, Mickey?" insisted Mike.

Cohen's response: "I have killed no men that in the first place [that] didn't deserve killing."

Cohen certainly had his share of enemies. Among his most prominent current nemeses was Los Angeles police chief William Parker, and Cohen made no bones about his distaste for him. "He's a known alcoholic. He's been disgusting. He's an old degenerate. In other words, he's a sadistic degenerate of the worst type . . ."

Mike was startled by the scathing tirade that poured forth from his guest, but he did nothing to stop it. In fact, Mike egged him on—asking the mobster to repeat the name of the object of his contempt, which Cohen did gladly, before going on to slander other top officials in the Los Angeles Police Department.

This was live television. The pronouncements uttered by Cohen were transmitted unedited over the airwaves, with no attempts to qualify them.

In his 1984 memoir, *Close Encounters*, Mike imagined what he *wishes* he had said to Cohen in the interview: "You're calling him a sadistic degenerate and that's undoubtedly actionable. I want to dissociate myself from all such statements unless you can prove to me at this instant that he is indeed a sadistic degenerate."[6] But that didn't happen.

"I'm afraid I was hypnotized," Mike admits.[7] "I was caught up in the drama of the moment."[8]

Ted Yates and Mike reviewed the program the moment they were off the air. They knew they were in trouble. They confronted Cohen, who downplayed the whole affair. "Mike, Ted, forget it . . . [Parker] wouldn't dare touch me. He won't sue. I have so much on this guy, he wouldn't dare sue."[9]

Mike and Ted hardly felt reassured. While Cohen might have information to protect himself from retribution, the network and its employees were fair game. Indeed, the next day Chief Parker held a press conference in which he declared: "I am concerned about the authority of a television station to use that type of slander."

While the mood at the network turned panicky, one man was feeling vindicated that the Wallace team had stumbled so quickly. John Charles Daly, who served as president of ABC News and also anchored the evening newscast, had warned his superiors against hiring Mike in the first place. Daly contended that Mike was an interviewer, not a journalist, and that he and his team were bound to bring trouble to the network.

The Wallace team, for their part, detested Daly. "John Daly was a prim, priggish, professorial, goyish guy," says Ramrus. "He was the anti-Wallace. Wallace was the anti–John Daly."[10]

Daly was threatened by Mike's skyrocketing reputation and took special delight when the ABC brass decided to offer an apology during the following week's telecast. ABC president Oliver Treyz made a personal appearance on the air along with Leonard Goldenson, the same man who had urged Wallace to make "the building shake." The contrite duo went on air in front of a sheepish Mike Wallace, declaring:

Last Sunday night something most unfortunate, unexpected and profoundly regrettable occurred while Mr. Wallace was questioning Mickey Cohen. Leonard Goldenson joins me most earnestly in stating that the American Broadcasting Company retracts and withdraws in full all statements made on last Sunday's program concerning the Los Angeles city government, and specifically Police Chief William Parker… The American Broadcasting Company deeply regrets the matter and offers its sincere apologies.

Then Mike lamely chimed in with: "I join sincerely and earnestly in the statement of retraction and apology." But it was not enough to mollify Chief Parker, who promptly filed a $2-million lawsuit against ABC. Captain James Hamilton, another officer who had been defamed, sued ABC for an additional $1 million. And the dominoes began to fall.

Mike had been scheduled to appear as the "mystery guest" on the CBS panel show, *What's My Line?* But, in the wake of the mushrooming Cohen scandal, CBS retracted its offer, due in large measure to the fact that the show's moderator was none other than Mike's detractor, John Daly. (In these early days of television, it was not unheard of for a news anchor on one network to host a game show on a competing network.)

"When [the producers] asked my opinion about using Mike Wallace as the mystery guest," John Daly told *The New York Times*, "I said I thought it would be an unwise decision. 'What's My Line?' is an ad lib program and there would be no way to assure that the Mickey Cohen matter would not be raised."[11]

Mike had had just about enough of Daly's shenanigans. As Ramrus explains: "Mike was not the sort of guy to let these sleights go by. He confronted them."[12]

So he called Daly and proposed a lunch to iron out their differences. But Daly declined, declaring: "Mr. Wallace, I'm very sorry but I cannot break bread with you."

"He didn't want any part of Wallace," says Ramrus.

The press, for its part, was also cooling on the once unstoppable Mike. *Times* critic Jack Gould, a long-standing and vocal supporter of Mike's since his arrival in New York, ran a highly critical piece whose premise was that *The Mike Wallace Interview* simply did not have the same quality as the local show, *Night Beat*—precisely what Mike had feared. While Gould praised Wallace for his contribution to "forthright discussion" on the airwaves, he criticized him both for being too soft in the first three shows and too sensationalistic in the Mickey Cohen episode:

Mature television journalism dictates precautions in an instance such as this. This type of interview at the very least should be done on film so that the journalist can retain control over what he is reporting. Reportorial fearlessness does not mean abdication of responsibility...

Then Gould concluded:

The great virtue of Mr. Wallace's local program has been its relaxed quality. He has not operated under any compulsion to regard his presentation as a contest which he always has to win. On the network, however, he has assumed more of the role of a prosecuting attorney who has to prove a point. There is a tension and a combativeness which has not shown Mr. Wallace at his best; he may disown any inclination to sensationalism but his approach may create the environment in which it thrives.

The lawsuits against ABC were eventually settled out of court—Parker received $45,000, Hamilton $22,500—but the insurance company decided they could no longer underwrite the show. After a desperate series of calls by the ABC legal department, Lloyds of London agreed to take over the coverage, but only under strict and humiliating conditions.

"Every night we went on the air, a lawyer would sit in the studio where, facing me, he would hold up cue cards at sensitive moments warning me to BE CAREFUL or STOP or RETREAT," wrote Mike in his memoir. "Like a baby with its bib and a dog with its leash, I was judged to be in need of a legal teleprompter."[13]

And that wasn't the only indignity the team had to face. "We had to submit our questions in advance to someone upstairs and they assigned us someone by the name of Don Coe," explains Al Ramrus. "Don Coe was a fat, flabby fool."[14]

One week they were set to interview Frank Lloyd Wright, and Coe objected to a question regarding a house that Wright designed but never built for Arthur Miller and Marilyn Monroe. The question was: "What do you think of Marilyn Monroe's architecture?"

"You can't ask that because it's an indecent question," declared Coe.

"We ignored it, of course," said Ramrus. "But that's the level of stupidity and ignorance that we had to deal with."

It made Mike and Ted more determined than ever to push the limits of the medium, and they decided to take their cameras on the road to Little Rock, Arkansas—frontline in the struggle for desegregation of the public schools. Despite the 1954 Supreme Court ruling mandating integration, Governor Orville Faubus deployed the Arkansas National Guard to prevent Negro students from entering Central High School in Little Rock in the fall of 1957.

Faubus was an interesting character. He came from humble origins, born in a log cabin to a socialist father who distrusted capitalism, declaring that both blacks and whites were its victims. Yet despite this upbringing, Faubus became increasingly right-wing as a politician, especially when it served his ambitions. In 1957, he decided to stand up to President Eisenhower and defy the federal desegregation law. The impasse lasted eighteen days, until the president federalized the Arkansas National Guard and sent in federal troops to enforce integration. It made Faubus a local hero and a national news story.

So Wallace and his team descended on the Governor's Mansion in Little Rock to hear it from the horse's mouth. But the governor dodged and evaded each pointed inquiry, refusing to state his personal view on integration. Mike continued to push.

"Governor, do you ever sit in this Executive Mansion now and read newspapers with your name in the headlines and say to yourself: 'Orville Faubus, hillbilly from Greasy Creek, Arkansas, who had got out of high school just twenty-three years ago, at the age of twenty-four, who would have imagined this?' And do you say to yourself, 'I wish I weren't here'?"

The governor calmly repeated his assertion that you cannot change the hearts of people by force of law. "When people feel that [desegregation] is being forced down their throat, against their will, then they naturally react. The American people have always been that way, Mr. Wallace."

Though the governor had judiciously avoided declaring his own views on the subject of desegregation, Mike's interview was nonetheless riveting and made national news, including a front page story in *The New York Times*. It landed Mike on the cover of *Newsweek*, too—a fact that Mike took pleasure rubbing in the face of John Daly.

Encouraged by their success in Little Rock, Mike and Ted soon set their sights on another political story, this one potentially even more explosive. It would require a rather more ambitious road trip—braving the backwoods of Cuba to interview a mysterious bearded revolutionary named Fidel Castro, who was in hiding with his loyal band of guerillas.

Before the Cuban Revolution, Castro remained a quixotic figure, whose ambitions to overthrow the government of Fulgencio Batista were considered to be a pipe dream, at best. Yet Mike and Ted sensed that Castro could be a big story. It was the height of the Cold War, after all, and if Castro succeeded he would establish a communist state within a stone's throw of the United States. Thus, Ted Yates made contact with some Cuban exiles in Miami who guaranteed they could deliver Fidel. There was only one problem—it would cost money to get Mike and his crew to a remote jungle hideout in Cuba, and the person who controlled the purse strings at ABC News was none other than John Daly, who promptly vetoed the idea in a condescending lecture:

"Wallace, Yates. This is simply another indication that you people just don't know what you're up to. Fidel Castro is a has-been. He's no longer a figure of importance."[15]

Sensing the gauntlet had been thrown down, Mike decided to finance the trip himself. He ordered his secretary, Rita Quinn, to round up mosquito repellant, canteens and other jungle gear. Adventurer Ted Yates was in heaven as they boarded the plane for Miami.

But their contacts failed to pan out. For days, they waited in their Miami hotel, hoping that a true conduit to Castro would emerge. "It was like waiting for Godot," grumbled Mike.[16] The channel to Fidel failed to materialize and, after days of twiddling their thumbs, the Wallace team was forced to return empty-handed to New York.

It was not to be their last overseas wild-goose chase, however. Months later, they found themselves in similar circumstances in the Middle East— on Mike's first visit to the hotspot. Certain Arabs in New York had led Mike to believe that they could arrange an interview with Egyptian president Gamal Abdel Nasser, the most powerful figure in the region. Such an interview, like the one attempted with Fidel Castro, would have been considered a journalistic coup.

"Mike was grasping at every opportunity to strengthen his credentials as a journalist," says Gary Paul Gates.[17]

Thus, Mike, along with Ted Yates and Al Ramrus, enthusiastically set off for Cairo, where they were picked up by a shady character with a gun. Yates felt right in his element.

But this mission, much like the jaunt to Miami, was to be entirely devoid of action. Their Egyptian hosts counseled patience—things move slowly in the Middle East.

"They were urged to relax, take in the pyramids," recounts Gary Paul Gates, "and in due course they would be given an appointment with President Nasser."[18]

It never happened. Nasser had no intention of granting an interview to this second-string reporter from America, a Jew no less. They sat waiting in Cairo for ten days, then packed their bags.

"It was terribly humiliating to fly home with our tail between our legs," remembers Ramrus.[19]

Mike returned to the ABC newsroom with two strikes against him. And the third came soon enough. The subject this time was fellow journalist Drew Pearson.

Pearson, born in a Quaker household in 1897, was a generation older than Mike. Balding, with a bushy moustache, he projected a mild, grandfatherly air. But that belied his reputation as one of the most hard-hitting and controversial reporters in Washington.

He was dubbed "the greatest muckraker of all time" in the *Chicago Tribune Book World* by Robert Sherrill, who went on to say: "Woodward and Bernstein may have toppled Richard Nixon, but as practitioners of muckraking they are drab apprentices compared to Pearson."[20]

Politicians, justifiably terrified of Drew Pearson, would viciously attack his credibility and credentials. President Roosevelt had called him a chronic liar; President Truman, a son of a bitch and a vicious liar; and Tennessee senator Kenneth McKellar filled up nearly six pages of the Congressional Record, calling Pearson every type of liar in the book: ". . . ignorant liar, a pusillanimous liar, a peewee liar, a liar during his manhood, a liar by profession, a liar in the day time, and a liar in the night time. A revolving, constitutional, unmitigated, infamous liar . . ." The litany was endless.

During the 1950s' Red Scare, Pearson was one of the few reporters aside from Edward R. Murrow to take Senator Joseph McCarthy repeatedly to task, in dozens of news columns and innumerable radio broadcasts, for creating an atmosphere of mass paranoia. So persistent were Pearson's attacks that an inebriated McCarthy once muttered to Assistant Attorney General Joe Keenan that he was considering "bumping Pearson off."[21]

Arthur Cooper of *Newsweek* stated simply that Pearson was "that rare combination of showman and newsman, and every day his pungent blend of punditry and titillating gossip would set off quaking shocks on the Washington seismograph . . . It is unlikely—and this may not be a bad thing—that any newsman will ever again wield as much influence as Pearson."[22]

Until Mike Wallace, that is. Indeed, Pearson was Mike's kind of reporter, and Mike was thrilled to have him on the show. Perhaps a little too thrilled.

After his opening plug for Parliament Cigarettes, the show's sponsor, Mike launched into a discussion of global politics, then turned the conversation to a young presidential hopeful—and walked straight into a minefield:

> MIKE: Mr. Nixon would seem to be the glamour boy of the Republican Party, the Democratic glamour boy would seem to be Senator Jack Kennedy. In your column on October 27th, you wrote that Senator Kennedy's, and I quote, "Millionaire McCarthyite father, crusty old Joseph P. Kennedy . . . is spending a fortune on a publicity machine to make Jack's name well-known. No candidate in history," you wrote, "has ever had so much money spent on a public relations advance buildup" end quote. What significance do you see in this, aside from the fact that Joe Kennedy would like to see Jack Kennedy President of the United States?
>
> PEARSON: Well, I don't know exactly what other significance other than the fact that I don't believe he should have a synthetic public relations buildup for any job of that kind. Jack Kennedy is a fine young fellow, a very personable fellow, but he isn't as good as that public relations campaign makes him out to be. He is the only man in history that I know who won a Pulitzer Prize on a book which was ghostwritten for him, which indicates the kind of public relations buildup he's had.
>
> MIKE: Who wrote the book for him?
>
> PEARSON: I don't recall at the present moment, I . . .

MIKE: You know for a fact, Drew . . . ?

PEARSON: Yes.

MIKE: That the book?

PEARSON: I do know.

MIKE: *Profiles in Courage* was written for Senator Kennedy, by somebody else?

PEARSON: I do.

MIKE: And he got a Pulitzer Prize for it, and . . .

PEARSON: He did.

MIKE: And he has never acknowledged the fact?

PEARSON: No, he has not. There's a little wisecrack around the Senate about Jack, who is a very handsome young man as you know, who some of his colleagues say, "Jack, I wish you had a little bit . . . uh . . . less profile and more courage . . ."

It was another contentious bombshell dropped on national television before Mike Wallace, who had no idea at the time whether Drew Pearson's accusation had merit. Though denied for decades by the Kennedys and their allies, it is now widely accepted that John F. Kennedy did not, in fact, primarily author the book for which he accepted the 1957 Pulitzer Prize.

The book profiled eight senators, from John Quincy Adams to Robert Taft, during pivotal moments of their careers in which they demonstrated remarkable political bravery. Largely ghostwritten by Ted Sorensen, chief speechwriter to then junior senator John F. Kennedy, the first draft was rejected by the publisher Harper & Brothers, so the Kennedy team secretly sent it to Georgetown University Professor Jules Davids. One year prior, Davids had delivered a lecture on political bravery in a continuing education class attended by the senator's wife, Jacqueline. It is she who, in consultation with Professor Davids, first came up with the idea of proposing the subject of political courage to her husband as a potential book topic.

Now, one year later, when the Kennedy team realized their manuscript needed revision, they naturally returned to Davids, who agreed to help edit it. The book was finally published on January 1, 1956.

Crediting John F. Kennedy as its sole author, it received wide acclaim and quickly became a bestseller. The book was awarded the 1957 Pulitzer Prize for biography, which established Kennedy, till then considered promising but lacking in gravitas, as one of the Democratic Party's leading lights, setting the stage for his ambitions in 1960 to become the youngest elected president in U.S. history.

But Kennedy's political trajectory could easily have been derailed on December 7, 1957, when Drew Pearson "outed" him on *The Mike Wallace Interview*. Shortly after the broadcast, Senator Kennedy marched into the office of attorney Clark Clifford, a highly influential Washington power broker, who would serve as confidante and counsel to four U.S. presidents.

Kennedy began: "I've written a book, as you know, *Profiles in Courage*. Drew Pearson said I didn't write the book and it's terribly upsetting to me."[23]

As if on cue, the phone rang in the office for Senator Kennedy. He listened in grim silence for a moment, then said, "Father, I'll put Clark on," and handed over the receiver.

"This is Ambassador Kennedy," came the booming voice of multimillionaire bootlegger-gone-legit Joseph P. Kennedy, who, twenty years prior, had been appointed by President Roosevelt as Ambassador to the Court of St. James's, an honorific he made sure was not forgotten.

"Yes, Mr. Ambassador?" responded Clifford.

"Sue the bastards for fifty million dollars," he snarled.

Clifford laughed and assured the elder Kennedy that they would certainly look into the matter. But Joe Kennedy was not kidding. "Sue the bastards for fifty million dollars," he repeated.

The following day, Clifford, along with a team of other lawyers including Bobby Kennedy, marched into the office of ABC President Oliver Treyz, presenting detailed evidence to support John Kennedy's authorship of the book and demanding an on-air apology. Treyz had good reason to be worried. Given his controversial news-gathering and reporting techniques, Drew Pearson had been involved in numerous libel cases throughout his career. And, while Pearson had only lost one case, Treyz did not want to take any chances.

Not only did Treyz cave in to the Kennedy ultimatum, he even agreed to have Clifford draft the retraction. Then Treyz himself read the mea culpa on the air, saying, among other things, "We deeply regret this error and feel that it does a grave injustice to a distinguished public servant and author."

Mike fumed in silent humiliation. "I was furious at my employers for the way they caved in to the Kennedys."[24]

In Mike's eyes, this was different from the Mickey Cohen episode. Drew Pearson was no raffish gangster spewing forth a torrent of abusive slander. Pearson had made a measured allegation about an ambitious public figure— which, it turned out, was largely true. But the episode became another failure for Mike.

Explains Gary Paul Gates: "The experience at ABC [was] severely damaging to Wallace, who . . . had come to be regarded in many circles as a reckless hip-shooter whose thirst for sensationalism had embarrassed his network."[25]

The wind had been knocked out of Mike's sails and he found himself in the doldrums. His interviews lacked energy. He had lost his fire. In one interview, he asked actor Peter Ustinov, "Does it worry you that you are only a *minor* genius?" It a question that Mike might well have been asking himself.

The coup de grace came when the Philip Morris company, longtime underwriter of *The Mike Wallace Interview*, declared that it would no longer sponsor the show. "I reached the conclusion that there was no real future for me at ABC," sighed Mike philosophically, ". . . as long as John Daly remained in charge of the news operation."[26]

So he began searching for another job.

Chapter Seven

Floundering

T he situation in late 1958 could hardly have been more disheartening. Though Mike already had one foot out the door, the terms of his contract forced him to remain at ABC in a lame-duck capacity; the network kept paying him, but John Daly made sure he was given no other news assignments.[1] As described in a subsequent *TV Guide* story: "In less than two years, the young man with the fearless spirit had plunged from a position of glory to a position of silent pariahdom."[2]

In July of 1958, *The New York Times* ran a piece with the headline: WALLACE FUTURE ON TV IN QUESTION. "Mike Wallace's career as a television interviewer appears to be at the crossroads," began the column, which went on to quote Mike as having "no plans for the future"[3]—an almost unfathomable statement for someone as career-minded as Mike, yet a first hint, perhaps, of the depression that would one day nearly consume him.

Some Wallace supporters, like gadfly author Philip Wiley, whom Mike had interviewed on *Night Beat*, saw Wallace's defeat as a symptom of "entrenched cowardice" on the part of the TV establishment. Mike had been destroyed, he said, by "men who were so unmanly that they made themselves intellectual nothings to prevent the risk of offending anybody."[4]

But while Mike was down, he was certainly not out. The blow was nothing compared to those that would soon befall him, and like a seasoned pugilist he would soon get to his feet, regroup and come out swinging. This new round happened to coincide with a rightward shift in Mike's political thinking, for this is the moment that he crossed paths with the philosophy of Ayn Rand.

Mike had hired an old journalistic acquaintance, Edith Efron, to help him write a newspaper column, *Mike Wallace Asks*, published weekly in *The New York Post*. Like most New York Jewish intellectuals at the time, Efron's politics ran liberal. In researching a particular column, she happened to interview Ayn Rand, whose *Atlas Shrugged* had just been published, espousing its philosophy of "Objectivism." Rand boldly declared that the moral purpose of life is the pursuit of one's own happiness and self-interest, and that the only social system consistent with this morality is absolute respect for individual rights embodied in pure laissez-faire capitalism.

Efron was, surprisingly, impressed by the encounter with Rand and, after reading her work, found herself drifting from liberal to libertarian. Excited by her new credo, Efron tried to foist *Atlas Shrugged* upon fellow Wallace staffer Al Ramrus, who was appalled.

"To me [Ayn Rand] was the equivalent of the anti-Christ," remembers Ramrus. "I never read her because intellectuals did not read Ayn Rand. She was so beneath me to read."[5]

But Efron would not relent. Ramrus explains: "Edith pressured me into reading the novel and I went through a similar conversion. Even Rita Quinn, our secretary, joined the ranks. Now, Mike found himself surrounded by conservatives, libertarians, heretics . . . His entire fucking staff!"

This was highly unusual at the time. As Ramrus wrote about this period:

It's almost impossible now to imagine what it was like then. With the occasional exception of a William F. Buckley appearance (and he was regarded not seriously but as an exotic weirdo, which, in a way, he was) you never heard on radio or TV anything other than praise for the welfare system, public education, government control of the airwaves, high taxation, the whole

statist package. To deviate from this in network news probably meant not get-
ting a job or losing a job.

Nobody had to ask about one's political opinions. It was correctly taken
for granted that everyone was a nice little liberal with a good heart and beau-
tiful soul. The liberal orthodoxy was as pervasive as the Muslim orthodoxy
in Saudi Arabia.

Ted [Yates] was an exception, a political conservative, but not a militant
or a crusader. Ted had exceptionally sensitive social antennae and could steer
his way through almost any delicate area without stirring up trouble or gen-
erating conflict.[6]

Yates kept his politics to himself. Mike, for his part, had been an out-
spoken conventional liberal up to this point. But the environment could
not help but rub off on him. Mike would eventually interview Ayn Rand,
in her first television appearance. And the conservatives in his midst would
ultimately affect Mike's presidential voting record in the decade to come.
Despite their common Brookline heritage, he remained singularly unimpressed with (and suspicious of) John Kennedy, voting instead for Richard
Nixon in 1960 and again in 1968. In private, he even admitted to certain
colleagues that he voted for Barry Goldwater in 1964.[7]

Along with this political shift came a personal one—a rapprochement
with his estranged sons, Peter and Chris, now fifteen and eleven. They had
been living in Chicago with their mother, Norma (Kappy) Kaphan, and
rarely saw their father.

Peter was a bright and sensitive young man, well aware of his father's
fame and misfortune, but he lacked a real relationship with this largely
mythic Mike Wallace. The opportunity came when Kappy remarried a
man from New York named William Leonard, who would later become a
pivotal figure in Mike's ascent in television news by paving the way for him
at CBS. (In decades to come, Leonard, as president of CBS News, would
become Mike's boss and one day field the Oval Office call from Jimmy
Carter, imploring the network to kill an embarrassing *60 Minutes* story
about covert operations in Iran.) Back in 1957 when he began courting

Norma, Leonard had Mike's dream job: working as a TV and radio newsman for CBS. In fact, their biographies have some striking similarities.

Born two years after Mike, Leonard, like Wallace, served in the Navy after graduating from college, then entered the nascent world of radio broadcasting as host of a successful magazine-show about New York City. But Leonard, more unassuming and modest than Mike, did not have nearly his charisma and doggedness, a fact that was welcomed by Norma Kaphan who needed a more stable and reliable mate.

Leonard suffered from serious health issues, however. As recounted in his 1987 memoir: "In October 1956, at the age of forty, I had a fairly severe heart attack. I was in the hospital for nearly six weeks, unable to continue my radio or television programs, certainly for months, and, for all I knew at the time, perhaps forever. By this time my first wife and I had separated and I was living in Manhattan, my income, as well as my health, somewhat less than blossoming."[8]

But Norma saw something in Bill Leonard that she fell in love with. He was a kind, generous man, loyal to a fault and a committed father— with *six sons* already from marriage number one.

Bill and Norma were wed in May 1957. As Leonard modestly admits: "I was no great prospect. Not only was I in questionable health, but also I brought with me the part-year responsibility for six young boys."[9] It was quite the brood.

"After our wedding we set upon our honeymoon to a lakeside cottage near Goshen, New York, lent by a friend," remembers Leonard. "Some honeymoon: Kappy and I and *eight* boys—for with us also were her two sons, Peter and Chris, who soon became as close to me as any of my own."

Indeed, Leonard was a stabilizing force and mentor in the lives of the Wallace boys during their formative years. He also encouraged them to develop a relationship with their biological father, and Peter had an advantage in that regard, for he was old enough to remember Mike from his childhood in Chicago. To Chris, however, Mike remained a virtual stranger. Peter nudged his younger sibling to try and reach out to their dad, as did

Bill Leonard. Now that they all lived in New York, Mike was able to spend more time with his sons.

It was awkward, at first, between Chris and Mike. Mike found he had much more in common with Peter, a gifted writer with journalistic aspirations. An excellent student, Peter was admitted to Yale in 1959. But while his sons were beginning to thrive, Mike's own prospects seemed to be dimming.

When his contract finally expired at ABC, the choices were few. The networks wanted nothing to do with Mike Wallace. Luckily, Ted Cott, his former employer at Channel 5, now found himself at another local New York station, Channel 13, where he needed a news team.

It takes courage for a man as ambitious as Mike to accept a highly visible demotion from his coast-to-coast perch at a major network back to relative anonymity on local airwaves. But that's exactly what he did. And this is where he and Ted Yates parted ways.

Says Al Ramrus, who followed Mike to Channel 13: "[Ted] and Mike really started to rub each other the wrong way towards the end. Ted was very ambitious, [and] we found ourselves in this stagnant puddle."[10]

Yates, with a growing family to support, went to work for NBC, where he would produce *David Brinkley's Journal*, the first television "news magazine," predating *60 Minutes* by more than a half decade. This pioneering show would go on to win two Emmys and a Peabody Award, the highest accolade in TV journalism, after which Yates would become a correspondent in his own right, known for his fearless reporting from war zones.

Ted Cott, meanwhile, offered Mike another desk job, the anchor slot of the Channel 13 nightly news broadcast. He also wanted to continue a version of the interview show, both as a local broadcast and also in syndication. In this third iteration, however, Mike's interview program lost its magic. With Yates gone, producing chores fell to Al Ramrus, who managed to secure a slate of colorful guests, including Ayn Rand. But something was missing. As Gary Paul Gates puts it: "This 'last hurrah' phase of *The Mike Wallace Interview* was something of an anti-climax . . . the program had become a victim of its own success. The interviews no longer conveyed the freshness and shock value that had made *Night Beat* such a conversation piece."[11]

While the interview show fizzled, a small but significant milestone was achieved on the evening newscast. Ted Cott had decided to allow the program to run thirty minutes rather than the fifteen-minute format that was the industry norm. Thus, though it was only a local newscast, Mike became the first reporter to anchor a half-hour news show. But hardly anyone noticed—his audience was miniscule and sponsors were scarce, putting financial pressure on Channel 13. Mike realized he was on a sinking ship and began to look for other opportunities.

Even though tobacco giant Philip Morris had dropped its sponsorship of his previous show at ABC, Mike had managed to remain on friendly terms with company president Joseph Cullman, who realized that Mike could still be a valuable pitchman for them. He was, in the eyes of the nation, inexorably linked to a brand. On *The Mike Wallace Interview*, each show had begun with: "My name is Mike Wallace . . . the cigarette is Philip Morris." This was followed by an enticing POV shot of a cigarette being lit and entering the "mouth" of the viewer. Mike proceeded to wax on the virtues of the Philip Morris brand for the better part of a minute, extolling its "manly mildness," its packaging, its size, and concluding: "probably the best natural smoke you've ever tasted."

Mike chain-smoked for the duration of the interview—his cigarette, the only prop on an otherwise spartan set. Mike used it to punctuate a line of questioning, jabbing the cigarette at a defensive guest, letting the smoke swirl menacingly or languidly, depending on the mood of the interrogation. It was the ultimate example of product placement—a highly visible consumer product, used and clearly enjoyed by the star of the show.

Other newsmen at the time were known to smoke, most notably Edward R. Murrow, who wound up dying of lung cancer. The cigarette in hand was a defining part of Murrow's onscreen persona. Yet Murrow never signed a contract with a tobacco company to promote a particular brand.

Mike's financial arrangement with Philip Morris was unique, and it tainted his credibility as an unbiased newsman. As Katie Couric has noted, "Wallace was a paid spokesman, long after other reporters had given up those jobs because of conflicts of interest."[12]

Mike remained unaware of the extent to which this association would prove to be a professional liability; in just a few years it would nearly sabotage his attempt to join CBS. But in 1960, as work dried up at Channel 13 and with personal expenses mounting, Mike signed a new contract with Philip Morris, agreeing to film a series of stand-alone commercials to be splashed across the airwaves. Mike's wife, Lorraine, who had gone to great lengths to improve his health through diet and exercise, must have been unhappy about the whole idea. She had lost her beloved father in November 1959. With her children, Tony and Pauline, away at boarding school, Lorraine now found herself largely alone in their twelve-room house in Sneden's Landing, with little to do.

Mike, likewise, was getting bored at Channel 13, and began looking for moonlighting gigs. He soon found himself with three additional employers. As Mike describes one of them: "A rather unimposing, blondish, slight and pale young man came into my newsroom . . . to tell me he had exclusive rights to some Soviet space footage that had never before been seen in the United States . . . I was skeptical . . . If they were available, the television news networks would surely have them."[13]

This "outsider" happened to be David Wolper, who would go on to be one of the most successful independent producers in television. His production of the miniseries *Roots* became one of the highest-rated television events of all time, nominated for an astonishing thirty-six Emmy Awards. But when Wolper crossed paths with Mike he was a young upstart, pitching his debut production; and Mike Wallace wasn't even his first choice to narrate *The Race for Space*.

Wolper had previously approached Walter Cronkite of CBS, then Chet Huntley of NBC, both of whom had been told by their networks that they couldn't work with an "outsider." Mike was not particularly overjoyed to be accepting a network hand-me-down as an assignment, but this is where he found himself in 1960, as his employer Channel 13 began to falter under mounting financial woes.

The Race for Space wound up receiving an Oscar nomination and becoming a hit in syndication, giving Mike some visibility on the national stage. He and Wolper collaborated again on the Peabody Award–winning series *Biography*, which featured half-hour profiles of well-known figures from Adolf Hitler to Babe Ruth. But *Biography*, like *The Race for Space*, was a syndicated program, which meant that Wolper had to sell it market-by-market to local stations. Though this series offered additional exposure for Mike, it was not the same as being on a network.

An offer trickled in the following year for another syndicated show, *PM East*, this time for the Westinghouse broadcast group, for which Mike had previously done a series of travelogues from across America. Yet to Mike's chagrin (and Lorraine's horror), *PM East* was a variety chat show with an attractive female co-host, Canadian Joyce Davidson. It's not that Lorraine was afraid of losing her husband to Davidson, who was married to a highly possessive and controlling husband, producer David Susskind. It's that Lorraine rightly thought *PM East* was beneath Mike, another *Mike and Buff* enterprise.

"Lorraine was embarrassed by it," says Al Ramrus, "to see her husband doing that kind of work. Mike felt terrible. It was humiliating . . . trying to compete with Jack Parr, previously Steve Allen, but he couldn't make jokes. It was just awful."[14]

PM East was scheduled to go head-to-head with *The Tonight Show*, another reason that nerves were frayed from the start. Although he had no formal title on the show, David Susskind appeared with regularity in the control room, demanding tighter close-ups of his wife and insisting that she not be photographed in the same frame as Mike. The show's producers walked a fine line when dealing with Susskind. They couldn't very well throw him out and risk losing Davidson. Susskind, who would go on to win twenty-seven Emmy Awards for his television work, was a major force in the East Coast branch of the television industry in the 1950s—perhaps *the* major force, according to the Museum of Broadcast Communications, which wrote of Susskind: "Some might say that his achievements were only surpassed by his arrogance."[15]

Needless to say, there was no love lost between Susskind and Wallace, who was equally put off by his high-maintenance wife. Marlene Sanders, who had been one of Mike's loyal staffers since *Night Beat*, was likewise disenchanted by Davidson: "The thing that really bugged me about Joyce was that we would prepare these scripts, you know, we were used to working with Mike and we would prepare material for him, background, and she would never even look at it.

"Mike really disliked her intensely and they were not the greatest happy couple on the set," continues Saunders. "He was supposedly a serious newsman and then he'd have to interview the band leader or some comic and I guess he didn't feel like that was the right image."[16]

The *PM East* experience marked a career low, though it was not entirely without redemption. The show provided a career boost for two young entertainers who would go on to become icons in their respective fields, recognized the world over. The first was Woody Allen. The other was Barbra Streisand.

It seems almost perfect in retrospect that Mike would encounter the young, fearless, supremely talented and iconoclastic Barbra Streisand during this particularly moribund chapter of his career. The two, after all, had much in common. Growing up feeling misunderstood in Jewish homes with overbearing mothers, self-conscious about their looks, they both went on to reach the top of their respective fields, becoming highly controlling, prone to temper tantrums, and utter perfectionists when it came to their work.

Mike claimed to despise Barbra the moment he set eyes upon her. But he must have been, on some level, secretly fascinated by her, for she mirrored to him his lost youth and squandered potential. Barbra ended up making more than a dozen appearances on *PM East* and her relationship with Mike would ultimately span a half century.

Back in 1960, the teenage Streisand had developed quite a following, particularly among the gay community in Greenwich Village. The talent booker for *PM East* thought she would make a good guest for the show and summoned Al Ramrus to make the necessary arrangements.

"Okay, I'll go talk to her," he said.[17]

"You can't go talk to her because she doesn't live anywhere."

"Well, how am I going to talk to her?" Ramrus asked.

"She'll call you."

The following night, according to Ramrus: "About two in the morning the phone rings. 'Hi, Al! Barbra.'

"She kept me on the phone for about two hours. She was like a fictional character . . . so colorful, so funny. I had no idea that she could sing.

"The next day she came for rehearsal and sang 'Happy Days Are Here Again,' but instead of cheerful she sang it with anger and ferocity," recalls Ramrus. "I remember turning to Mike and saying: 'She is going to be a great star.' Well Mike pooh-poohed it, he just didn't get her. She was not attractive, she was funny-looking with the nose and the crooked teeth. When he would try to interview her, she was much too smart and agile, so he couldn't sink his teeth into her."

Recalls Mike: "She had this big bunch of keys on a key ring. I said, 'What's that all about?' And she said, 'Well, I sleep around.' I said, 'What do you mean "I sleep around"?' She said, 'I have a bunch of friends who have apartments and I live over in Brooklyn. When I work sometimes I want to stay in Manhattan and these are the keys to their apartments.' "

The first of Streisand's fourteen appearances on *PM East* took place on July 12, 1961. Mike began as follows: "New York is just full of unusual and interesting girls who are starting out in show business, but few of them have the style as early as this young lady. She's nineteen years old. Her name is Barbra Streisand. . . . what are you going to sing?"

"The Kinsey Report," deadpanned Barbra.

The audience loved it. Mike shifted uneasily in his chair. Later, he asked her, "What do you want to be when you grow up, Barbra?"

She smirked. "A fireman," to chuckles from the crowd.

Streisand, in fact, was a natural entertainer, and her ease in the limelight seemed to exacerbate Mike's confusion and frustration with the state of his own career. Was he destined never to be a bona fide newsman? Did he simply have to accept the fact that he'd always be forced back into the role of TV entertainer, a role he despised?

Every so often, Mike would try to resurrect the flavor of *Night Beat* by asking a probing question of his guests, but it inevitably ended disastrously. He once queried Burt Lancaster about his legendary temper, which prompted the star to rise seething from his seat and storm off the set, the first and only time this happened to Mike Wallace.

With Mike floundering and unsure, the producers of *PM East* were forced to hire an acting coach to help him find an appropriate tone for his ad lib. They brought in Abe Burrows, the famed Broadway director who had directed Mike in *Reclining Figure;* Burrows became a sidekick to Mike, feeding him lines and comedic opportunities, much like Ed McMahon would do for Johnny Carson. The whole affair became increasingly humiliating for Mike.

The *PM East* talent bookers' persistence in inviting Barbra Streisand repeatedly to appear on the show seemed to turn Mike's mood even more foul. At some point, Streisand rented a little apartment above Oscar's Fish Store, which was around the corner from the *PM East* studio.

Recalls Marlene Sanders: "She used to come on the set and she was kind of kooky. She would bring this big bag of stuff with her and occasionally would open this big bag and eat a sandwich on the set and Mike just *hated* that! He thought it was awful. But then she'd get up and sing and blow everybody away."[18]

Three decades later, in 1991, Mike and Barbra would once again face off on the small screen. He was at the top of his game as the star of *60 Minutes;* she had just released a retrospective album of her thirty-year singing career and was promoting *The Prince of Tides*, her latest film as a star and director. The interview began with reminiscences of the *PM East* days with a walk to her old Greenwich Village apartment above Oscar's Fish

Store. Then, the broadcast cut to a spirited clip from one of the 1961 episodes, in which Mike tries to get Barbra to talk about her affinity with Zen Buddhism, which she had confided to him off camera. Streisand evades, Mike persists, then she says: "I used to like you. [Big laugh from audience] No, this is the truth; I really like what he does. A lot of people don't. [Another laugh] It's the truth! But I like you. I like the fact that you are provoking. But don't provoke *me*." [Guffaws from the crowd.]

With this set-up, Mike launched into the 1991 interview:

MIKE: You know something, I really didn't like you back thirty years ago. And I don't think you liked me either.

STREISAND: I thought you were mean, I thought you were very mean.

MIKE: I didn't think that you paid much attention to me because you were totally self-absorbed back thirty years ago.

STREISAND: Wait, wait. I resent this. I resent this. You invite me as a guest on your show and . . . we would talk about all kinds of subjects that interested me, right? So you were using me as a guest on your show to talk. Now how do you dare call me self-involved?

MIKE: Self-involved is one thing, self-absorbed is—you know something, twenty to thirty years of psychoanalysis, I say to myself, what is that she's trying to find out that takes twenty to thirty years??

STREISAND: I'm a slow learner.

"Self-absorption" was the personality trait that Mike detested most—both in himself and in others[19]—and in Mike's eyes, Barbra seemed to epitomize it. Later in the broadcast, Mike steered the conversation to Barbra's relationship with her parents, bringing her to tears by quoting her mother as saying, "Barbra doesn't have time to be close to anyone."

"You like this," says Streisand to Mike, "that forty million people have to see me like—do this?"

Mike did not respond. But, of course, Streisand was dead right. This was Mike in his element, probing the dark recesses of his interviewees' psyches, searching for answers to questions which he dared not ask of himself. Years later, while addressing a forum of journalists in Chicago in 1996, Mike would replay that clip with unabashed pride. After watching the question sink in, Barbra welling up and asking, "You like this, that forty million people see me like—do this?" Mike turned to the crowd, admitting gleefully, "And you know what? I did."[20]

The episode caused an irreparable rift in the relationship between Mike and Barbra, with a flurry of recriminating letters back and forth, followed by a decade of silence. Many years later, when Mike was interviewed by his *60 Minutes* colleagues upon announcing his retirement after forty years on the show, he would publicly apologize to Streisand for his harsh treatment of her. He would also admit that he had once attempted suicide.

Back in 1961, when those bleak feelings had not yet emerged, Mike's encounter with Streisand held up a mirror to him in ways that made Mike feel uncomfortable. She seemed to represent a freedom and self-assuredness that Mike longed to recapture. Barbra, at nineteen, was bursting with undiscovered potential and ready to seize the world by storm. Mike, at forty-three, was burnt out, nearly washed up, staring midlife in the face and desperate for resurrection.

It would come soon enough, but not before a truly devastating turn of fortune.

Chapter Eight

Death & Rebirth

P eter Wallace gazed out across the shimmering Gulf of Corinth. The nearby hills were dotted with wandering sheep, struggling to find patches to graze upon in this rugged, rocky landscape. He trained his binoculars farther up the slope to the distant Mega Spileo monastery, set dramatically like an eagle's nest against the sheer cliffs of the Peloponnesus peninsula. Secluded and virtually inaccessible, this remote sanctuary had been founded sixteen centuries prior as a simple hermitage in a cave. If one wanted a life of complete renunciation, this place was ideal. Over the last millennium, the monastery had been destroyed by fires and rebuilt nearly half a dozen times. During World War II, German occupying forces seized the mountaintop structure as a strategic lookout point, killing all the residents, a grim reminder that even men of God are not immune to the forces of evil.

What leads a man to renounce the world in search of God? The thought may have passed through Peter's mind. Despite being Jewish, part of him was actually drawn to the idea of monasticism.[1]

Peter had arrived in Greece on August 3, 1962, exactly one month shy of his twentieth birthday. An undergraduate at Yale, he had just completed his sophomore year with honors and had attended summer school in Grenoble, France. Now he was spending a few weeks backpacking across Europe, with plans to meet up with some friends in Greece. The friends were late, but Peter didn't mind. In fact, he was enjoying the solitude. It gave him time to think about his place in the world. There was something magical about this landscape. The Apostle Paul had spent eighteen months roaming these Corinthian hills before writing his epistles. Peter loved history, particularly Greek history.

As his father explained: "Pete had always wanted to go to Greece, since the time he was a kid. He used to dress in sheets like togas, make swords out of wood and shields from garbage can covers."[2]

Despite the early divorce of his parents, Peter had grown into a fine young man, in part because of the stabilizing influence of stepfather Bill Leonard, who worked at CBS News as a producer and correspondent. Under the combined influence of his father and stepfather, Peter had begun to express an interest in journalism. He'd worked for Bill Leonard during the 1960 presidential conventions and for Mike as a copy boy at Channel 13, but his aspirations were not in television. As a gifted writer and researcher, Peter's ambition was to go into print work, as a "real" reporter. As CBS News producer Av Westin puts it: "Television for many in those days was still not regarded as the journalist's dream."[3] It was print work that won you a Pulitzer.

So, for the past two years, Peter had been on staff at the *Yale Daily News*, the oldest college newspaper in the country. Mike was deeply proud of him, and perhaps, on some level, living vicariously through Peter. Having accepted that he himself might never be viewed as a bona fide journalist, Mike suspected the profession would be more welcoming to his Yale-educated progeny. Indeed, sons have a way of fulfilling the dreams of their fathers— but the outcome of this particularly story would end up horrifying everyone.

Like Peter, Mike had also spent the summer of 1962 traveling overseas. On assignment for Westinghouse, he had visited eight foreign capitals for a radio series entitled *Around the World in 40 Days*. It was an overseas reprise of *Closeup U.S.A.*, a series Mike had worked on two years earlier for Westinghouse, wherein he had driven across the United States, filing daily reports from around the nation.

Says Gary Paul Gates, "It was a richly rewarding experience [for Mike]. It marked the first time in his broadcasting career that he had a chance to work extensively as a correspondent in the field."[4]

Now, two years later, he was at it again—this time abroad. The prospect unsettled him somewhat, for his two prior overseas outings as a reporter—when he attempted and failed to land interviews with both Fidel Castro in Cuba and Gamal Nasser in Egypt—had resulted in humiliating fiascos. This time he would be on an even more ambitious itinerary, including Tokyo, Taipei, Hong Kong, Saigon, New Delhi, Cairo, Nairobi and London—though the reporting would be hardly more than a glorified travelogue. Still, globe-trotting at this pace required focus and stamina. Such a schedule would become almost commonplace during Mike's tenure at *60 Minutes*, but in 1962 it somewhat daunted him. He was glad, therefore, to have the company of his multicultural wife, fluent in French, conversant in Spanish and utterly charming. That summer marked one of the few times that Lorraine would join Mike on assignment. In the decades to come, his endless weeks on the road would cause friction between them and ultimately doom their marriage.

As they flew to India, Mike's mind was still in Saigon, where he had filed his last story. The United States had only 11,300 troops stationed in Vietnam in 1962, acting as advisors and support personnel, so it was not yet a full-fledged combat zone. But Mike was aware of its geopolitical importance as a pivotal frontline in the Cold War, and he was disappointed by how little his week in Saigon had yielded. He had tried to no avail to secure an interview with Nationalist leader Ngo Dinh Diem—Mike simply did not have the journalistic credentials to be taken seriously at that time. Says Gary Paul Gates, "His professional life that summer was at a low ebb . . . he was merely dabbling on the fringes of journalism."[5]

So Mike had to settle, instead, for Ngo's sister-in-law Ngo Dinh Nhu, "the Dragon Lady." As interviews go, it was fairly uneventful—and he was not pleased. Lorraine told him to take a deep breath and let it go. But Wallace would not soon forget his week in Saigon, for it marked the beginning of a summer that would sink him into his first major depression.

When he returned to New York in late August, he received a call from Bill Leonard, stepfather to his children, explaining that he and Kappy had not heard from Peter in nearly a month. The boy had been fastidious about writing home once a week, so the sudden cessation of correspondence was worrisome. They had the name of a Greek youth hostel as his last known whereabouts. Mike mulled it over and, despite having just gotten off an airplane, decided to fly to Athens.

Arriving in Greece, Mike met with the American Consul, who was able to secure an address for the youth hostel and graciously offered to escort Mike in his search. They traveled fifty kilometers west from Athens by automobile and arrived at a small hostel outside Corinth. The entourage of Americans walked into the lobby where they were presented with evidence, which Mike found both hopeful and heartbreaking: Peter's bags.

The suitcases had been gathering dust in a storage room for the better part of a month, which was the last time Peter had been seen in those parts. He had left, it seemed, with a day pack—and never returned. With the help of a translator and a wallet photograph, Mike roamed the village, asking if anyone had spotted the missing American. A shepherd said he had seen the boy hiking toward the nearby monastery. They rounded up a pair of mules and the party set off, climbing the steep switchbacks in the blazing afternoon sun.

As Mike scanned the rugged landscape for signs of Peter, he spotted a crumbled ledge, where the rocks had given way in a mini-avalanche. Mike leaped off his mule and approached the precipice with caution and surging trepidation. He peered down into the abyss. There was his son.

Peter's twisted, lifeless body lay strewn fifty feet below on the craggy rocks, his clothing in tatters, his backpack dashed open. Mike found himself short of breath, his mind reeling. Was it intentional . . . could it have been a suicide? Not Peter. Not like this. This was an accident. A terrible, grisly accident.

Mike spun to the American Consul, whose face was grim and deeply compassionate. For a father to discover his own son like this—the tragedy is almost unfathomable.

Although Mike was emotionally ravaged, the group had to go back into town and hire some men to build a wooden casket. It was dark by the time they finished. As he rode in a truck behind the one carrying the casket, he felt an annihilating sense of doom and mushrooming panic: would he ever come to terms with the senselessness of Peter's death? The healing process would, in fact, take the better part of his life.

Mike flew back to New York to convey the devastating news in person to his ex-wife, Kappy. Bill Leonard took Mike aside and thanked him. If Mike hadn't followed his instincts to search for Peter in person, they might never have known what had become of him—which would have been far worse.

The grief-stricken family returned to Greece for the funeral, a sizable entourage including Mike, Kappy and their surviving son Chris, who was fourteen at the time and utterly shell-shocked at the loss of the older brother whom he idolized. They had made the decision to bury Peter, Grecophile that he was, on the mountainside where he had died. Bill Leonard was in attendance along with his son Andrew, the eldest of six from his previous marriage, and the one who had grown closest to stepbrother Peter. Notably absent were Loraine and her children, Pauline and Anthony. While Mike would have liked to have had them along, it would have proven awkward for Kappy.

Descending upon the tiny hill town, the family made arrangements to acquire a small plot of land and hired a blacksmith to construct a wrought-iron perimeter fence. The local Greek Orthodox priest from the Church of St. Demetrios, Father Anastassios Papageorigiou, officiated at the interment. With flies buzzing and goats bleating on the surrounding hillside, the experience felt entirely surreal to Mike. His foundation had been shaken at its core.

The pain of Peter's death was so intense that Mike could barely speak of it. Even now he gropes for words to describe his feelings, but they don't come easily. "You can imagine," he says. "It was the worst thing that ever happened to me."[6]

When he returned home to Lorraine in September 1962, he had changed. With the many misgivings Mike had about his career, he had had great journalistic hopes for Peter. The boy's death had left Mike paralyzed. When Mark Goodson, a TV producer and former employer, offered Mike the hosting job for a new game show, *Match Game*, Mike turned him down flat. He just couldn't bring himself simply to jump, once again, at the next opportunity on the television treadmill.

As Gary Paul Gates explains it: "His customary justification for accepting those jobs—that he had the future of his kids to consider—had a rather hollow ring now that Peter was gone."[7]

As he had done in other difficult periods, Mike forced himself to look squarely at his life's purpose. His mind went back to an earlier period of despondency, following the breakup of his second marriage to Buff Cobb and the ill-fated stint as a Broadway actor. He had concluded back then that his life was going nowhere and had resolved to make some significant changes. That's when Mike went to work for Ted Cott at the news division of Channel 5, where he had crossed paths with Ted Yates with whom he created *Night Beat*. And shortly thereafter Mike had met Lorraine.

In her quiet wisdom, Lorraine had known all along what made Mike tick. She could see that he thrived when working as a journalist, and suffered, ultimately, when he dabbled in all those other television entertainment roles he seemed incapable, at times, of turning down. She encouraged Mike, *this* time, to stick to his guns and hold out for a job for which he was worthy. And she was not alone in her advice.

Remembers Mike: "There was a man named Arthur Goldsmith, an older man of some means . . . an old bachelor whom we'd met at a dinner party. He used to say: 'You are wasting yourself. You're capable of more. You're better than what you're doing.' I remember saying: 'I'm too old, I'm too far along . . . time has passed me by to make these kinds of changes.' "[8]

And that was even before the loss of Peter. Now his perspective had changed entirely. "Lorraine and I talked about it and talked about it for such a long time . . . We talked about . . . concentrating on work that was more worthwhile and somehow I had been reluctant to do or afraid or unwilling to do."[9]

At forty-four years old, Mike figured it was now or never. He typed letters to the presidents of the three network news divisions, declaring his intention to devote himself exclusively to journalism. Then came the rub. No one was interested.

Mike's image had been deeply tainted, more so than he even realized, by his career choices. All the game shows, chat shows and quiz shows were now coming back to haunt him. Even more damaging were the myriad commercials where Mike had endorsed everything from Fluffo shortening to Peter Pan peanut butter. Worst of all, of course, were the cigarettes.

Several years prior, when David Wolper had tried to sell *The Race for Space*, narrated by Mike, to the networks, it was Mike's association with Philip Morris that had quashed any interest at CBS. Wolper was told by a blunt CBS news executive: "We wouldn't want the man who measures the quarter inch filter on a Parliament cigarette measuring the missile gap between the Soviets and the Americans."[10]

In the 1950s, smokers and smoking were ubiquitous—but things had begun to change in the ensuing decade. Beginning in 1962, after pressure from public health groups, President Kennedy authorized the Surgeon General's Office to take on the task of reviewing literature on smoking and health and begin issuing periodic reports.

In the upheaval following Peter's death, Mike decided formally to terminate his relationship with Philip Morris, which he hoped would enhance his journalistic credibility, but it would also eliminate his last remaining source of income, a gamble he was prepared to take in the tumultuous fall of 1962.

Unfortunately, the move didn't help—for it wasn't merely the association with cigarettes that tainted Mike, it was the seeming recklessness and bravura of his onscreen persona that had network executives worried. His reputation was still smarting from the Mickey Cohen libel suit and other controversies. Simply stated, no one wanted to work with Mike; his mood went from despondency to despair.

As Gary Paul Gates puts it: "Wallace thrived on work—it was tantamount to a psychic need—but now, for the first time, he had nothing to do, nowhere to go . . . The long, empty hours of sitting around at home waiting for the phone to ring made each day a misery."[11]

Mike dreaded running into acquaintances who would invariably ask what he was up to, which would force him to admit he had no job and no prospects. His life, according to Gates, had become "a social embarrassment."[12] So Mike went into a self-imposed hibernation, holing himself up in his home—which only worsened his isolation and anguish.

Lorraine was deeply nurturing and remained confident that things would turn around. Support came from other quarters, as well. In this bleak period, dozens of strangers wrote letters of sympathy to Mike, reassuring him that he was not alone—they, too, had lost grown children in freak accidents. But it wasn't any comfort to Mike, who, as the days became gray and cold in the winter of 1962, sank deeper and deeper into depression.

For someone who made a habit of being keenly aware of his net worth, Mike found himself sitting numbly, watching the digits hemorrhage from his bank account in the service of their substantial overhead. But what was he to do? No one would hire him as a newsman. And he just couldn't bring himself to put on his huckster hat and sell out again.

The holiday season came and went, but there was little rejoicing in the Wallace household. The weather was brutal that winter, one of the coldest Januaries on record. Then, in February 1963, a reprieve finally arrived in the form of a phone call from California. A Los Angeles TV station, KTLA, was interested in hiring Mike to anchor their local newscast. It was another demotion to the local airwaves, not exactly what he had hoped for. Plus, it would mean moving the household to California, where Lorraine had been raised and had a series of less than fond memories, including two failed marriages. Nonetheless, she was game to do whatever was necessary to get her husband back on his feet.

Mike tried to remain philosophical about it: "Maybe if I go to the minors, the majors will take a look."[13] But he had other reservations—accepting the job would put him three thousand miles away from Chris, who needed Mike more than ever now that his brother was gone. Peter's death drove home to Mike what an absentee father he had been all of these years. He knew he couldn't change things overnight, but he owed it to Chris at least to try. Tensions between the households were beginning to thaw. The shared grief over Peter's death had started to heal the rift between Mike and his ex-wife. Her husband, Bill Leonard, accustomed to getting an earful from Kappy regarding how Mike had mistreated her, noticed a change in Kappy's feelings towards Mike, which were shifting to pity and even compassion.

Wallace was a changed man, no longer interested in chasing big TV paydays. He had given up commercial endorsements and other non-journalistic pursuits, intent on dedicating himself entirely to the news. With Bill Leonard as the likely conduit, the information reached CBS News President Dick Salant who mulled it over and decided to bring Mike in for a meeting.

Mike had no way of knowing as he entered the CBS newsroom on this day that it would become his home for the next half century. Mike entered the opulent office of CBS News President Richard Salant. The two men already knew each other from Mike's days at *Night Beat*, where Salant had appeared on the show as a guest.

"Like so many idiots before and after me, I just knew that I was smarter than Mike and that he couldn't lay a glove on me," remembers Salant. "Sure enough, he lacerated me. But he did it fair and square. It was the essence of Mike: he didn't bully; he just cut through my obfuscations, exposed my fallacies, and got to the heart of the issues. *He* didn't win; the cause of an informed public did."[14]

Salant admired Mike, but he was nearly alone at CBS: "Some of my news colleagues had doubts about the non-journalistic portions of Mike's résumé. They believed he had forfeited the right to reenter journalism because he had acted in a play, he had done some entertainment shows on television and he had made television commercials for Parliament cigarettes. Whatever Mike had done, I knew that my journalistic résumé was much skimpier than his."

Salant was a Harvard-educated lawyer, who had graduated with honors and served as editor of the *Harvard Law Review*. What he lacked in journalistic credentials, he made up for in deal-making acumen. His first question to Mike in that meeting was: "If you're that serious, will you go to work for $40,000 a year?"

Mike nodded quietly. That was one quarter of what he had been making.

"Good," said Salant. "We'll give you a five-minute radio show called *Personal Close-up*, and maybe some local news."

The two men shook hands. For the first time in months, Mike's fortunes seemed to be turning around. He would remember this moment for the rest of his life. Some forty years hence, Mike would dedicate his 2005 memoir, *Between You and Me*, to his first boss at CBS, writing: "To Dick Salant, who, back in 1963 as President of CBS News, gave me the job and the life he knew I yearned for."

One wonders what fate would have befallen Mike Wallace but for this bold decision by Salant. It's doubtful, given the size of Mike's talent and personality, he would have languished on local airwaves for long. But without this admittance to CBS, there would have been no *60 Minutes*, which ultimately turned Mike into a legend.

It would not be easy, however. Indeed, when he first walked through the doors of CBS News, most of his colleagues assumed he would fail. This, after all, was the realm of the Edward R. Murrows and Walter Cronkites. No one expected him to join their ranks.

Now it was up to Mike to prove them wrong.

Chapter Nine

Network News

The business of network news was and remains cutthroat. There is competition not just between rival networks but within the newsroom itself, among correspondents and their respective staffs. It's important to cultivate allies in this environment, and that made it especially difficult for Mike when he first joined CBS in 1963. Whereas in his previous network news stint at ABC he had but a single nemesis in John Daly, here at CBS many were rooting for Mike to fail.

Nonetheless, it was an exhilarating time to be a part of the Columbia Broadcasting System, which had dominated the ratings battle since 1955 and was well on its way to earning its crown as the "Tiffany Network." The man behind its success, William S. Paley, has been described by *The New York Times* as "a 20th-century visionary with the ambitions of a 19th-century robber-baron;"[1] or, as producer Don Hewitt put it, "Part P.T. Barnum, part Henry Luce."[2]

Though NBC had a substantial head start on CBS when Paley took control of the fledgling radio network in 1928, the twenty-seven-year-old shrewdly decided to concentrate his efforts on news and public affairs to give his venture an aura of class and respectability. The gambit paid off with Edward R. Murrow's stellar reporting during World War II, which established CBS as the leader in broadcast journalism.

Next, Paley set his sights on usurping NBC's dominance in entertainment programming. Despite a long-standing gentlemen's agreement not to poach talent from his NBC counterpart, General David Sarnoff, Paley used persuasion, flattery and hard cash to lure Jack Benny, Amos 'n' Andy and other stars into the CBS fold. By the late 1950s, with shows like *Gunsmoke* and *I Love Lucy*, CBS began a decades-long streak as leader of the ratings wars. But with this rise on the entertainment side came an ironic slip in the news division, as CBS fell into second place behind perennial rival NBC. The problem was that the CBS star reporter, Edward R. Murrow, was a radio man who did not particularly like the newfangled medium of television.

"This instrument can teach, it can illuminate; yes, and it even can inspire," Murrow said in his memorable 1948 keynote address to the Radio-Television News Directors Association in Chicago. "But it can do so only to the extent that humans are determined to use it to those ends. Otherwise, it's nothing but wires and lights in a box."

Murrow's distaste for TV's commercial underpinning would eventually lead to his resignation from the network. Thus, CBS had to stake its hopes on another man, Douglas Edwards, who, as the small world of broadcasting would have it, had worked with Mike in the early 1940s back in Detroit.

Mike Wallace and Doug Edwards had been the two "Cunningham News Aces" on WXYZ, reading headlines in a news segment sponsored by the Cunningham Drugstore chain. But, while Edwards found his way to CBS and became the nation's first news "anchorman" (a term that CBS coined) Mike had taken a meandering path through an eclectic mélange of radio and television work, often on local airwaves.

The two would not be together for long at CBS. By the time Mike showed up, Edwards had been on the air for fourteen years and the network's news division was mired in second place, where it had been some time, trailing the flashier *Huntley-Brinkley Report* on NBC. One of Dick

Salant's first moves when he took over the reins of CBS News was to axe the "old-school" Doug Edwards and fill the anchor chair with a real newsman: Walter Cronkite.

Cronkite had been a respected print reporter, like his competitor at NBC, David Brinkley, who was considered a first-class writer. Brinkley, one of the most popular newsmen in America, had also been hosting the very first television "news magazine," *David Brinkley's Journal*, a half-hour program that covered topics in greater depth, a format that would later inspire *60 Minutes*. In another small-world coincidence, the producer of *David Brinkley's Journal* was none other than Mike's former partner, Ted Yates, who was now at NBC.

Mike needed another Ted Yates, desperately. Would he find one at CBS? Maybe. But meanwhile he kept his head down, trying his best to ignore the sniggers and sneers. He worked diligently on his radio series, *Personal Close-up*, interviewing in his first few weeks on the job an impressive list of guests, including Jimmy Hoffa, Jack Benny, Moshe Dayan, Noël Coward and Gloria Steinem. So successful was Mike on this show that it would eventually be rechristened *Mike Wallace at Large*, and would become a CBS radio staple for the following two decades.

But the television side of the CBS newsroom remained unimpressed. Radio interviews, after all, had been Mike's mainstay—he could do them in his sleep. The naysayers still had serious doubts about whether he could perform as a bona fide CBS journalist in front of a television camera. The opportunity to prove himself would come soon enough.

In the spring of 1963, Mike was summoned to a meeting in Dick Salant's office, where he was introduced to a thirty-something named Av Westin. Westin, who had recently been recalled from a two-year stint at the CBS bureau in London, was a rising star in the news division. He had been at CBS since 1948, starting as a radio copy boy. When Westin learned how to use a tape recorder, he was quickly dispatched into the field. Back in those frontier days, one week's experience qualified you as an expert. Before he knew it, Westin found himself producing and directing TV news segments.

"When we went out, we were the new kids on the block and there was no one to tell us how to do it," he recalls. "Whatever we did turned out to be the way it was done."[3]

Westin became one of Dick Salant's favorite producers at the network, so, when Salant introduced Mike to Av, it was with these words: "Mike, this is Av Westin and you listen to what he says."[4] The subtext was clear: this guy is your ticket to becoming legitimate.

"Flattering words," demurs the modest Westin. But Salant had clearly recognized that Westin had an uncanny savvy about the power of television. Two decades hence, Westin would begin his 1982 memoir[5] with these lines:

> *Television news has changed the way America is governed.*
> *Television news has changed the way America votes.*
> *Television news has changed the way America thinks.*

Av Westin would have a profound effect on Mike's career at CBS. Indeed, in his own 1984 memoir, Mike groups Westin with Ted Yates and *60 Minutes* creator Don Hewitt as "one of three men . . . who came into my life at critical points and formed strong working relationships with me that were not only productive at the time, but also had positive and lasting effects on much that followed."[6]

When they first met in Salant's office, however, Westin had no idea who Mike was. Westin had spent the last few years abroad, so he had not followed the success and scandals of *Night Beat* and *The Mike Wallace Interview*. Nonetheless, Westin took an instant liking to Mike, and the feeling was mutual—which was exactly what Salant had hoped for. Dick Salant had an important mission in mind for them: to create a midmorning news show, the *CBS Morning News*.

It was a bolder move than it would appear at first, for the network at the time did little, if any, broadcasting during the morning hours. It generally went off the air after the morning show at 9 A.M. and did not resume network programming until the soaps at 1 P.M., with the morning filled with shows from local affiliates. Indeed, for the network to reclaim a slot for the *CBS Morning News* from 10 A.M. to 10:30, smack in the middle of that four-hour block, did not sit well with some of the affiliates. And they were further disgruntled by another network landgrab, this one in the evening. William S. Paley, determined to reestablish the preeminence of his network's news division, had decided to expand *CBS Evening News* from fifteen minutes to a half hour.

There was a lot of hand-wringing about this move within the newsroom. Says Av Westin, "They were concerned that audiences would be bored, or, in the words of one writer who later left to return to newspapering: 'Viewers would be *newsed* out.' "[7]

Mike watched in silent amusement as his CBS colleagues worried themselves sick with how they would fill those extra fifteen minutes, for he knew that Walter Cronkite would not, in fact, be the first anchorman to carry a half hour of news. It was Mike who had actually pioneered the format four years prior at Channel 13, albeit on the local airwaves. (Mike had also been a trailblazer in the first color broadcast of a talk show, with *Mike and Buff.*)

When news spread that Mike was getting the anchor slot on the *CBS Morning News* show, the animosity toward him reached a fevered pitch. Says Westin, "There was plenty of back-of-the-hand snickering in the CBS newsroom about hiring this 'actor anchorman.' Mike still had, according to the people in the hallway, the reek of Parliament Cigarettes on him."[8]

News writer Joan Snyder was even more blunt: "We were all quite contemptuous. Why on earth, we wondered, had this sleazy Madison Avenue pitchman been chosen to anchor a CBS News broadcast? As long as we were going camp, I would have preferred Johnny, the Philip Morris bellhop."[9]

Yet there was a double standard at work as to what constituted a "proper" CBS news broadcast. Consider that the first CBS morning news show, which was launched in 1954, featured a lion puppet named Charlemagne, who would discuss the news with the original host, none other than Walter Cronkite himself. And Cronkite makes no apologies about the puppet:

"Charlemagne . . . was a witty, erudite and acerbic critic of the daily scene. In our two- to three minute spot, I led Charlemagne into a totally ad-lib discussion of the day's news that was remarkable for its depth. A puppet can render opinions on people and things that a human commentator would not feel free to utter. It was one of the highlights of the show, and I was, and am, proud of it."[10]

Cronkite also delivered commercial messages on the show, including spots for cigarettes, which would have him lighting up on air and declaring with a look of satisfaction: "Ahhh . . . Winston tastes good like a cigarette should."

And CBS was not alone in mixing cigarettes with the news. At NBC, before the era of Chet Huntley and David Brinkley, John Cameron Swayze anchored the *Camel News Caravan*, underwritten by Camel Cigarettes. At the time, Swayze also hosted a children's program and appeared as a regular panelist on *Who Said That?*, a quiz show.

So why was Wallace held to a different standard? Several factors conspired to tilt the bias against him. For one, this was a new decade. Whereas the medium of television was still somewhat nascent in the 1950s, when Cronkite ad-libbed with Charlemagne, the 1960s would usher in the systematic use of color and other technological advances, and the unwritten rules of conduct would get codified.

It was also, perhaps, a matter of degree. Whereas Edward R. Murrow smoked on the air and Cronkite endorsed cigarettes, it was all contained within the news program itself. Mike had taken it a step further by appearing in stand-alone cigarette commercials that could and would be aired at all hours of the day. Acting in a Broadway comedy was likewise considered having crossed the line. But perhaps the unspoken motive for his detractors at CBS was that Mike, in his previous stints in TV news, had pushed the limits of the medium in both content and style, courted controversy and grabbed headlines. Indeed, some were secretly envious.

Particularly hostile among the newsroom staffers was Harry Reasoner, who was second only to Cronkite in the CBS News pecking order. His

Saturday night show, the *Eleven O'clock News With Harry Reasoner,* which had the good fortune of going on air right after top-rated *Gunsmoke,* was the most watched news show on television.

Reasoner, with whom Mike would eventually be teamed up on *60 Minutes,* had every reason to be mad. Not only had he been passed over to anchor the morning news show, but his own morning program, *Calendar,* had been cancelled to make room for the new program. "Harry looked at me," Mike would say, "like I was a hair in his soup."[11]

The *CBS Morning News* was scheduled to debut at the same time as the expanded evening news show with Walter Cronkite. In preparation for the dual launch, CBS News employees were invited to a celebratory brunch at the home of Blair Clark, Dick Salant's deputy. Mike and Av Westin were, of course, on the guest list, but they could hardly have felt less welcome. The entire focus of the event sat squarely on Walter Cronkite and the evening broadcast, with nothing whatsoever said about the morning news.

"Wallace and Westin were obliged to sit below the salt," says Gary Paul Gates. "They resented being treated like stepchildren whose views and concerns were of no interest to the rest of the family."[12]

"Stepchildren?" quips Westin. "We weren't even in the room as far as the brass at that table were concerned."[13]

Mike and Av Westin stormed out of the luncheon, like men on a mission. They waved away the limousine that was waiting to take them back to the office and chose to walk instead, venting the entire way about how they had been snubbed and how determined they were to make something noteworthy of the morning news show. The experience served to bond them.

"They were both proud and ambitious men," says Gary Paul Gates, "who welcomed the fire of competition."[14]

At one point along the purposeful walk, they passed a noisy construction site, with jackhammers going full blast. Mike stopped and shouted at the top of his lungs: "We'll show those bastards! Damn it! We'll show those fuckers how to do it!"[15]

Westin grinned in agreement and shook Mike's hand, which sealed the pact between them. But now what? Everything was stacked against them. They had a skeleton staff, most of whom disdained their anchorman, and very little money, hardly enough even to hire a field crew.

Mike and Westin discussed the predicament at length in the ensuing days. They reasoned that their audience demographic at 10 A.M. on a weekday was likely to be homemakers busy with chores—with the television on in the background.

"Grab 'em by the ears," Westin declared suddenly. "We have to grab them by the ears!"[16]

Mike, with his radio background, understood exactly what Westin meant. Their audience would probably be multitasking, while listening but not necessarily watching the screen. It was important to have strongly written copy that would catch their attention and draw their eyes. Thus, Westin and Mike became uncompromising about the writing of the show. With his experience as an actor, Mike had developed a keen sense of what makes a story work. "News is drama," he said in a 1964 magazine interview. "If you look closely, every interesting news story is built around a value conflict."[17]

Westin also had very specific ideas about how he wanted to shape the content of the morning news show. During his time in London, he had frequently watched a BBC program called *The Tonight Show* (no relationship to the eponymous American program), which mixed headline stories with inquisitive pieces of an informative nature. It was inspiring to Westin.

"We should broaden the traditional definition of what is news," Westin had written in a passionate memo to Dick Salant. ". . . information need not be tied directly to today's news. Analytical features should anticipate events so that they can be on the air before the headlines."[18]

Westin sold Mike on the idea of producing public interest stories involving food safety, health care costs and other consumer issues. Though such segments are commonplace on today's airwaves, it was a radical departure to program these "back of the book" pieces in the early '60s, where newscasts lasted only fifteen minutes and typically covered front-page headlines and nothing more.

Like Ted Yates, Westin, who retained editorial control of the program, was inclined to push the envelope when it came to subject matter. The broadcast dealt quite openly with matters such as menopause, Pap smears, alcoholism, boredom—issues that might be of interest to the show's largely female audience.

"Birth control, infidelity, venereal disease, we did them all," explains Westin. "We became the publishers of record, if you will, of a lot of sociological research that was being done at universities."[19]

Long before the sexual revolution took hold in the late '60s, this constituted a daring move by Westin. It was news you could use—though that phrase had a negative connotation back then. As Westin puts it: " 'News you can use' was something that local did."[20]

But the Wallace/Westin team stuck to their guns, and it paid off. The show received high ratings, a nearly 30 percent bump from the Harry Reasoner show it had replaced. Reasoner began to realize that the usurper Mike Wallace was here to stay.

With his career on the mend, things began to look up for Mike on the home front, too. Lorraine had started painting again, following a period of aimlessness after the death of her father. The focus of her work, fittingly, was to bring light into areas of darkness, designing colorful paintings for collectors to hang in windowless vestibules. With growing demand for her work, Lorraine opened a small gallery on the Upper East Side and started getting out of the house with regularity. Mike was proud of her increasing independence.

In this period, Mike also reached out to his son, Chris. He took the teenager for lunch one day at Toots Shor's Restaurant, a famed watering hole for media and sports figures. Young Chris followed his father through the vestibule, where the maître d' seemed to recognize Mike. A patron called out as they were escorted to their table: "Hey Mike, how ya doing?" It wasn't just any patron. This was Joe DiMaggio. Chris's eyes widened in awe: *Joe DiMaggio knows my father?* It proved the breakthrough moment for their relationship. Both Mike and Chris were passionate about sports (and highly competitive), which helped to bring them together.

Years later, when Mike was named "Man of the Year" in 1989 by Chicago's Museum of Broadcast Communications, Chris regaled the gathering with stories about the perils of being Mike's son. "Adolescence is tough enough," he told the $200-a-plate dinner crowd at the Chicago Hilton, "without having the world's best investigative reporter as your father. How would you like to come home late from a date to find Mike Wallace laying in wait behind the door?"

In point of fact, it was the congenial Bill Leonard who would have been waiting behind the door—for Chris lived with his mother and stepdad throughout his teenage years. But Leonard went out of his way to provide chances for Mike and Chris to deepen their relationship—and, in 1964, thanks to Leonard, father and son found themselves working together.

Leonard had recently been put in charge of what was perhaps the most combative arena in all of network news: the presidential election cycle, where networks pulled out all the stops to get a leg up on the competition. "In those days," says Leonard, "convention and election coverage seemed to set the tone for audience preference in news for months, even years afterwards."[21] It could make or break the entire news division.

CBS had been trounced in 1960 by the golden team of Huntley-Brinkley at NBC, and they were desperate to get back into the game in 1964—so desperate that Don Hewitt, who directed the convention coverage, once impersonated a sheriff to glean information about NBC and was later caught stealing a binder outlining NBC's strategy, which would lead to his temporary demotion within the news division.

Leonard, for his part, had been relying on new and untested computer programs to predict election outcomes in advance of the official tabulation of votes. But Walter Cronkite distrusted this new technology, and that was a problem. The team badly needed something to make their coverage more exciting. Explains Leonard: "The ratings showed that Walter, good as he was, couldn't hold an audience hour after hour, particularly during a convention that lacked much action or suspense."[22]

Though Bill Leonard was, technically speaking, Cronkite's boss, it was a delicate relationship, given Cronkite's growing star power and the fact that he had just been named managing editor of CBS News. The two men had considerable history together. Back in 1952, when Cronkite first began to anchor CBS's coverage of presidential conventions, Leonard had worked under him as a floor reporter. This highly visible job was coveted amongst correspondents eager to make a name for themselves. In terms of national visibility, floor reporting at a convention was second only to the anchor chair itself.

In 1964, the CBS convention coverage team consisted of Walter Cronkite as anchorman, with Dan Rather, Roger Mudd and Martin Agronsky on the floor. Though Mike pined to be in their company, he remained far too low on the CBS totem to stand a chance, and it riled him. After all, in 1960, he had *anchored* the convention coverage, though that was off-network in syndication for Westinghouse Broadcasting, which didn't help him in the major league news game, where Mike had no cachet. Further irking Mike was the fact that his own sixteen-year-old son, Chris, would be working at the conventions as Walter Cronkite's assistant, a dream summer job made possible by stepfather Bill Leonard. Mike decided to get as close to the action as he could by taking his *Morning News* show on the road to San Francisco for the week of the Republican National Convention. It proved a fortuitous decision, putting Mike in the right place at the right time.

The year 1964 was a landmark in GOP convention lore. It marked the moment Barry Goldwater ushered in the modern conservative movement when he defeated moderate Nelson Rockefeller for the Republican presidential nomination. A tension-filled convention, it was one of the most acrimonious on record, with moderates and conservatives lashing out at one another across the floor. Rockefeller was loudly booed when he took the podium, even screamed at by conservatives in the galleries. The keynote speech was delivered by Ronald Reagan, who had recently abandoned formally the Democratic Party to join the Republicans. And when Richard Nixon finally introduced Goldwater to the frenzied crowd, he hailed him as "Mr. Conservative" and "Mr. Republican."

The CBS news booth had its share of fireworks, too. Bill Leonard found himself in a battle for control of the broadcast with his anchor, Walter Cronkite. In an attempt to add some life to their coverage, Leonard spontaneously decided to bring news analyst Eric Sevareid into the booth for color commentary—a move that had Cronkite fuming. Chris Wallace found himself subjected to icy stares from Cronkite every time he brought him coffee.

Feeling the tumultuous convention spinning out of control, Leonard made a second impulsive decision—to add another floor reporter. The closest available candidate happened to be Mike Wallace, who was in town, serendipitously, with his morning news show. Like a battlefield general bestowing a sudden promotion on the most capable man within earshot, Mike got another break from Bill Leonard—a decision that would likely have been questioned back at headquarters. Mike jumped right in, grabbing a microphone and headset, and joining Dan Rather and Roger Mudd on the convention floor. But there was one problem: Cronkite began refusing to cut away from himself in the booth.

As Leonard remembers it: "Through our director, Don Hewitt, I would ask Walter every now and then to hand things over to one of the floor reporters. As often as not, he'd keep talking. It finally became more and more obvious that he was digging in his heels . . . I went into his anchor booth, smoking mad, and told him that when he got an order to switch to the floor I expected him to carry it out."

Cronkite responded by storming out of the booth. When all was said and done, CBS once again got clobbered by rival NBC in its convention coverage. And Leonard had to return to New York to answer to the CBS brass. He had every reason to be nervous—Dick Salant had recently been fired as president of the news division because of CBS's seeming inability to overtake NBC in the ratings war.

Leonard braced himself as he entered "Black Rock," the just-opened

CBS corporate headquarters building designed by Eero Saarinen—an imposing monolith of ink-black granite. He took the elevator to the corporate floor and entered the chairman's executive suite, where William S. Paley was waiting to interrogate him along with CBS president Frank Stanton.

"What the hell happened to Walter?" barked Stanton.[23]

"I thought the idea was that Walter was going to do a little less, and you were going to spread the load around, so the pace would pick up," growled Paley. "Wasn't that the idea?"

"Well, sir," stammered Leonard. "That *was* the idea but Walter sort of . . . I guess you could say . . . resisted it."

"Did you actually give him *orders* and he wouldn't carry them *out*?" demanded the chairman.

There was no getting around it: Cronkite had gone rogue. So Paley, being Paley, did the unthinkable—he removed Walter Cronkite from the anchor chair for the upcoming Democratic National Convention, replacing him with Roger Mudd and Robert Trout. This seismic shakeup had an ancillary benefit for Mike: his field promotion to floor reporter managed to slip under the radar, without the usual scrutiny from Black Rock. So one month later, he was back at it in Atlantic City for the Democratic National Convention, which helped him gain the exposure and credibility within CBS news that he so badly craved.

The convention itself was fairly humdrum. President Johnson predictably secured the nomination by a landslide and CBS news was, once again, walloped by their perennial adversary, NBC. But something happened that fall, as Chris Wallace returned to his senior year in high school and Mike to his day job, anchoring the morning show. The CBS newsroom once again regrouped, getting back to basics and returning Cronkite to his rightful anchor chair for the coverage of election night. Though Mike was not yet officially part of primetime news at CBS, he was managing to secure some airtime in the evening hours by virtue of being a part of the election coverage unit. Cronkite, having had his knuckles rapped, rose to the challenge, accepted the new technological innovations . . . and somehow, third time was the charm.

Election night was a landslide—both for President Johnson, and for CBS, too. Not only did the network come out atop the ratings, it received a rave review for its coverage from influential *New York Times* critic Jack Gould:

CBS BY A LANDSLIDE
Network's Coverage of the Election
Called Far Superior to Its Rivals'

The Columbia Broadcasting System turned in a superb journalistic beat last night, running away with the major honors in reporting President Johnson's election victory.

In clarity of presentation the network led all the way, and in speed it was way up front for at least an hour and a half. In a medium where time is of the essence, the performance of CBS was of landslide proportions...

Bill Leonard and his reliance on computer analysis, which worked without a hitch this time, was singled out for praise. Everyone in the CBS newsroom breathed a big sigh of relief. Says Leonard, "We were the best. We knew it. *The New York Times* confirmed it."[24]

And Mike Wallace was part of the team that made it happen.

Chapter Ten

Blood Looks Very Red on Color TV

C hris Wallace had been bitten by the journalistic bug. Being part of the election coverage team was one the most exhilarating experiences he'd ever had. He realized, of course, that it could be a tall order to become a journalist in this media family. Yet Chris applied himself at school, determined as ever to emerge from the still-lingering shadow of his overachieving late brother, Peter—not to mention the formidable and perennially looming one of his father. Neither of them was one to shy away from challenge or competition. In fact, before the decade was up, both father and son would be arrested for being a little too aggressive in their pursuit of a news story.

Under the guidance of alumni uncle Irving, Chris was accepted into Harvard, which he entered in September 1965—an interesting time to be on campus. Timothy Leary had been conducting experiments with psychedelics and would soon be exhorting students to "Turn on, tune in, drop out." To the horror of the establishment, Harvard Yard increasingly became the site of student sit-ins for civil rights and rallies to end the escalating U.S. involvement in Vietnam.

It was an interesting time to be a reporter, too—especially one on television. Brutality and mayhem play much more vividly as moving images than they do in newsprint. In fact, the stories of the day helped to establish the dominance of television as our primary source for news—and Mike covered all of them, albeit mainly from his desk as the *Morning News* anchor. But he also found himself frequently dispatched to the field—an unintended consequence of the fact the Wallace/Westin *Morning News* team had been ostracized by the rest of the news division. By necessity they had become efficient, inventive and self-reliant at producing the news.

As with many of the early Wallace enterprises, the members of Mike's staff developed a certain hubris about what they were capable of accomplishing, a quality that got noticed at Black Rock. Thus, when it came to producing news specials, the CBS brass often turned to the *Morning News* crew as the go-to team. For example, after the murder of three civil rights workers in Mississippi rocked the nation in 1964, it was Mike and Westin who were sent to cover the story.

"By moving [Mike] into that kind of arena, it gave him strengthened credentials," comments Westin.[1] Mike was increasingly seen as the voice for national stories of considerable gravitas. But in 1965, the *Morning News* show became a victim of its own success. With their solid ratings, Mike and Westin had proved that there was a consistent audience and considerable profits to be made in the midmorning timeslot. Bill Paley realized that he could earn even more money and cut expenses to boot by airing reruns of *I Love Lucy* in lieu of the *CBS Morning News*. Thus, despite outrage and vociferous protests from Mike and Av Westin, their show was shifted to the ungodly airtime of 7 A.M.

Even in the previous midmorning timeslot, Mike had been setting his alarm for 4:30 A.M. to get to the studio in time for the many hours of prep that precede a news broadcast. Now he found himself squarely in the graveyard shift. He was forced for the first time in his life to start taking sleeping pills in order to get to sleep by 7 P.M., a habit that wreaked havoc on his home life and one that he had enormous difficulty shaking, even many years after moving on to other assignments.

For Westin, who was required to be on the set several hours *before*

Mike, this new timeslot proved untenable. After a stint running the CBS Special Assignments desk, he eventually left the network to become executive director of the Public Broadcast Laboratory, an effort funded by the Ford Foundation to prove the need for public broadcasting. Westin staffed the venture with a number of bright and ambitious young interns, one of whom was the not-yet-twenty Chris Wallace.

Meanwhile, Chris's forty-eight-year-old father had left the *Morning News* in exhaustion during the summer of 1966 to join the ranks of general assignment reporters, a demotion in his career path but one that at least normalized his working hours and lifestyle. The biggest story of the day remained Vietnam, and Mike would be sent there soon enough. But first he latched onto another evolving story—the resurrection of Richard Nixon as a political contender.

Nixon had all but disappeared since suffering back-to-back defeats, to John F. Kennedy in the 1960 Presidential Election and to Pat Brown in the California gubernatorial race of 1962. Nixon had a terrible relationship with the media, television in particular. He self-destructed in the first televised presidential debate broadcast by CBS and directed by Don Hewitt, after having refused Hewitt's strong suggestion that he put on makeup. The result, as described by Theodore H. White, was that Nixon appeared "half-slouched, his 'Lazy Shaves' powder faintly streaked with sweat, his eyes exaggerated hollows of blackness, his jaws, jowls and face drooping"—whereas the well-tanned Kennedy "appeared to be the pillar of robust good health."[2]

Then, after his humiliating 1962 loss in the California governor's race, Nixon further embarrassed himself in front of 100 reporters at the Beverly Hilton Hotel, when he lashed out at the media, declaring, "You don't have Nixon to kick around any more, because, gentlemen, this is my last press conference."

But five years later in 1967, the tenacious Mr. Nixon was back, and Mike became one of the first reporters to take him seriously. "I did not find him cold or double-dealing or paranoid or any of the other negative things I had heard or read about him over the years," wrote Mike. "I was impressed by his intelligence, his grasp of history and his clear understanding of the difficult problems he would face in the White House . . . I grew to respect him and even to feel a kind of affection for him."[3]

Nixon, who had been hounded by muckraking journalists like Jack Anderson for his entire career, was desperate for an ally within the press corps and gave Mike special access to his campaign, inviting him, for instance, to sit up front on the chartered campaign plane.

In the early days of August, 1968, Nixon staffers declared a media moratorium while the candidate worked in seclusion on his acceptance speech to be delivered at the Republican National Convention—but Nixon allowed an exception when Mike requested an interview. It made Mike brim with pride to brush past his competitors from NBC and ABC who were pacing impatiently in the wings, and to scoop them for an exclusive chat with the reclusive Mr. Nixon—a piece that ultimately ran as the highlight of CBS's coverage of the convention's opening day. Mike did a fine job as a floor reporter, as well. In fact, *Time* magazine singled out his work in a review of the convention coverage that year.

Mike made national headlines again a few weeks later at the infamous Democratic Convention in Chicago, which featured demonstrations in the streets, mass rioting and police violence. The country was in turmoil following the recent assassinations of Martin Luther King and Robert Kennedy. Some 10,000 demonstrators converged on Chicago, where they were met by 23,000 police officers and National Guardsmen under the command of Mayor Richard Daley, who was hell-bent on maintaining law and order in his city. But with tensions mounting steadily, skirmishes broke out between the protestors and police, who used tear gas and Mace against them. As violence escalated, hippies, innocent bystanders and even reporters were brutally beaten by police armed with batons. And the mayhem was captured and broadcast nationwide by television reporters who had descended upon the city in great numbers. The disturbances even spread to the convention floor, where one of Mayor Daley's goons punched Dan Rather in the stomach, knocking him down.

"It looks like we've got a bunch of thugs in here," said Walter Cronkite, clearly fuming while on the air. "If this sort of thing continues, it makes us, in our anger, want to just turn off our cameras and pack up our microphones and our typewriters and get the devil out of this town and leave the Democrats to their agony."

It did continue. The following night it was Mike's turn to be assaulted, when he approached a delegate who was being dragged off the floor for speaking rudely to a security agent.

"Stay away!" shouted a police officer. "This is none of your business."[4]

"Certainly it's my business," retorted Mike. "This is a public place."

The policeman narrowed his eyes. Mike shifted tactics, trying to ingratiate him with a friendly smile. "Officer, what are you getting so upset about?" Mike made the mistake of softening his remark by chucking the officer under the chin. Physical contact was all it took.

The cop responded by slugging Mike squarely across the jaw. A second cop, clearly rattled by the mounting confrontation, jumped in and declared to Mike: "You're under arrest!"

"*I'm* under arrest? *Me?*" Mike frowned incredulously. "What have I done?"

"Assaulting an officer!" said the second policeman.

Thus, to his astonishment, Mike was dragged off by the duo under the glare of a dozen cameras, further cementing his reputation as a dogged and unrelenting reporter. The incarceration lasted less than a day, but made headlines across the country.

One year later, it was Chris's turn to land in jail. He was a Harvard senior at this point, cutting his teeth as a correspondent for campus radio station WHRB. Like many universities across the country, Harvard had seen burgeoning student protests and rallies against the Vietnam War. When Defense Secretary Robert S. McNamara came to speak at the Institute of Politics in 1967, 800 students blocked his car and McNamara was forced to escape through the university's underground tunnel system. Later that year, 300 students imprisoned an executive from napalm manufacturer Dow Chemical who had come to campus on a recruiting trip.

By 1969, protests reached a furious pitch when students occupied

University Hall. The demonstrators were committed to nonviolent resistance, but in the early hours of April 10, 1969, university administrators made the unprecedented decision to call in city and state police. The cops charged with billy clubs and Mace to remove the demonstrators, and arrested them by the dozens. The use of force outraged the Cambridge community, including many who did not support the takeover. Sit-ins like this were not unique to Cambridge, but, as one participant put it, "Like it or not, whatever goes on at Harvard gets a lot of attention."[5]

Chris Wallace was among those taken into custody by Cambridge Police, his tape recorder confiscated. But, ingeniously, Chris used his one phone call to contact the campus radio station. He asked his WHRB colleagues to record the call and filed his story from prison, a stunt that must have made his father proud. They were clearly cut from the same cloth.

Meanwhile, over at NBC, the fearless Ted Yates had become a correspondent in his own right. In those violent times, networks needed reporters like Yates who were willing to go at a moment's notice to the frontlines. As a marine veteran of the Korean War, not only was Yates trained to maintain his composure in danger zones, he actually thrived on the adrenaline. "I take a lot of killing," he once said.[6]

As the leader of an elite NBC documentary unit, Yates became a prized reporter for areas of conflict. Yates's crew was a hard-drinking lot who worked long hours and endured unthinkable hardships in pursuit of their stories. They traveled to menacing, inhospitable places, were often shot at, threatened by contaminated water, swarmed by impoverished masses, and even on occasion forced to take up arms to complete a story.

In 1964, they produced a prescient documentary entitled *Vietnam: It's a Mad War*, which depicted the iconic horrors of Vietnam long before other broadcasts dared to do so. Bloodied, shell-shocked soldiers, bodies in ditches, anxious river patrols, the ritualistic killing of beasts of burden by jungle tribesmen—imagery that years later would be adopted by Francis Ford Coppola in his seminal movie *Apocalypse Now*. The pictures were horrifying and unforgettable. As a BBC commentator remarked, "Blood looks very red on the colour television screen."[7]

Mike, who had already been to Vietnam during the summer that Peter died, was dispatched there again in 1967, this time for a two-month tour. The stakes were dramatically higher now, the number of U.S. troops having swelled to 400,000, with 11,000 casualties that year alone. Needless to say, it was a dangerous and demanding assignment. And, as Gary Paul Gates noted: "At the age of 49, Mike Wallace was a little long in the tooth to be running around combat zones . . . Most reporters then in Vietnam were endowed with younger legs and quicker reflexes."[8]

But junior correspondents tended to be uniform in their condemnation of the war, filing stories full of doom and pessimism that didn't always sit well with the older viewers back home who made up a substantial portion of the CBS audience. That's why the news division dispatched Mike, a veteran of WWII, who would perhaps be inclined to present more "balanced" reporting on the U.S. intervention in South East Asia. This hope was shared by military commanders on the ground, who were eager, like Mr. Nixon, to recruit a potential ally in the press corps. Thus, Mike was given a red-carpet welcome, greeted in person on the tarmac by the impressive figure of General William Childs Westmoreland, commander of U.S. forces in Vietnam.

"Westy," a decorated veteran of WWII and Korea, had graduated at the top of his class at West Point and gone on to receive an MBA from Harvard Business School. He was the very model of the modern corporate warrior who firmly believed that the outcome in Vietnam was simply a matter of deploying sufficient resources to ensure decisive victory. He met Mike with a bone-crushing handshake, escorted him to a waiting jeep and took him on a daylong tour of firebases, forward positions and field briefings. Mike realized that he was being fed a rosy picture of the conflict, but certainly appreciated the personal attention from the top man in the theater of operations. He had no idea that, fifteen years hence, General West-moreland would sue him for a cool $120 million and drag Mike through a humiliating trial that would nearly finish him.

That was another story—a *60 Minutes* piece which would air in 1982. These eight weeks in 1967 were a different matter altogether; they actu-ally provided a substantial boost to Mike's professional reputation. This was due, in part, to the fact that Mike had the airwaves to himself. AFTRA (American Federation of Television and Radio Artists), a union represent-ing all on-air talent including newscasters, had just called for a strike against the networks. This meant all of Mike's colleagues at home, includ-ing Walter Cronkite, were forbidden from going on the air; their positions were filled temporarily by management personnel. But AFTRA did not have jurisdiction overseas, so Mike was able to file daily reports.

With no competing stories, Mike's dispatches received prominent air-time, often leading the evening newscast. For those not already familiar with Mike's distinctive face and commanding voice, he now became etched in the public imagination as the fearless reporter who brought the war into living rooms across America in vivid and gruesome color—practically every night, the lead story of the evening broadcast.

While in Vietnam, Mike did not cross paths with his intrepid former partner Ted Yates, and he would also miss him by several weeks in an-other hotspot later that year. He would, in fact, never see him again.

I n June of 1967, war broke out in the Middle East between Israel and Jordan. Ted Yates, not surprisingly, was the first journalist on the ground, ensconced with his crew in Jerusalem even before the first shot was fired. On June 5, the men were eating breakfast at the Intercontinental Hotel when the so-called "Six-Day War" erupted.

Cameraman Jim Norling remembers the scene: "About 11:00 a.m., as I was looking out through the large plate glass windows, I suddenly saw a large plume of smoke and debris rising high above the city. It was strange—not a sound through the windows—just this single column of smoke. We all jumped up and ran outside. By this time it seemed that everything had hit the fan and we had a grandstand seat."[9]

"Get the camera," shouted Yates. "I want to do a standup."

Norling darted back inside the hotel to get his Arriflex and tripod, while soundman Al Hoagland grabbed the Nagra tape recorder. Gunfire was erupting throughout East Jerusalem, echoing up and down the narrow streets.

Norling continues his account: "We had just gotten back outside when bullets began to come in our direction."

He dove to the ground alongside Yates, who had taken cover to survey the situation.

"Ted and I were lying shoulder to shoulder with Al a few feet away to our left. The Israelis must have seen us [wearing khakis] and thought we were Jordanians, for the bullets began to fly around us thick and fast. Our only protection was a six-inch curb of the driveway."

Fred Tepper, the lighting electrician, and associate producer Bob Rogers were pinned down behind a car in the driveway. Bullets ricocheted off the concrete pavement.

"I heard what sounded like a baseball bat hitting something," said Norling, "and Ted convulsed and slumped back down. I saw that he had taken a hit in the head."

When the gunfire subsided, the crew dragged Yates into the hotel and onto a desk. The head wound was severe. A makeshift bandage was applied. Bob Rogers flagged down an ambulance and rushed his boss to a nearby hospital. The bullet had entered Yates's forehead, traveled down the back of his skull, and exited through his neck. The staff surgeon tried to operate— but it was hopeless.

Mike was back in New York when he got the devastating news that his former partner had died. He called Ted's widow, Mary, who was in a state of shock, left suddenly alone with three young boys. Mary knew that something like this was a possibility, given Ted's penchant for seeking out danger—but the reality hit her hard. That afternoon, a shaken Mike eulogized Ted on his radio show, *Personal Close-up*:

"He wanted to know everything. He feared nothing. He was convinced that no serious harm could come to him. I don't think he understood fear in the sense that most of us do. He was just not afflicted by it. But it was not a foolish bravado. He was simply different from most of us."[10]

Ted Yates was gone. But Mike's relationship with the Yates family was far from over. Years later, they would quite literally save his life.

Chapter Eleven

Good Cop, Bad Cop

L ike many enterprises that achieve lasting fame and widespread recognition, *60 Minutes* came about through a confluence of elements that created a perfect storm. As is also typical, it had more than its share of naysayers. The show was vetoed more than once by the president of CBS News, who also very nearly nixed Mike Wallace as co-host. Mike himself had serious reservations about the assignment, given all that was happening during the volatile summer of 1968.

The country, by and large, was turning against the war in Vietnam and Mike was not particularly surprised that Richard Nixon appeared poised to become the nation's thirty-seventh president. He had been following the former vice president for quite some time, and now, with Nixon's victory all but assured, Mike was gunning for the coveted assignment of White House Correspondent for CBS News, a position then occupied by competitor Dan Rather. As it turned out, Mike received a more unexpected offer.

"The boss would like you to join up," declared Len Garment, a former law partner of Nixon's who was now working on his campaign.[1]

"To do *what*, exactly?" asked Mike.

"We're not sure . . . we're not that well organized," admitted Garment. "But I imagine it would be press secretary or communications director, or something like that."

Mike was intrigued. This was far more alluring than the prospect of filming nightly stand-ups in front of the White House lawn; this meant full access to the inner workings of the Oval Office. But it was not the only offer on Mike's desk that summer. He had also been considering a radical idea from CBS producer Don Hewitt for a one-hour news program with a rather perfunctory name: *60 Minutes.*

Hewitt had already been wooing one anchor for his show, the smooth and genteel Sunday night anchor Harry Reasoner, and now he was court-ing Mike as a potential co-anchor, to add some spice to the mix. As Wal-lace biographer Gary Paul Gates explains it: "[Hewitt] recognized at once that the broadcast would take on an added dimension if Reasoner was given a foil to play off, a heavy who would wear the black hat and patrol the dark alleys in search of stories while Harry, all smiles and charm, worked the sunny side of the street. And once they had defined the role in those terms, Hewitt and Leonard had no trouble deciding who should play Darth Vader to Reasoner's Obi-Wan Kenobi."[2]

According to Mike, the idea for dual anchormen came originally from CBS vice president Bill Leonard—the husband of Mike's first wife—though others have claimed that the suggestion was from Leonard's deputy. Yet in 1968, Mike remained unsure about the whole proposition, still tempted by the offer to join the Nixon White House. So Mike decided to call Hewitt and fill him in on the conversation he had had with Len Garment.

"Kid, guess what?" said Mike. Though Mike was fifty and Hewitt not far behind him, they were both still "kids" and would continue to call each other by that moniker for another four decades. ("Mike calls everybody 'kid,'" jokes Hewitt. "I think he called his father 'kid.'")[3]

"Leonard Garment just called me," Mike continued. "They're offer-ing me the job of Nixon's press secretary."

"Are you out of your mind?" barked Hewitt. "You don't take a job like that *after* you've been Mike Wallace. You take a job like that so after it's over you can *get to be* Mike Wallace."[4]

Mike took it in, aware that Hewitt was flattering him, for Mike had not yet become the iconic figure of *60 Minutes* fame. Mike was wise enough, however, never to dismiss an idea from Don Hewitt, the man who had, for all intents and purposes, invented the wheel in television news, despite being a college dropout.

In the 1950s, it was Hewitt who put into practice the use of tele-prompters in newscasts so that anchormen would not have to look down at written copy. It was Hewitt who created the "chyron," superimposed text on the lower third of the screen to convey additional information. It was Hewitt who pioneered the use of "B-roll," cutaway footage over which a newscaster would narrate the story. And Hewitt, not surprisingly, ended up directing every major news broadcast at CBS, from national convention coverage to the first televised presidential debate, which paved the way for John F. Kennedy to enter the White House.

In the mid-'60s, Hewitt was taken off breaking news for a while and given the task of producing documentary specials. Even here, he broke new ground. Hewitt resolved that any news specials he produced would have high entertainment value in addition to their newsworthiness. "Why don't we try to package sixty minutes of reality as attractively as Holly-wood packages sixty minutes of make-believe?" he had asked CBS News president Dick Salant, who took less than ten seconds to dismiss the idea.[5] Explains Bill Leonard: "To Dick Salant, the term 'show business' was like syphilis: he didn't want to catch it. Even a story that smacked of 'human interest' was hardly worth our precious air time."[6]

But Hewitt would not relent. Leonard, who, as vice president of CBS News, was Hewitt's immediate superior, found himself on the receiving end of myriad memos detailing Hewitt's evolving vision for *60 Minutes*. "The magazine should be very 'with it,'" wrote Hewitt in one of them. "And in today's world being 'with it' connotes a certain amount of irreverence for established institutions."[7]

He began to envision his brainchild as the broadcast equivalent of *Life* magazine—part gloss, part substance. "We have documentaries—the broadcast equivalent of a book. We have the evening news broadcasts— the broadcast counterpart of a newspaper. But we have no counterpart of a magazine," Hewitt pitched his bosses.

But Salant remained unimpressed: "I told Don and Bill that they had a lousy idea and it would never work."[8]

During a heated discussion in early 1968, Leonard provoked Salant with the remark: "You know, Dick, this is the first time I've ever heard you and Fred Friendly agree on anything."[9] He knew full well that there was no love lost between Salant and Friendly, an executive who had briefly replaced him as president of CBS News. Salant had very little regard for the executive decisions Friendly had made in his absence.

"Is that true?" shot back Salant. "Did Fred turn down something like this?"

Hewitt nodded vigorously. "And for exactly the same reasons," goaded Leonard.

Their strategy worked. Salant, despite himself, agreed to fund a pilot for *60 Minutes*, with Harry Reasoner as host. But both Hewitt and Leonard thought the program would be better suited to two hosts playing off one another. When Mike's name was proposed, Salant again balked.

In his words: "The suggestion that there be a double anchor—Mike Wallace added to Harry Reasoner—was all wrong. There was no reason for a double anchor—what was each one supposed to do? Also, Wallace and Reasoner were not a good combination—their 'chemistry' was not right."[10]

Hewitt rolled his eyes in exasperation. Yes, Mike and Harry were polar opposites. That was precisely the point—Wallace would provide the vinegar to Reasoner's oil. It was not the first time, in fact, that they had been on screen together. After Av Westin departed the morning news program and moved to the special assignments desk, he was given the task of producing a pair of public service programs on the "National Citizenship

Test" and the "National Health Test." Westin wanted Mike to host the shows but his superiors decided that Mike should be paired with Harry Reasoner, considered more congenial and affable. Indeed, their styles could not have been more different.

The son of Midwestern schoolteachers, Reasoner had a plain manner, neither forced nor faked, that appealed to viewers. As Don Hewitt has described him: "Harry Reasoner was not the only broadcaster from the Midwest, but he was the only broadcaster who brought the Midwest with him to television. He not only had craggy good looks but also that Iowa sense of what's important."[11] But Reasoner was also something of a bon vivant, with a taste for cigars, fast cars and a reputation as a skirt chaser.

"Romanic feelings towards women were not the only indulgences Harry enjoyed," wrote Douglass K. Daniel, Reasoner's biographer. "He treated himself to a drink before each broadcast, an act that had become almost a ritual for him. As early as eight or eight-thirty in the morning he would seek a drinking companion."[12] Reasoner made no qualms about it, declaring: "There's nothing less moral about having a drink at eleven o'clock in the morning than there is at eleven o'clock at night."[13]

By contrast, while Mike enjoyed the occasional cocktail, health-conscious Lorraine made sure that he limited himself to a single round. Though he remained hooked on cigarettes, Mike did not particularly care for cigars, Reasoner's mainstay. And while Reasoner—despite a wife and seven kids in Connecticut—was dating Angie Dickinson (among numerous others), Wallace remained loyal and utterly faithful to Lorraine.

Between his Bacchanalian hobbies and movie-star girlfriend, Reasoner didn't have a lot of time to chase after stories and had developed a reputation at CBS for being lazy, which he did little to dispel. His leisurely lunches at Le Biarritz were invariably lubricated with martinis and followed by an afternoon nap on the sofa in his office. Hypercompetitive Mike probably hadn't napped since he was in diapers. He was, in fact, utterly perplexed by Reasoner's glib and lackadaisical attitude.

In 1967, Mike had been given the task of filling in as anchor of the

Sunday evening news, when Reasoner was sent for a three-week tour of Vietnam. To Mike's shock, Reasoner signed off his final broadcast before the brief hiatus as follows: "I haven't been in Vietnam since 1953, so I'll have to study up on it. I understand the French have left."[14]

Moments after they were off the air, Mike called Reasoner with a severe reprimand, demanding to know how he had the nerve and bad taste to jest about a news story in which Americans were dying. Reasoner simply shrugged it off. Then he received another call—this one from the President of the United States.

Reasoner thought at first that it was another call from Wallace, playing games with him. But then he heard the unmistakable Texas drawl of Lyndon Baines Johnson. The president declared that he would be assisting Reasoner in his study of Vietnam and invited the correspondent to the White House for a personal briefing. Such was the desperate need of the Commander-in-Chief to influence the media's increasingly pessimistic take on the deepening quagmire in Vietnam.

Whatever Mike made of him, Reasoner was taken seriously by the White House and by the public, too. He brought talent to the table that could not be dismissed; his screen persona was affable in a natural, unself-conscious way. And there was his skill with words—many considered Reasoner to be the best writer in the newsroom. So, with Mike's talent for interviewing and his fearlessness as a reporter, it seemed that he and Reasoner had complementary skills that could make for a solid team for *60 Minutes*. But while Dick Salant had been persuaded to buy the show, the ultimate decision-maker just didn't see adding Mike as a co-host.

Thus, Bill Leonard was forced, once again, to win him over. He composed a passionate and persuasive memo on behalf of Wallace, but without Mike's knowledge—and Salant ultimately relented. As he remembers it: "Bill and Don, thank goodness, patted me on the head, said, 'There, there; we know what we're doing, wait and see,' and went on their way."[15]

Convincing Salant was only half the battle. Hewitt now had to persuade his star correspondents that it was in their interest to share the *60*

Minutes stage. Both Reasoner and Mike were decidedly lukewarm in their embrace of the enterprise, with remarkably similar recollections of how they reacted to Hewitt's proposal.

Reasoner's account: "In 1968, when Hewitt told me about this idea he had for a television magazine, I figured what the hell. I wasn't doing anything very exciting at the time and I figured I owed him for our early days together on the Douglas Edwards News. Even if it never got on the air—and it probably wouldn't—I didn't have anything to lose. It wasn't going to have much effect on my career, one way or the other, to do a pilot, so I said yes."[16]

Mike's account: "In the spring of 1968, when Hewitt came to me with his grandiose scheme, I kept my reservations to myself. I didn't want to rain on his parade, and, besides, when Don Hewitt is in full cry, there is no resisting him . . . I figured if the network executives gave us the go ahead, *60 Minutes* would run for at least a season, maybe two, enough to make it a worthwhile experience."[17]

Neither Reasoner nor Wallace could possibly have foreseen that *60 Minutes* would go on to run for forty-three years—and counting. Nor could they have imagined that it would become the most profitable television series of all time. Yet Hewitt's brainchild might never have gotten off the ground had one or both of this unlikely duo declined to participate.

With seniority over Mike, Reasoner began as top dog on the program, though it would not be long before he was eclipsed by the formidable presence of Mike Wallace. For Mike's part, having committed to *60 Minutes*, he now had to close the loop with Nixon. On the last night of the 1968 Republican Convention, Wallace told the future president that he would be declining his offer to join him at the White House, and would instead be working on "this new feature program."

"Nixon was dumbfounded," recalls Mike, "he looked at me as if I'd gone bonkers."[18]

Nixon then attempted to set Mike straight: "I'd call that a big mistake. We're going to win this thing, Mike, and when we get to the White House, we're going to take some great trips."[19] Though not particularly enticing at the time, Mike believes it was a veiled reference to Nixon's historic plans to be the first U.S. president to visit the communist capitals of Moscow and Beijing.

Mike, too, was about to embark on the trip of his life, and this was not to be his last encounter with Richard Nixon. Indeed, in his four decades as the star of the most influential news program on television, Mike would conduct interviews not only with the thirty-seventh president but with nearly every newsmaker of the late twentieth century.

Chapter Twelve

Rough Beginnings

W hat about setting up cameras inside Nixon's suite at the Hilton on the night of the balloting?" proposed Mike. "We could film him as he watches himself being nominated."[1]

It was Mike's very first story idea for the maiden episode of the show that would consume him for the next four decades—and Don Hewitt thought it was great.

"Terrific," he responded. "We'll do the same in Chicago with [Democratic nominee] Hubert [Humphrey], then play them back to back on the first show. Great idea."

Mike's relationship with Nixon helped pave the way for the filming request to be granted. Thus, CBS News cameras captured a moment that had never been seen by the television public: a candidate in his private quarters with his family, witnessing the long-awaited triumph of his nomination for president. As Mike remembers it: "Nixon conducted a kind of on-camera political seminar for his family . . . as the balloting unfolded."

During the shoot, Don Hewitt noted that, when the big moment finally arrived, Nixon's cronies jumped up to congratulate him, but Pat Nixon was left all alone in one corner—a fact that Hewitt happened to mention to Hubert Humphrey, before they filmed with him. So when his turn came around at the Democratic Convention, Humphrey made sure to leap up and kiss his wife, first and foremost. Only trouble was that Muriel Humphrey happened to be on the convention floor at the time, not in the hotel suite where CBS was filming with her husband. So Humphrey dashed over and kissed the TV screen where Muriel's face appeared in an emotional close-up. It was a moment made for television. And it was this CBS exclusive that kicked off the first broadcast of *60 Minutes* on September 24, 1968.

Though the opening had some pizzazz, the remainder of the show was not particularly riveting, and lacked focus—hardly what one might have expected for the launch of the most profitable TV program of all time. After the Nixon-Humphrey segment, the program moved on to Mike interviewing Attorney General Ramsey Clark, the nation's top law enforcement official. In attempting to recapture his *Night Beat* edge, Mike provoked Clark with: "Dick Gregory has said that today's cop is yesterday's nigger. Do you understand that?"

"I think what he means is that the policeman today is a man who is put upon from every standpoint," responded Clark, maintaining his composure. "He's not paid well, he's not trained well. He finds little opportunity to improve himself."

This was followed by an odd interstitial segment called "Digressions," featuring two silhouette puppet figures called Ipso and Facto. The bit, written and voiced by Andy Rooney and senior producer Palmer Williams, was intended to be funny but proved simply to be bizarre:

IPSO: I know how cops feel.

FACTO: Not being a cop, you can't possibly know how they feel.

IPSO: Not being me, how do you know whether I know how the cops feel?

FACTO: Not being me, how do you know whether I know how you know or not?

Ipso: Thank you.

Facto: Thank you.

This curious routine, neither newsworthy nor particularly amusing, would not survive the first season, as Don Hewitt and his staff refined the *60 Minutes* formula. The pilot episode also featured a short film, *Why Man Creates*, by designer Saul Bass, along with some humorous commentary by newspaper columnist Art Buchwald, all of which added to the hodgepodge feeling of the broadcast.

At the show's close, Mike attempted to sum up the eclectic lineup as follows: "There you have our first *60 Minutes* broadcast. Looking back, it had quite a range, as the problems and interests of our lives have quite a range. Our perception of reality roams, in a given day, from the light to the heavy, from warmth to menace, and if this broadcast does what we hope it will do, it will report reality."

The unfocused broadcast received mixed reviews and was trounced by the competition. "The stories were dated," dismissed *Variety*, "and the magazine format, lifted from print, pretentious."

The New York Times began on a more positive note: "The Columbia Broadcasting System's new alternate-week news magazine, '60 Minutes,' is something television has long needed." But then, a qualification: "Last night's edition explored only a few of the many possibilities open to an imaginative editor."[2]

The pilot episode garnered around 13 million viewers, which would be monumental by today's standards. But its competition, *That's Life!* with Robert Morse on ABC and Rock Hudson in *Blindfold* on NBC, had more than double the viewership. Still, given the modest production costs for *60 Minutes*, the CBS brass were content enough with the results.

Mike, for his part, thought the writing was on the wall: "I figured that *60 Minutes* would be lucky to make it through a couple of seasons in prime time."[3]

The second episode, which aired two weeks later, had Mike reuniting with Richard Nixon, now just four weeks away from the general election.

Mike, despite his affinity for the Nixon candidacy—indeed because of it—was determined not to be seen as throwing softball questions.

> **MIKE:** There are those who suggest you were awed, almost overawed by Jack Kennedy's money, social grace, position.
>
> **NIXON:** Oh, I don't buy that. I think everybody tries to rewrite history in terms of what the book should read, but while I do not have money and perhaps while I am not blessed with a particular social grace, I have a confidence that comes from a different source . . . Believe me, when you've gone through the fires of having to work your way through school, of having to fight campaigns with no money, of having to do it all on your own, you come out a pretty strong man and you're not in awe of anybody.
>
> **MIKE:** There's been so much talk in recent years of style and of charisma. No one suggests that either you or your opponent, Hubert Humphrey, have a good deal of it. Have you given no thought to this aspect of campaigning and of leading?
>
> **NIXON:** Well, when style and charisma connotes the idea of contriving, of public relations, I don't buy it at all. As I look back on the history of this country, some of our great leaders would not have been perhaps great television personalities, but they were great presidents because of what they stood for . . . The most important thing about a public man is not whether he's loved or disliked but whether he's respected. And I hope to restore respect to the presidency at all levels by my conduct.

Back then, Mike did not, of course, recognize the profound irony of Nixon's response, given the disgrace that would later befall the Nixon presidency in the wake of Watergate and other scandals. Nonetheless, Mike kept trying to prod and provoke the candidate:

> **MIKE:** The name "Nixon" is anathema to millions of American voters. To them Richard Nixon is a political opportunist to whom

the desired political end has justified just about any political means. How does Richard Nixon, if elected by a majority, go about reconciling the doubts of the skeptics?

NIXON: I do have, based on a hard political career going back over 22 years, some people in this country who consider me as anathema, as you pointed out. But on the other hand, I believe that I have the kind of leadership qualities that can unite this country and that at least can win the respect if not the affection of those who have a very bad picture of Richard Nixon.

There were no shocking revelations in the interview, but neither did Nixon dodge any of Mike's questions. According to journalist David Blum, a media critic of the times: "[Mike's] patented methods still provoked his subject to respond with his own version of the truth . . . Wallace used his seductive powers as an interviewer to draw out the inner Nixon." And this type of piece soon became a *60 Minutes* mainstay: "the newsmaker interview with gravitas."[4]

Wallace appeared in another segment on that second episode, this one so sensationalistic that it bordered on tabloid journalism. It concerned the development of biological weapons, and Mike recorded his stand-up covered head to toe in full Hazmat protective gear, complete with gas mask and ventilator.

"In wars of the future, one breath could mean instant death. An invisible odorless cloud could be lethal," warned Mike theatrically from within his protective gear. "The uniform I'm wearing was especially designed to protect a man against nerve gas. The mask protects against both gas and biological agents. If chemical and biological weapons are used in wars of the future, a man will have to have a uniform like this just to stay alive in order to fight."

The segment featured a montage of tanks, chemical factories and other ominous imagery, unabashedly trying to alarm the audience. All of this, says Blum, was part of Hewitt's plan for "*60 Minutes* to get noticed at any cost, by delivering stories that begged, even demanded, to be watched."[5]

Mike became an integral part of that plan—for he, like Hewitt, was determined to get to the top and more than willing to play whatever role was needed, whether interviewer of substance or journalistic showman.

Reasoner was a different animal altogether. Though equally ambitious, his style was more laconic—and that sometimes got him into trouble. Having tried to shake the "lazy" rap without much success, it was not a good time at CBS for Reasoner. The public liked him well enough—a recent poll of favorite anchormen had placed Reasoner second after Cronkite, and *before* their competitors at both NBC and ABC. But Bill Leonard had recently removed Reasoner from the CBS election coverage team, after an uninspired performance during the 1966 midterms.

In 1968, Reasoner, Hewitt and Mike found themselves in the same boat—they all needed to reinvent themselves. And, although Reasoner and Mike competed for stories and prominence, it never got nasty, because each was comfortable in his unique role. They knew that the acceptance and success of *60 Minutes* depended upon them becoming "performers" on some level, higher-relief versions of themselves who together could make a dynamic duo. Mike became the barracuda, the heavy, the eviscerator; Reasoner, the epicure, the waggish commentator, the connoisseur. Like Kirk & Spock or Starsky & Hutch, they formed an unstoppable team.

Though both correspondents had a staff of three producers who did almost all the journalistic legwork, Hewitt's formula relied on cultivating the myth that the correspondents were doing all of their own reporting, and bringing something of themselves to the stories they covered. Harry presented an "Essay on Whiskey," for example, that was, in fact, written and produced by Andy Rooney. Mike took special delight in introducing the piece with a raised eyebrow, noting, "I don't believe that in all the years that I've known Harry I have ever seen him devote himself to a story more completely and with more apparent pleasure. Herewith that report."

"The droll treatment of offbeat subjects was Harry's forte," explains Gary Paul Gates. ". . . whiskey, small cars and miniskirts—journalistic side dishes that he served to viewers with his own special brand of 'wry.' "[6]

Mike and Harry played nicely off one another. In one report by

Reasoner, Mike made an unexpected appearance, crashing into his partner's stand-up. It was a story about young, middle-class panhandlers who
had begun to crop up in numbers on New York sidewalks. Mike happened
upon Reasoner as he was recording his on-camera close on Fifty-second
Street, across from New York's posh 21 Club:

> REASONER: The trouble with panhandling as a career is that
> you cannot expand indefinitely, and there are no fringe benefits
> like hospitalization or a pension . . .

Then, Reasoner threw in a dash of irony, delivered with his signature
wispy smile and twinkling eyes:

> REASONER: But it has certain advantages for young people:
> healthful work in open air, flexible hours and a chance to meet a
> lot of interesting people . . .

Mike, ever the prankster, decided that was his cue to barge into the scene
in the middle of filming and demand brazenly:

> MIKE: Pardon me, sir, I wonder if you could let me have a hun-
> dred dollars for lunch at the "21"?

Reasoner, always quick on his feet, didn't miss a beat in his "haughty"
rebuttal:

> REASONER: Why don't you get a decent job—like me?

Later in the season, Mike and Harry paired up in a segment called
"Playing the Money Game," in which they played an illustrative board game
while economist Adam Smith explained the international monetary system.

But it was not all fun and games. During the second season, the pair took *60 Minutes* on its first international trip, and assumed adversarial roles in reporting on the tensions in the Middle East—Mike represented the Israeli viewpoint, while Reasoner told the Arab side of the conflict. It was an interesting innovation in primetime news reporting. Reasoner explained: "We could become somewhat less objective, we were briefly advocates, knowing that the other side would have its advocate, too."[7]

Just a few months later they broadcast a follow-up piece on the Middle Eastern conflict, in which they flipped sides. Mike and Harry took a similar two-sided approach in reporting the war between Biafra and Nigeria, where they had to contend with harsh third-world conditions. Though Mike ended up getting a fairly reasonable hotel room in Lagos, Reasoner notes, "This was not a case of Mike choosing the cushy side of the story; we flipped a coin. His coin, as I remember it."[8]

In fact, Mike ended up contracting dysentery and spending the majority of his two-week trip making debilitating excursions to the lavatory. Reasoner also had his challenges on the assignment; he and his crew came under fire in rebel territory in southern Nigeria.

But the formula had proved successful, and they repeated it a third time to cover the conflict in Northern Ireland, with Reasoner taking the Catholic side of the equation, and Mike, the Protestant. Then, for the second time in his career, Mike boarded a plane with the hopes of interviewing Fidel Castro. Don Hewitt, always eager to meet a head of state, accompanied him to Havana. Their ramshackle hotel rooms were like prison cells, with toilets in the room but no toilet seats. So Hewitt worked his magic: "I bribed the maid to remove the seat from the room of a Romanian bigwig who had the room next door. That night I knocked on Mike's door and presented it to him. We have been fast friends ever since."[9]

Yet, despite Hewitt's prowess as a producer, the Castro piece never materialized—just as it had failed to happen for Mike in 1957 when he attempted to interview Fidel for *The Mike Wallace Interview*.

He did, however, manage to interview another overseas radical that year: Black Panther leader Elridge Cleaver, a fugitive from the law who was living in exile in Algeria. Mike's interview made headlines across America and, as a further measure of its success, had its outtakes subpoenaed by the Justice Department.

Another controversial Wallace piece from that second season involved an interview with Paul Meadlo, a twenty-two-year-old Vietnam War veteran who claimed to have been ordered to fire upon women and children in a 1968 raid of a Vietnamese village. Based on reporting by Pulitzer Prize—winner Seymour Hersh, this electrifying segment made the front page of *The New York Times*—and Mike knew that *60 Minutes* was on the right track. The offices were flooded with irate calls and letters in response to the piece. Mike, who had specifically asked Meadlo about "shooting babies," became an involuntary poster boy for the antiwar movement.

Despite all of its promise, however, the program was not an early success—but neither was it an abject failure. In the first season, it wound up finishing eighty-third out of 103 primetime shows; in the second season, slightly worse at # 92. As *Variety* put it dryly: [*60 Minutes*] showed great promise . . . [and] should easily capture the thinking man's home in the Nielsen sample—both of them."

In the program's defense, the competition in its initial Tuesday night timeslot at 10 P.M. was fierce: *Marcus Welby, MD*, one of the most popular shows on television. CBS was content to concede the hour, given that *60 Minutes*—which broadcast every other week—cost less than $100,000 to produce, only one fifth the budget of most dramatic programming at the time.

As Bill Leonard sees it: "The history of *60 Minutes* has been recounted many times, with writers often implying that the series was not a success at first but gradually grew into something wildly popular . . . As far as we who were running CBS News were concerned, it was a smash almost immediately. Within two seasons it had won a Peabody and a DuPont Award, and from the very first year its ratings were somewhat better than the documentaries that aired on our other Tuesday nights."[10]

The beauty of those early years at *60 Minutes* was that Hewitt and his correspondents could essentially do as they pleased, experimenting with form and format until they got it right. As Mike explains it: "In other magazine broadcasts . . . [stories] are assigned by a central desk. The correspondents on *60 Minutes* and their producers come up with their own stories. There's a kind of creative tension between teams to get the best stories that we can get."

Ideas percolated from the ground up and, after being fleshed out, they were pitched in a one-page summary known as the "Blue Sheet," which went to Don Hewitt for approval. Once approved by Hewitt, that story became the protected domain of the correspondent who originated it, and could not be encroached upon.

The system seemed to work. "I was thoroughly enjoying myself," declared Mike. ". . . Harry and I were having a fine time as a team."[11]

But, as the third season rolled around in 1970, and the show was beginning to find its voice and gain momentum, the unthinkable happened: Reasoner decided to call it quits. He left CBS for a more lucrative offer at ABC, which was trying to establish a credible news division. Mike was shocked by Reasoner's sudden departure, but not Bill Leonard. He knew that Harry had had one foot out the door ever since his removal from the election coverage unit in 1966.[12]

Reasoner had been hurt and saddened by the whole affair. When it came time to renegotiate his contract, which was set to expire in November, 1970, CBS refused to offer Reasoner even a single penny in increased compensation. They were, in effect, asking him to leave. CBS had by now established dominance over NBC in all areas of programming including the news division, now firmly under the stewardship of Walter Cronkite, whose electrifying coverage of the 1969 lunar landing had cinched his position as the nation's top TV news man. With legendary correspondents like Eric Sevareid and Charles Kuralt waiting in the wings, the CBS brass didn't feel like they needed to hold on to Harry Reasoner. And so he went.

It was, in Reasoner's words: "the most wrenching experience I had ever had . . . I was heartsick."[13]

When Reasoner announced his departure from CBS, he received personal good wishes not only from President Nixon, but also from Hubert

Humphrey and former president Lyndon Johnson, who wrote: "CBS will be a lonelier place without you."[14]

No one was feeling it more than Mike, who had grown fond of his collaboration with Reasoner, particularly since his partner's low-key style had allowed Mike to seize the top perch. Now he'd have to contend with another potential rival, and it was anyone's guess who that would be.

This marked the start of a period of tumult for Mike that would build steadily for the next decade until it became overwhelming. As CBS News scrambled to fill Reasoner's vacated shoes, they recruited Dan Rather to take his post at the *Sunday Night News*. Roger Mudd took over Reasoner's other gig as the regular substitute for Walter Cronkite and they still had to staff Harry's *60 Minutes* chair. Reasoner remarked dryly: "If I were so lazy, why did it take three people to replace me?"[15]

And, for Reasoner, ABC would never fully replace CBS in his heart. It speaks volumes that in the eight years from 1970 to 1978 that Reasoner worked at ABC, he continued to have his hair cut at the little barbershop in the basement of the CBS News building on West 57th Street, while nine floors above frenzied staffers would be racing to catch up with Don Hewitt in his relentless drive to the top.

Reasoner would ultimately return to *60 Minutes*, just as the program seized the crown as the number one show on television. But it was not the place he had left, and no one felt it more than Mike. The atmosphere by then would be toxic.

Chapter Thirteen

To Hell with Wallace

T *hank God it wasn't Mike*, thought Don Hewitt, when he learned of Harry's intention to leave the network. Reasoner may have begun as the show's star attraction, but it was certainly no surprise to Hewitt that he had been quickly been overtaken by the larger-than-life presence of Mike Wallace.

As Hewitt puts it: "Mike is, quite frankly, the best thing that ever happened to a television set—certainly the best thing that ever happened to my television set. He's a tiger, the kind of journalist that comes along once in a lifetime."[1]

Now came the daunting question of who could present a match for him. Though Mike might well have been able to carry *60 Minutes* on his own for a stretch, it would have fundamentally changed the nature of the show. The program depended on the synergy of two viewpoints, two personalities. But CBS management had considerable difficulty finding someone who was willing to team up with Mike.

Bill Leonard's first choice to play Mike's foil was an unlikely one: Charles Kuralt, whose bald, pudgy figure made him perhaps Reasoner's antithesis. Kuralt had been called "TV's rumpled Everyman" and was renowned for a sonorous voice and eloquent commentary on his Peabody

Award–winning travelogue series, *On the Road*. But Kuralt declined the offer to join *60 Minutes*, which surprised Leonard. In retrospect, given recent revelations that Kuralt led a secret double-life during his three decades' tenure at CBS, harboring a second hidden family in Montana, it is understandable why he might have wanted to remain the master of his own solitary, itinerant beat, rather than being forced into the far more scrutinized schedule of *60 Minutes*.

Leonard's second choice was likewise reluctant, not terribly attractive nor particularly well-known, but nonetheless an outstanding reporter. Morley Safer had distinguished himself with a series of stellar reports from Vietnam. His 1965 piece on U.S. Marines burning down a South Vietnamese village with their cigarette lighters had earned Safer a George Polk Award and a colorful reaction from President Johnson, who called up CBS president Frank Stanton the morning after the broadcast, demanding, "Frank, are you trying to fuck with me?"[2]

"Who is this?" Stanton asked, still half-asleep.

"Frank, this is your President, and yesterday your boys shat on the American flag."

As Don Hewitt saw the situation: "The truth about Vietnam was that someone had indeed 'shat' on the American flag. But it wasn't Frank Stanton. And it wasn't Morley Safer."[3]

Safer, in fact, had showed extraordinary courage under fire. In the course of reporting another story in Vietnam, he and two CBS cameramen were shot down in a helicopter by Vietcong ground fire. All of the passengers miraculously escaped injury, as did the exposed film. In 1967, Safer pulled off an equally gutsy coup in China, where, using his Canadian passport and posing as a wealthy tourist, he filmed an entire one-hour undercover documentary—a stunt that could easily have landed him behind bars.

But by 1970, Safer was out of the hot spots and ensconced in a far cushier beat as the London bureau chief for CBS News, an exalted office formerly occupied by such legends as Edward R. Murrow, Eric Sevareid and Charles Collingwood, among others. And he was living up to them.

"Safer's pieces from Europe had two outstanding qualities," explains

Leonard. "First, they were exceedingly well written. Second, they *moved.* Most reporters tend to stand in one place and let the camera wander around. With Morley, one got the sense that *he* was really covering the story and that the camera had better hurry to keep up with him."[4]

Safer loved his life in London. His wife had recently completed renovations on their dream home, an Edwardian brownstone on one of London's prettiest squares. A dandyish dresser with a taste for life's fineries, Morley had just turned forty and was happily married with a baby daughter and an antique Rolls Royce—acquired off winnings from a high-stakes poker game in Saigon. When the call came from Bill Leonard, Safer was on assignment in Paris covering preparations for the funeral of Charles de Gaulle, and about to feed his report via satellite to New York.

"I couldn't imagine what Leonard could want," remembers Safer. "I assumed, as all reporters assume, that when the brass calls you, it is because you've screwed up."[5]

But that was not the case. "How would you like to move to New York and take Reasoner's place, be the co-editor of *60 Minutes*?" asked Leonard directly.

Safer's reply was: "Shit! This is the phone call I'd like to get five years from now."

"We can't wait five years," said Leonard. "Reasoner is leaving on Monday. Come tomorrow."

Safer's head was spinning. "I can't come tomorrow! Tomorrow we're burying de Gaulle."

"Okay, the day after," allowed Leonard. "Have a nice funeral."

Safer was beside himself. "Why would I want to give up the dignity and importance of reporting for Walter Cronkite for the dubious honor of working for a fledgling television magazine that would surely have no staying power, that only went on the air every other Tuesday against the lovable *Marcus Welby, M.D.*, and was run by the certifiably insane Don Hewitt? This proposition had all the appeal of winning an expenses paid vacation to Lagos."[6]

But ultimately Safer agreed, on the condition that he receive a contractual guarantee that when *60 Minutes* folded, as everyone expected it would, he would be given his old job back in London. Thus, Safer spent exactly one night in his newly refurbished house before departing for New York, where he and Mike would make history.

Mike, for his part, welcomed the addition to the team. After spending an evening with Safer and his wife, Jane, in London, Mike had come away convinced that Morley would pose no threat to his dominance at *60 Minutes*. As journalist David Blum writes: "Safer's position as newcomer would allow Wallace to exercise his muscle as senior partner and become the most famous face on *60 Minutes*. Safer, of course, had other ideas."[7]

The dueling began from day one. Unlike Reasoner, Safer was no pushover, and his willpower took Mike by surprise. As Mike remembers it: "Morley Safer and I were pals, we came to CBS about the same time, '63. And I didn't know him well, but when I'd do a piece out of London or when I'd travel or when he came to New York or whatever, we were friends."[8]

But friendships didn't count for much at *60 Minutes*. The working structure of the shop demanded a considerable degree of assertiveness on the part of the correspondents and their teams. As Mike recalls: "There was a struggle for turf, which is perfectly healthy, and Hewitt did nothing to dissolve it because this was a creative tension, it's the kind of tension that Ben Bradlee used to preach . . . at the *Washington Post*."[9]

Hewitt had banned all meetings and memos as a matter of principle to encourage individual initiative—and also because he simply didn't have the attention span to sit through a meeting. Most decisions were made quite literally on the fly, marching down hallways, often to the men's room—or inside. (There were hardly any women on staff in those early days.) Profanity abounded as part of the macho culture.

"Come here and fucking look at this!" Hewitt would scream at the top of his lungs, bounding out from a screening room.[10] The *60 Minutes* staffers would be expected to file in obediently from their respective cubicles and cram into the room, where Hewitt would hold forth on the merits of a story he deemed worthy, which was something of a rarity. Hewitt was a stickler for details and demanded the utmost from all who worked for him, including Mike, whom he had a particular way of motivating.

Mike's 1935 high school yearbook portrait. *(Courtesy of the University of Michigan, Bentley Historical Library—Mike Wallace Papers: Box 9, Formal Portraits; photographer: J. E. Purdy & Co., Boston, MA)*

Mike and Buff in 1951 on the set of their CBS show, with his and her matching mugs (plus one for their "Guest"). *(CBS Photo Archive/Getty Images)*

Mike and Buff in "traditional" Irish garb dancing a jig for a 1952 St. Patrick's Day episode of their show. *(CBS Photo Archive/Getty Images)*

Mike performing on the CBS radio program, *On a Sunday Afternoon* (1954). *(CBS Photo Archive/Getty Images)*

Mike hosting *Big Surprise*, a quiz show, in 1956. *(Photo by Hulton Archive/Getty Images)*

Mike and Lorraine playing violin and guitar at their Sneden's Landing home in 1957. *(Courtesy of the University of Michigan, Bentley Historical Library—UM Alumni Association Collection: Box 147, Mike Wallace Folder)*

Mike and Lorraine
drinking tea at Sneden's
Landing. *(Ed Feingersh,
photographer,* Look *Magazine
Collection, Library of Congress, Prints & Photographs
Division, LC-L9-57-7172-D
#21)*

Interviewing Lee Edwards,
Imperial Wizard of the Ku
Klux Klan, on *Night Beat,*
in 1957. *(Courtesy of the
University of Michigan, Bent-
ley Historical Library—UM
Alumni Association Collection:
Box 147, Mike Wallace Folder,
photographer: Gary Wagner,
New York, NY)*

Hosting a live event in front of an audience in 1957. *(Courtesy of the University of Michigan, Bentley Historical Library—Mike Wallace Papers: Box 9, Informal Portraits; photographer: Wagner International Photos, New York, NY)*

Enjoying a lighter moment with Sammy Davis Jr. *(Courtesy of the University of Michigan, Bentley Historical Library—Mike Wallace Papers: Box 9, Mike Wallace with Guests)*

Reporting from a trench
in Vietnam, 1967.
*(CBS Photo Archive/Getty
Images)*

Harry Reasoner, Don Hewitt, and Mike Wallace on the
set of *60 Minutes*, 1968. *(CBS Photo Archive/Getty Images)*

Mike being ambushed by reporters while picketing during a Writers Guild strike at CBS. *(Photo by Bill Foley/Time & Life Pictures/Getty Images)*

Mike and Mary attending a 2004 charity event in New York City.

As Hewitt wrote later in his 2001 memoir: "For more than three decades, Mike and I have had the same conversation. He'll record a narration and invariably ask: 'How was it, kid?' For more than three decades, I've given him the same answer: 'I'll give you an A. Want to try it again and see if you can get an A-plus?' He always does—and he always gets an A-plus."[11]

Hewitt had recognized early on that Mike was a perfectionist who would stop at nothing to get it right, competitive to the point of compulsion. Now it appeared that Morley Safer was cut from the same cloth—another over-achiever, ready to step up and fight, especially when the gauntlet is thrown down. In this case, the gauntlet happened to belong to Mike Wallace.

"It graveled him that I was getting more attention than he at that time," says Mike. "I was much better known in New York than he was and had a bigger 'name,' if you will, than he did, and he found that a little bit difficult to deal with."[12]

"The competition began immediately," explains David Blum, "resulting in fierce fighting over ideas, producers and position on the broadcast, and raging battles between the two men, with hallway screaming matches, of the 'Fuck you!' 'No, fuck you!' variety, alternating with extended periods of angry silence."[13] Safer proudly kept an old 1968 campaign button on his office wall that read: *To Hell with Wallace.*[14]

"Every program should have one sweetheart and one son of a bitch," he once explained, without specifying which position he claimed for himself. Mike, for his part, made no apologies for his strong personality: "I had no intention of becoming the Ed Sullivan of news shows."[15]

In truth, both Mike and Morley felt threatened by the other. "I was envious of his grace at writing," admits Mike.[16] Though he had become a keen editor in his years anchoring the *CBS Morning News,* Mike did not have the gift of turning a phrase like both Safer and Reasoner. Mike was feeling particularly sensitive about this shortcoming in the fall of 1970, for he had been recently approached by Harper & Row to write his first book.

"The fact is that you should probably be writing a book at this stage of your life and career," came a note from the publisher.[17] It was to be ghost-written, naturally, given Mike's busy schedule and the feeling that he did not have a natural writing talent like Morley Safer. This point in particular did not sit well with Mike, for the volume that Harper & Row had proposed for him was to be entitled *Profiles in Journalistic Courage*, a collection of portraits of legends of the Fourth Estate such as Peter Zenger, Harry Ashmore, David Halberstam and George Polk. The title, of course, was a reference to *Profiles in Courage*, the Pulitzer Prize–winning biography that had played a role in Mike's early career. It was during a 1957 broadcast of *The Mike Wallace Interview* that Mike's guest, journalist Drew Pearson, had dropped a bombshell: *Profiles in Courage* was not, in fact, the work of John F. Kennedy, who accepted the Pulitzer for it, but instead had been ghostwritten for him by Ted Sorensen and others. Thus, in the early 1970s, when the idea of *Profiles in Journalistic Courage* was proposed, Mike was understandably touchy about hiring a ghostwriter. The book never came to pass.

The written word, however, remained a critical ingredient of Mike's day job. As Don Hewitt explained it: "The words you hear and not the pictures you see are essentially what *60 Minutes* is all about. In television, if you don't know how to communicate with words, you're in the wrong business."[18]

Mike relied primarily on his producers to write the copy of his stories, lending an editorial hand where needed. Safer, on the other hand, was never far from a typewriter, which would continue to be his preferred means for expression long after everyone around him had turned to computers. In fact, by the 1990s, Safer wound up the proud owner of six manual typewriters, having stocked up on a product that was surely destined for obsolescence.

In November 1970, when he took over his new office at *60 Minutes* and sat down before his beloved typewriter, Safer knew he needed to come crashing out of the gates in order to stand a chance against Mike Wallace. One story in particular might give him a significant leg up: Vietnam. Though Mike had done his share of reporting from the war zone, it didn't compare to Safer's two-year, award-winning tour in Saigon. As Mike puts it: "Safer *owned* Vietnam."

But what could Safer report about the nearly seven-year-old conflict that hadn't already been covered? And how to work within the *60 Minutes*

magazine format, which did not lend itself to breaking news? Safer had a
thought. Why not go back to the very beginning?

And so he wrote:

*The date: August 4, 1964. For most people it triggers no particular emotion.
It is not December 7, 1941. But August 4 is important whether you remember
the date or not. It was on that date in the Gulf of Tonkin, off the coast of North
Vietnam, that the war in Vietnam really began. And the incident that began it
has become as controversial as the war itself. The U.S. destroyers* Maddox *and*
Turner Joy *were attacked by Communist torpedo boats. Or were they?*

Within hours of this alleged attack, President Johnson would issue the
order to bomb North Vietnam, and, days later, Congress would pass the Gulf
of Tonkin Resolution, giving the president the authority to take the country to war. But what if, as some suspected, the Tonkin incident had been
largely fabricated?

Safer's idea was to go back and interview the naval commanders actually involved in the incident and review the cable communications between
the fleet and Washington. He knew he needed a top-notch producer unafraid
of potentially explosive subjects. That man was Joe Wershba.

By far the most experienced and talented producer in the shop at the
time, Wershba had been at CBS News since 1944, during the era of Edward R. Murrow. Safer wanted him because he was a producer willing to
take on the highest levels of government. Mike, feeling an intrusion on his
turf, went ballistic when he heard that Wershba would be working with
Safer, but there was little he could do about it once Don Hewitt had approved the "Blue Sheet" for the Vietnam story.

Safer was given the green light for "What Really Happened at the
Gulf of Tonkin?" at the end of 1970. He and Wershba went to work on it in
early 1971, interviewing, among others, Captain John Herrick, a naval officer who was aboard the U.S.S. *Maddox* the night of the alleged attack by
North Vietnamese PT boats. But Herrick painted a confused and ambiguous

picture of the events, as evidenced by the many cables he sent that evening to the pentagon:

ENTIRE ACTION LEAVES MANY DOUBTS EXCEPT FOR APPARENT ATTEMPED AMBUSH AT BEGINNING. SUGGEST THOROUGH RECONNAISSANCE IN DAYLIGHT BY AIRCRAFT.

The hawks in Washington, itching to go to war, were in no mood to wait for daylight and pressed President Johnson to order an aerial bombing raid against North Vietnam, even when Captain Herrick continued to express his serious reservations that retaliation was justified. In his final cable of that fateful evening, Herrick wrote:

MADDOX SCORED NO KNOWN HITS . . . NO KNOW DAMAGE OR PERSONNEL CASUALTIES . . . SUBSEQUENT MADDOX TORPEDO REPORTS WERE DOUBTFUL IN THAT IT IS SUPPOSED THAT SONAR MAN WAS HEARING SHIP'S OWN PROPELLER BEAT.

Despite the obvious confusion on the battlefield, President Johnson chose that night to set into motion the events that would drag the nation into a decade-long quagmire that would claim some 60,000 American lives.

Safer and Wershba chose to stage their interview with Captain Herrick on the bridge of a destroyer. It was, in fact, the very ship where it had all begun—the U.S.S. *Maddox*, now used as a training vessel. This dramatic backdrop served to enhance the stakes in an already powerful and provocative story. The piece went on to win an Emmy Award for Joe Wershba and Morley Safer—the first Emmy for *60 Minutes*.

Mike bristled at being upstaged so soon, but took it in stride. Competition made him thrive—and he knew, with Safer in the house, that he would have to up his game considerably. He did.

Chapter Fourteen

Lacing Up the Gloves

W hile millions of Americans were enthralled by the March 16, 1971 broadcast of Morley Safer's "Gulf of Tonkin" piece, Lyndon Baines Johnson was not. The former president brooded sullenly as he watched the program with his wife, Lady Bird, at their ranch in Stonewall, Texas. Vietnam had been Johnson's albatross, eclipsing all that he had accomplished on the domestic front and forcing him to withdraw ignominiously from seeking reelection in 1968. He had tried at various points to imply that he had inherited the conflict in Vietnam from Kennedy, but this *60 Minutes* piece implied that the decision to escalate the war without provocation lay squarely on Johnson's shoulders. As Don Hewitt put it: "We pointed a finger at a president and suggested that he had played fast and loose with the people."[1]

Johnson crushed his cigarette butt in the ashtray and rose to pace the room. Lady Bird recognized the signs at once—her husband was hatching a plot. Johnson had recently learned that *60 Minutes* was planning to cover the inauguration of his Presidential Library in Austin. But it wouldn't be Safer— this time, CBS was sending Mike. Intent on controlling the story, Johnson decided to invite the correspondent and his team to stay at his ranch.

When word of the presidential summons arrived at West 57th Street,

Mike felt vindicated. While Safer may have been able to seize the Vietnam story on the ground, Mike was still king when it came to the big interviews. Hewitt jumped jubilantly into the fray and announced he would be accompanying Mike to Texas. Johnson, however, had an axe to grind with Hewitt over the "Gulf of Tonkin" piece, and would soon find an amusing way to humiliate him.

During his presidency, the six-foot-four-inch Texan had developed a particular brand of persuasion that became know as "The Johnson Treatment," a dizzying blend of badgering, cajolery, intimidation and horse-trading designed for one purpose only: to get his way. Johnson planned to apply the full measure of "The Treatment" to the arriving *60 Minutes* delegation in order to spin their story in his favor. But Johnson's plan came up against something he didn't expect and could not easily defend against: The Wallace Treatment. Not unlike the Johnson formula, Mike's technique would combine disarming flattery with sudden aggression.

Johnson took control of the first round with a heavy dose of Texas charm. He and his wife showed up in person to pick up the *60 Minutes* team at the Austin airport. Mike and Hewitt piously took the jump seats opposite Lyndon and Lady Bird Johnson in the presidential limousine. Mike knew there would be a price to pay for this magnanimous hospitality, and it came soon enough when Johnson declared that a certain topic would be off limits.

"I don't want to talk about Vietnam," he snarled at Hewitt. Then, knowing Mike's reputation for pushing limits and crossing boundaries, he turned to the correspondent and made sure to underscore his point. As Mike recalls it: "He said that if I brought up Vietnam while the cameras were rolling, he would cut off the tour on the spot and 'send [us] boys packing.'"

Mike and Hewitt exchanged a glance—without Vietnam the Johnson interview would be a dud. Knowing that Hewitt was depending upon him to turn the situation around, Mike retreated to his corner to prepare for Round Two. He knew it would be a tough fight. As Mike explains: "Throughout his long career in Washington, Lyndon Johnson had a well-earned reputation for being almost compulsive in his need to exert authority and dominate all who came into his presence."[2]

The next morning began bright and early. As Hewitt remembers it: "About 6 A.M., I heard a rooster crow and a knock on the door. It was LBJ himself, ready to take Mike and me on a tour of his 'spread.' Sure enough, parked outside was that big white Lincoln convertible that had become as much identified with him as the Stetson he wore."[3]

Mike and Hewitt climbed into the backseat. Johnson took the wheel and floored the accelerator. "We took off on the sightseeing ride at an alarming high speed," recalls Mike.[4] Johnson's aggressive driving became even more reckless when the former president began fumbling with one hand to unwrap a candy bar in the glove compartment.

"It was 6 A.M.," recalled Don Hewitt, "but the thirty-sixth President of the United States wanted a candy bar."[5]

Upon devouring his snack, Johnson slammed on the brakes alongside an outdoor trash can. He turned squarely to Don Hewitt and handed him the wrapper.

"You," he said. "Throw it in that can."

"Sir?" gasped Hewitt.

"Throw the wrapper in the garbage," Johnson repeated impatiently.

Hewitt actually caught Mike grinning at him as he sheepishly obeyed the presidential decree and delivered the offending refuse to the receptacle. It would have been demeaning enough, but then President Johnson hit the gas, leaving Hewitt in the dust and forcing him to trot breathlessly after the departing car. Hewitt took the episode in stride: "You haven't been put in your place until you've been put in your place by Lyndon Johnson."[6]

Round Three began as Johnson pulled up to the first stop on their tour: a tumbledown shack in the middle of Lyndon Johnson State Park. The lanky Texan emerged from his convertible and pressed a button that activated a loudspeaker hidden in a nearby tree, triggering a recording that went something like this:

The little old black lady who lived here was a midwife, and one night she got on her mule and rode ten miles down the road through thunder and lightning to deliver a little baby....[7]

"As the tree got to the punch line," recalls Hewitt, "LBJ turned to me and Mike in the backseat. I couldn't look him in the eye so I concentrated on the big ears sticking out from under his Stetson, as the tree said: 'And that little baby's name was Lyndon Baines Johnson.' "[8]

"There he was, looking right in our faces, and I didn't know what in the hell to say," Hewitt continued. "Mike, cool customer that he is, said: 'Mr. President, that's the loveliest story I ever heard.' Mike said it. Honest to God, he actually said, 'That's the loveliest story I ever heard.' How he kept a straight face I'll never know."[9]

But of course he did know. Mike had acted on Broadway. He could play it straight, play it cool, play it tough, friendly, furious and anything else that was required to get people to tell their story. Mike was well aware that most interviews began before the cameras started rolling, and had the skills to ingratiate himself and tenderize his subject in advance of the kill. President Johnson was getting the Wallace Treatment. Round Three: Wallace.

Round Four took place in the LBJ library where the CBS cameramen were lining up their shots for the interview. Hewitt pulled Mike aside to plot a strategy for getting Johnson to discuss Vietnam. "I think we should just spring it on him," whispered Hewitt.[10]

"No," responded Mike. "I want him to know it's coming so he can think about it and give us a cogent answer."

What both of them failed to realize was that Mike had a microphone on his lapel—he was *wired* and everything he said could be heard in the control room, where Lady Bird Johnson was waiting with a close aide. Soon thereafter, an infuriated President Johnson marched onto the set and barked: "Goddamnit, Mike, I've said all I'm going to say about the war, so forget about it."[11]

But Mike stood his ground. "You're wrong, Mr. President. You can't avoid it."

"I can avoid any goddamned thing I want to avoid!"

"You're wrong," Mike said again with astonishing calm. Hewitt could see the veins beginning to bulge on LBJ's neck, and backed away from the escalating confrontation. Then Mike shifted tactics and began to compliment the former president on his many achievements, particularly the passage of landmark civil rights legislation, and all the other accomplishments of LBJ's vision for America that became known as the "Great Society."

"But then everything turned sour, Mr. President," said Mike, "and you know why?"

"Why?" frowned Johnson.

"Because you let that war get out of hand. Vietnam fucked you, Mr. President, and so, I'm afraid you fucked the country. And you've got to talk about that."[12]

Johnson glared at Mike in shock and fury, then stormed off. Mike could scarcely believe those words had come out of his mouth. Hewitt took a deep breath, wondering if they should start packing up the cameras. But, after some time, Johnson returned to the set.

When the interview finally began, Mike decided not to press his luck on the Vietnam question. He tossed Johnson a few softballs, then raised the issue of presidential responsibility in the nuclear age.

Johnson cleared his throat and, looking squarely at Mike, said, "Throughout our history, our public has been prone to attach presidents' names to international difficulties. You will recall that the War of 1812 was branded as Mr. Madison's war and the Mexican War was Mr. Polk's war, the Civil War . . . was Mr. Lincoln's war, and World War I was Mr. Wilson's war, World War II was Mr. Roosevelt's war, Korea was Mr. Truman's war. But Kennedy was spared that. Vietnam was Mr. McNamara's war and then it became Mr. Johnson's war . . . I think it's very cruel to have that burden placed upon a president because he is trying to follow a course that he devoutly believes is in the best interest of his nation. And if those presidents hadn't stood up for what was right during those periods, we wouldn't have this country what it is today."

With that, Johnson stopped dead and looked squarely at Mike.

"Goddamnit, Mr. President, that was great!" exclaimed Mike, so excited that he couldn't resist giving the former president a playful shove.

"Is that what you were after?" Johnson allowed a smirk.

"Damn, right, Mr. President," Mike grinned back at him.

The bout of the titans was over. Verdict: Wallace, by TKO.

Both Mike and Morley Safer were beginning to hit their stride by the time the 1970–71 season of *60 Minutes* came to a close. In addition to Safer's Emmy, the show had also picked up a coveted Peabody Award for distinguished programming—the industry's most competitive honor. But the program continued to languish at the bottom of the ratings. It had declined steadily in viewership over the first three seasons and now ranked a dismal 101 out of 103 primetime shows. CBS considered pulling the plug, as it would for another three seasons, but decided instead to move the show outside the primetime schedule, so it would not affect the network's over- all average in terms of primetime viewers. The new time slot: Sunday eve- ning at 6 P.M. In a vote of confidence, however, the network decided to double the number of shows—the program would now run every week, rather than biweekly as it had in its Tuesday slot. Two factors conspired to keep *60 Minutes* in good stead at CBS: it still cost far less to produce than any other hour-long program, and, unlike breaking news coverage, many epi- sodes of *60 Minutes* could successfully be rerun, because its essays and profile pieces were not time sensitive.

If imitation is a measure of success, then *60 Minutes* was a winner even in its initial timeslot, where NBC had launched a rival show *First Tuesday*—one of many unsuccessful attempts to seize the newsmagazine crown from CBS. Don Hewitt worked ceaselessly to refine the show's for- mula with magazine-like touches, such as the inclusion of viewers' mail. *60 Minutes* became the first television program to devote airtime to reading mail from its audience—a feature that served to increase the loyalty of the fan base. The volume of mail climbed steadily and became an incubator for story ideas. As *60 Minutes* delved more into investigative pieces, some 20 percent of the stories came from ideas suggested in viewer mail, which delighted Mike, who began to perceive that the show had a mission.

"I was always after the hard story, the gritty story, the pointed story, because those are the ones I do best," said Mike. "Don wanted essays and features and humor."

In order to get the stories he was after, Mike had to recruit producers who shared his vision. In 1971, he teamed up with the first of three journalists who would produce Mike's most explosive and controversial pieces for *60 Minutes*. He was a young Canadian named Barry Lando.

Like Ted Yates and Av Westin before him, Lando would help Mike raise the level of his game by going after provocative subject matter and employing the type of reporting that became *60 Minutes'* trademark—the use of hidden cameras, ambush interviews and other undercover techniques employed for the first time in television news, often with severe aftershocks. Indeed, one of these Lando pieces would end up in litigation that went all the way to the Supreme Court, and set a precedent that has had an impact on all journalists since.*

Poring over the pages of the alternative press and other radical sources for ideas, Lando had a nose for provocative and riveting stories. In their very first assignment together, Lando and Mike produced a piece that contained, according to one journalist, "the first truly magical moment in the history of *60 Minutes*."[13]

It involved the touchy issue of school busing in Washington, D.C. While outwardly championing the policy as a way of racially balancing public education, many of the city's liberals, like Senator Edward Kennedy and Supreme Court Justice Thurgood Marshall, sent their own children to elite private schools in Georgetown, and refused to discuss the matter on camera. Lando decided to shine a spotlight on this hypocrisy by staking out the Senate Office Building with a camera crew and having Mike name the names.

They finally got a politician to agree to go on camera: liberal black delegate Walter Fauntroy, who represented the District of Columbia and whose children attended the Georgetown Day School. By pure chance, there happened to be a demonstration on the sidewalk where the outdoor interview

---

* In *Herbert v. Lando et al.*, which will be discussed at greater length in chapter 15, the Supreme Court ruled that plaintiffs in libel cases should be allowed to inquire as to the accused journalist's "state of mind."

was taking place, about the very issue they were discussing. It was a group of picketers in front of the Supreme Court bearing antibusing placards.

Quick to seize the moment, Lando signaled his correspondent, who waved over some protestors to join the conversation he was having. Just as Congressman Fauntroy was delicately trying to defend his decision to send his children to private school while advocating the policy of busing, Mike cut him off mid-sentence:[14]

> MIKE: May I interrupt you for a second? Ladies, would you come over here for just a second? We had no idea that you were coming. This is Congressman Fauntroy from the District of Columbia and we're talking about the very subject of busing at this instant. . . .

What followed could not have been more perfect, even if it had been scripted. The protestors began asking Mike's questions for him. Turning directly to the congressman, an outraged white mother demanded:

> WOMAN: May I ask you a question? Where do *their* children go to school? Private schools or public schools? Eliot Richardson, where does [sic] his kids go to school? Kennedy, where does his go to school?

Since the camera was rolling, the Congressman had no choice but to respond:

> FAUNTROY: Yes, the answer is, I believe, that all of them have their children in private schools . . .
>
> WOMAN: Then you're discriminating against me because I have my kids in public school . . .
>
> OTHER WOMAN: Now, you are our leaders and we ask you as our leaders to provide an example. If you truly believe that a child may get a quality education in a racially balanced school, we think you should step forward and say, "Here's my child, and I want to put him in a racially balanced school." That's all we ask.

Fauntroy, convinced he had been set up, was left speechless. The piece, entitled "Not to My Kid, You Don't," aired in November 1971, and earned Mike another feather in his cap.

Lando's second story with Mike was even more powerful. This one involved draft-dodgers and deserters who had fled to Canada. Mike and Lando traveled north across the border to meet and interview the self-proclaimed "refugees." While many remained defiant, some were scared and unsure of their future, particularly a young man named Ken Duff.

After returning home, Mike and Lando decided to track down his parents to film their side of the story. Mike came down particularly hard on Ken's mother, asking Mrs. Duff if she felt "ashamed" of her son's conduct, how she would react if he went to jail and what she had to say to the parents whose children served and died in Vietnam.

"At that point, Mrs. Duff's voice broke and she began to cry," Mike remembers. "She was, in fact, so distraught that I immediately called a halt to the interview. Nor did I do that only for her benefit, for in truth my own feelings were edging out of control. I've always tried to maintain emotional distance from the people I interview. But that was one time when the normal defense mechanisms failed me."

Mike found himself suddenly welling up for all the parents who had lost a child to a senseless tragedy. Perhaps he was back on that desolate mountain in Greece where nine years earlier he had discovered the broken body of his son.

"It turned out," notes journalist David Blum, "there was only so much Wallace's black hat could hide."[15]

As this deeply painful loss would continue to haunt Mike for decades to come, he would be forced to toughen his exterior, steel himself and hone a public image of fearlessness and bravura to mask this inner vulnerability. But one day that would all change.

Chapter Fifteen

Abuse of Power

WASHINGTON, D.C., June 19, 1972—One of the five men arrested early Saturday in the attempt to bug the Democratic National Committee headquarters is the salaried security coordinator for President Nixon's reelection committee...

So began a story filed by a pair of cub reporters working the Metro desk at the *Washington Post*—the first piece by Bob Woodward and Carl Bernstein on a scandal that would soon engulf the Nixon presidency and win the newspapermen multiple Pulitzer Prizes. But it took some time for other media to pick up on the Watergate story, particularly television news.

Mike had been especially slow on the draw. As Gary Paul Gates noted: "Wallace had become an apologist for Nixon, which revealed a certain perversity, a characteristic desire to go against the grain of fashionable opinion and liberal cant . . . Wallace disdained the elitist, cocktail party liberalism that flourished in Manhattan and Georgetown."[1]

There may have been a strategic calculation in cultivating this contrarian image, however, for it would later give Mike a distinct advantage in helping to secure access to some of the key players in the Watergate scandal, who were steering clear of Mike's left-leaning colleagues in the media. And playing devil's advocate was also largely a parlor game for Mike, who loved to test the mettle of those around him through provocation, and, later, intimidation. Like a boxer working the speed bag at his local gym, Mike was constantly honing his ability to get a rise out of anyone and everyone who crossed his path, including staffers who needed to develop impressively thick skins to survive Mike's near constant jabs. Indeed, as the full extent of Nixon's abuse of power became known, Mike, too, on his smaller stage at West 57th began to throw his weight around in ways that some found offensive. He was tough and mercurial, apt to reduce an underling to tears. To survive on his team, you had to be able to withstand his verbal tirades without taking them personally, and even argue back when need be. It took a certain personality.

One such personality was CBS News producer Marion Goldin. Based in Washington and a self-confessed "political junkie," Goldin had latched onto the Watergate story long before her peers. During the summer of 1972, she worked with Mike as an assistant on the coverage of the political conventions. While few at CBS, including Don Hewitt, were particularly focused on Watergate, Goldin quickly convinced Mike that the break-in and its aftermath was the story of the moment. The convention had been carefully orchestrated by Republican power brokers to be a "coronation" of incumbent President Richard Nixon, but Mike, with prompting from Goldin, veered off the playbook to seek out interviews with some of the unsavory characters whose names had been mentioned in Woodward's and Bernstein's reporting.

Says Goldin: "It was really a preview in many ways of the way Mike and I worked, because Don [Hewitt] was not always an ally. He was sometimes an adversary. Mike was famous for saying: 'We'll shove it down his throat.' And that's what we did with Watergate. The Watergate coverage began at that convention."[2]

Mike knew right then and there that, more than just as a convention assistant, he needed Goldin as a permanent member of his *60 Minutes* team. As she explains it: "One of the reasons that Mike wanted to work with me and Barry [Lando] was that he wanted to do tougher stuff than was in Don Hewitt's DNA. Don obviously had tremendous strengths but investigative news was not one of them."[3]

Many years later, Mike would tell Goldin: "You know, if it wasn't for you and Barry there would be no *60 Minutes*, because Don Hewitt has no moral compass."[4]

Thus, in 1972 Goldin joined Mike's staff at *60 Minutes*, the lone female producer in a high-testosterone fraternity of journalistic overachievers. It was not an easy environment; Goldin had to contend with rampant sexism, chauvinism and harassment. But she clearly valued the opportunity she had as a *60 Minutes* producer, so Goldin made it work. Six months would elapse before Goldin landed her first Watergate story—and it was a monster.

Tensions between the new administration and the news media had begun from the moment Nixon took office. The president held firm to the paranoid conviction that news organizations had been mistreating and misrepresenting him throughout his entire political career, and as Commander-in-Chief, he was determined to do something about it. Nixon considered CBS to be Enemy Number One. He loathed its White House correspondent, Dan Rather, with whom he often got testy during news conferences—a forum which the president did his best to avoid. A particularly volatile exchange between the two led Nixon to blurt: "I have never heard or seen such outrageous, vicious, distorted reporting in twenty-seven years of public life."[5]

By 1972, the relationship between the administration and CBS had deteriorated to the point that White House hatchet man Charles Colson told network president Frank Stanton that the Nixon administration would "bring CBS to its knees."[6] It was in this climate that Mike would take on the Watergate players, one by one, exposing their lies and establishing his reputation as television's ombudsman.

By the spring of 1973 the Watergate dominoes had begun to fall. White House Counsel John Dean had been fired and Nixon advisor John Ehrlichman and Chief of Staff H. R. Haldeman were forced to resign. Dean, who saw himself as a fall guy, had begun cooperating with prosecutors and was scheduled in late June to testify before the Senate committee investigating the Watergate crimes. That's when Mike received a phone call from Ehrlichman.

It was not a call he was expecting. Ehrlichman had been shunning the press for months, though Goldin and others in the media had not relented in their efforts to get him on the record. Knowing that John Dean's imminent testimony would be highly damaging to his reputation, Ehrlichman had decided to preempt it, and chose *60 Minutes* as his vehicle.

Like a team of prosecutors preparing to depose their star witness, Mike and Marion huddled together to mount a systematic plan of attack. First, they deconstructed Ehrlichman's motives in finally agreeing to the interview. It seemed clear that *60 Minutes* offered him long-form exposure on the national television stage. Mike, moreover, was probably seen by Ehrlichman as somewhat sympathetic to Nixon—and, as a Washington outsider, perhaps not as well-versed in the minutiae of the unfolding Watergate story.

"I must say that being sized up in that way—as a relatively safe interviewer, a soft touch—was an uncommon experience for me, and I was determined to disabuse Ehrlichman of that comforting notion," says Mike. "I prepared as thoroughly for the interview as for any I have ever done."[7]

Mike and Goldin spent an entire week holed up in her office, poring over reams of documents, briefing papers, wall charts and more. Ehrlichman, for his part, apparently did little to prepare for the pounding he was about to receive.

When the interview finally took place, there was nothing Ehrlichman could do but evade, deny, and claim lapses of memory—all of which came off just as badly as any words he might have spoken. What was worse, Mike and Goldin chose to film Ehrlichman in excruciating close-ups, which revealed every nervous tic and bead of sweat. Says Mike, "Ehrlichman came across not only as a liar but as a man who knew, even as he stammered through his answers, that he was being perceived as a liar. It was a devastating exercise in self-incrimination."[8]

Ehrlichman simply had no leg to stand on—particularly when it came to the infamous slush money and other covert funds. In one exchange, Mike asked: "Why would anybody in the Nixon administration—in the official Nixon family—want to defend, want to raise money to defend the guys who burglarized the Watergate?"

Ehrlichman's response: "Certainly for no reason of self-interest . . . There may have been a—a compassionate motive on somebody's part. I can't answer that."

Then Mike did what Mike does best—the one-word follow-up. He simply raised an eyebrow and repeated incredulously: "Compassionate?"

It sat there for a moment while a clearly flustered Ehrlichman tried to think his way out of the corner into which he had painted himself, then he attempted to redirect: "But the—the—in terms of self-interest, protecting one's own interest, and so on, that's a question that comes back to this whole cover-up thing. Cover up what? The White House had no interest, as such, in covering this thing up. It had no exposure."

In truth, the White House's exposure had been snowballing for some time—even more so now that Nixon's right-hand man, John Ehrlichman, sat squirming in the hot seat opposite Mike Wallace. The interview was broadcast in June 1973. While some criticized Mike for being too soft on Ehrlichman, by and large the public admired the broadcast for what it was—the first substantial interview with a major player at the epicenter of the biggest scandal in modern American politics. Fred Friendly, the network executive who had briefly served as president of CBS News in the mid-1960s, praised Mike for being the "best-prepared interviewer" he had ever seen. Mike, who has always been generous in acknowledging the legwork of his producers, gave the credit to Marion Goldin. John Ehrlichman, who had been so publicly exposed by the interview, would go on to be convicted on multiple counts of conspiracy, obstruction of justice and perjury for his role in the cover-up. And Mike would go on to confront many of the other players in the Watergate scandal, including Ehrlichman protégé Egil Krogh, whom he interviewed in prison, as well as Charles Colson, G. Gordon Liddy, and even disgraced Chief of Staff Bob Haldeman himself.

But CBS would be lambasted in the press for checkbook journalism on those last two interviews—for they paid $15,000 to get Liddy on camera, and for Haldeman, an astonishing $100,000. What made matters worse, was that neither interview was particularly revealing. As Mike explains it: "Liddy likened himself to a prisoner of war whose duty, even if tortured, was to disclose nothing more than his name, rank and serial number."[9]

Haldeman proved an even greater disappointment. "Throughout our long interview . . . he was unfailingly courteous as he calmly but deftly parried my attempts to pin him down on Watergate . . . I felt like a frustrated boxer trying to land a solid punch on an elusive, nimble-footed opponent. And the truth is, I barely laid a glove on him."[10]

When the dust finally settled on Watergate, it became clear to Mike that the contours of the media landscape had shifted. Having gotten a taste of the transformative power of investigative journalism, the public now craved more. Mike was determined to bring this type of journalism to *60 Minutes*. His producers Marion Goldin and Barry Lando were eager coconspirators.

Though both were based in Washington at the time, Lando had decided to leave the political stories to Goldin, choosing instead to focus on crime, corruption and injustice. In 1973, Lando hit upon a piece that had it all. The story involved Lieutenant Colonel Anthony Herbert, a highly decorated war hero who had enlisted at age seventeen, taken home some twenty-two medals for his service in Korea, and then, in a span of merely fifty-eight days, won the Silver Star and three Bronze Stars for service in Vietnam. He was by every measure the model of the American fighting man. The Army, in fact, had used his picture on the cover of its training manual and had sent Herbert on a promotional tour around the world. But everything changed in 1969, when Colonel Herbert was unceremoniously stripped of his command. The sudden and unexplained demotion seemed to come out of nowhere, until Herbert went public about reports he had filed that accused his superiors of war crimes in Vietnam for having covered up atrocities perpetrated by U.S. troops including looting, torture and summary executions.

It was a bombshell—and the media pounced on it. *The New York Times*

Sunday magazine ran a scathing indictment of the military entitled "How a Supersoldier Was Fired From His Command," which solidified Herbert's status as a heroic martyr in the eyes of the antiwar public. But there was one thing the public didn't know about Colonel Herbert: he had lied.

Though producer Barry Lando had initially believed Herbert's accounts of the events and had even considered coauthoring a book with him, his research uncovered serious inconsistencies in the officer's story. Lando also found sources who alleged that Herbert himself was capable of brutality. It was a story made for *60 Minutes*, particularly the way that Mike and Lando conspired to tell it: they set a canny trap that would make television history.

Taking a page from their earlier piece about bussing, which had shown the power of having two opposing views in direct confrontation, Mike and Lando decided to conduct the interview with Colonel Herbert while a second officer, Major Jim Grimshaw, waited in an adjacent room, ready to come out with contradictory testimony. It was the first use of a television trick that has since become ubiquitous on sensationalistic programs like *The Jerry Springer Show*.

Major Grimshaw had served in Vietnam as a company commander under Herbert, whom he greatly admired. "I would stick up for Tony Herbert for anything," he had told Mike when the *60 Minutes* team first approached him to be interviewed for the piece. "However, I feel that as an individual, let alone an Army officer, a man must have integrity. Therefore, I would not lie for him or for anybody else."[11]

According to Grimshaw, Colonel Anthony Herbert had fabricated important facts in *Soldier*, the book he wrote about his experiences in Vietnam. (Herbert had ultimately chosen to coauthor the book with *New York Times* journalist James Wooten and not Barry Lando, as first discussed.) However, though others besides Grimshaw had cast doubt on the veracity of Herbert's accusations against the Army, the Colonel had voluntarily subjected himself to a lie-detector test, which he had passed. He was, in Mike's words, "a very tough nut to crack."

When the two sat down for their interview in January 1973, Mike presented Colonel Herbert with substantial evidence to repudiate his claims that he had been dismissed for reporting war crimes in Vietnam. "I also questioned him about the stories we had heard that he himself had either committed or condoned mistreatment of Vietnamese," recalls Mike. "None of it seemed to faze him. He clung firmly to the position that all those who disagreed with him were either lying—were, in fact, part of the conspiracy—or were still in the service and under pressure to lie."

Then Mike revealed to Herbert that one of those who disagreed with him—Major Grimshaw—was waiting across the hall to join the interview.

"Bring him in," said Herbert, poker-faced. ". . . Ask him the same questions."

Grimshaw took his seat across from Mike and proceeded to discredit a great deal of what Herbert had said. He also insisted emphatically that he had not been pressured by his superiors or the Pentagon to do so. Herbert fumed silently.

Says Mike, "It was evident that Grimshaw's unexpected appearance had scored a palpable hit . . . Herbert did not exactly lose his composure—he was far too disciplined for that—but he was visibly shaken."

After the cameras stopped rolling, Herbert lashed out at producer Barry Lando, convinced that Lando had done a deliberate hatchet job on him for having been "spurned" as a collaborator on Herbert's book. It was another fantasy, of course—but one Lando believes to have partially motivated Herbert when he filed a $44 million libel lawsuit against Lando, Wallace and CBS. It would prove a long and grueling legal battle that would span thirteen years and produce a ruling that would significantly affect the protection of journalists under the First Amendment.

Though Mike was confident that they had done nothing improper as journalists, he must have felt uneasy about the whole thing. Certainly, there had been some theatricality about the way they had chosen to ambush Colonel Herbert.

In fact, in a 1971 article that Mike had written about television news, he freely admitted to the artifice of what he did: "Most television interviews are, at least in the nature of their staging, artificial."

Indeed, all of the reverse angles in those early *60 Minutes* interviews were fabricated after the fact, for there was only one cameraman on the set. Thus, all the cutaways of Mike listening, grimacing, nodding his head or raising an eyebrow had to be staged by turning the camera around after the interviewee had left.

But Mike remained unapologetic about it and a staunch defender of his often difficult job: "The television reporter/interviewer must somehow persuade the interviewee to forget all the paraphernalia, the lights, the camera, the technicians, the intervals for reloading film. He must persuade his subject to forget all that and perform as an accomplice in counterfeiting reality . . . a coconspirator in revealing something provocative and newsworthy."

"The Selling of Colonel Herbert," as the *60 Minutes* piece was named, certainly had been provocative and newsworthy. As far as the lawsuit went, CBS ultimately prevailed—but Herbert managed to score a key victory in a Supreme Court ruling, which established a precedent that is now part of the curriculum at journalism schools and has affected every reporter in the field since. The decision states that litigants suing journalists are entitled to "inquire into the editorial process or states of mind" of those involved in the alleged libel. This meant a plaintiff could potentially subpoena a reporter's field notes and other evidence that, prior to the landmark ruling, had been vigorously shielded by First Amendment protections. Despite this procedural triumph, however, the Herbert case would ultimately be dismissed because nothing in the *60 Minutes* piece was found to be libelous. But the victory was bittersweet.

"It cost CBS News a fortune to defend ourselves from Anthony Herbert's lawsuit," remembers Mike. "It cost Barry Lando, the producer, an emotional fortune. Barry once told me that he never went to sleep even one night without thinking about the libel suit. Because a libel suit against a reporter is very similar to a doctor facing a malpractice suit. All we have is our credibility, our integrity, and if that is called into question, the reporter suffers. A reporter has to be fair, has to be accurate, has to be thorough, has to be careful."[12]

Careful, indeed—for Mike and Barry Lando were about to introduce another weapon into their investigative arsenal, something that would come to define *60 Minutes,* and finally send its ratings through the roof: the use of the hidden camera.

Chapter Sixteen

Nowhere to Hide

T here has been much discussion as to what caused the meteoric ascendancy in the late 1970s of *60 Minutes* to become the most viewed and profitable show on television. Certainly, it must have been a combination of factors. Even after the 1971 move from a twice-monthly broadcast on Tuesday night to its weekly berth on Sunday evening, *60 Minutes* continued struggling to find its audience. The 6 P.M. broadcast was often preempted by Sunday afternoon football games that went into overtime, frustrating *60 Minutes'* viewers.

That all changed in 1975, when *60 Minutes* finally returned prime-time into the 7 P.M. Sunday night berth that it occupies to this day. That decision, which proved to be the most lucrative scheduling adjustment in television history, was largely motivated by a legal technicality. Since 1971, CBS and the other networks had been constrained by the FCC-mandated "Primetime Access Rule," which allowed them to broadcast only three hours of primetime shows per night, with the remaining time being allocated to affiliates for local news and other programming. The networks fought the rule for years to no avail. Then, in a 1975 amendment, the FCC decided to allow the networks to retain a fourth hour on Sundays, provided they use it for children's shows, documentaries or public affairs programming.

NBC promptly moved a family show to the coveted 7 P.M. Sunday slot— its highly-rated *Wonderful World of Disney*. ABC followed suit with its own established family show, *Swiss Family Robinson*. CBS, however, had nothing in its arsenal of existing programs. After a disastrous attempt to create an original children's show, which finished dead last in the weekly ratings, CBS came up with the idea of moving the broadcast of *60 Minutes* one hour later. It was a stroke of pure genius. By counter-programming a hard-edged documentary series against the family fare offered by its rivals, CBS began to woo increasing numbers of adult viewers.

The year 1975 was also marked by another important change at *60 Minutes*—the addition of a third correspondent. The show had been airing weekly since moving to Sunday, and the pressure on Morley and Mike to crank out stories had become almost unbearable. They were constantly on the road, changing time zones—so disoriented, sometimes, that they had to reach for the hotel matchbook to remember what city they were in. Mike did a piece on jetlag in 1973 in which he discovered, to his chagrin, that he flew more air miles annually than a typical TWA pilot. They desperately needed relief. That's when Dan Rather's name came up.

Morley Safer was not too keen about the idea—he didn't think a third correspondent was necessary and was worried about what the addition might do to the program's chemistry. Mike, on the other hand, relished the added competition—that's what drove him to excel.

"Listen, my friend," he told Rather, "we are going to have a third correspondent. We all want it to be you. There is no second choice."[1]

Rather was already a star-on-the-rise at CBS, having distinguished himself as Nixon's most vocal antagonist in the White House pressroom. But, like all the *60 Minutes* reporters before him, including Mike, Rather had some initial reservations about the assignment. It was his wife, Jean, who ultimately persuaded him to join the team.

With three correspondents, *60 Minutes* was now able to run year round, without a summer hiatus—a fact that helped to increase loyalty among its viewers. According to Mike, another factor in the 1970s that conspired in *60 Minutes'* favor was the Yom Kippur War, when Egypt and Syria launched a surprise attack on Israel on October 6, 1973.

The audacious offensive on the holiest day in Judaism caught the Israelis off guard. President Nixon, relieved to have an international crisis on his hands to deflect attention from the ballooning Watergate imbroglio, responded by sending 20,000 tons of tanks, artillery and ammunition to resupply the Israeli army. The Arabs, in retaliation, decided through OPEC to enforce an oil embargo against the United States, causing long lines at the pump, rationing of gasoline and a quadrupling in oil prices. This meant that Americans were much more likely to be housebound on Sunday evenings— when *60 Minutes* was broadcast.

As Mike puts it: "People no longer had the gas to drive to grandma's house on a Sunday afternoon. They had to stay home. And they began to fiddle around with the dials and see what was on . . . And this was at the time of Watergate . . . when we were doing investigative pieces that nobody else was doing on television."[2]

Indeed, the *60 Minutes* formula dovetailed perfectly with the national zeitgeist, and Mike came to occupy a unique perch as the nation's foremost investigator, uncovering corruption and injustice wherever they lurked, and doing it in a way that was highly cinematic, with clandestine filming techniques like hidden cameras.

It was not the first time such devices had been featured on television. Alan Funt had introduced hidden cameras on his seminal 1948 show, *Candid Camera*. But *60 Minutes* marked the first time the technique was used in the gathering of television news. It would bring the viewing public to places and situations they had never seen. For a story about child pornography, for example, Barry Lando walked into a porn shop with an undercover cameraman who filmed clandestinely as the producer made a casual purchase of illegal kiddie porn.

From a technological standpoint, it was no small feat. Unlike today where one can record high-definition video on a mobile phone, *60 Minutes* pieces in the 1970s were photographed entirely on 16mm. Magazines of film had to be loaded and unloaded in a darkroom or changing bag. Some smaller cameras allowed the use of "daylight spools," which could be loaded outside a darkroom, but these too required careful threading and only lasted a few minutes. On top of it all, the smaller cameras needed to be wound up by hand between takes. Because the cameras were also quite noisy, *60 Minutes* cameramen created special foam-insulated bags with discreet cutouts for the camera lens. Like a crew of criminals preparing for a heist, the team would stake out the location and rehearse their plan meticulously, testing their hidden camera in a dry run and adjusting their choreography to ensure the best angles.

For one such caper, Lando borrowed a tool from police interrogation rooms: the one-way mirror. The story in this case was an exposé of Medicaid fraud in the Chicago area, where several laboratories were suspected of running a kickback scheme to secure contracts. It worked as follows: if local physicians agreed to funnel their blood work to these establishments, the labs would then kickback a significant portion of the federal money they collected from Medicaid reimbursements.

A traditional news approach to telling this story might have involved interviews with various participants and law enforcement officials—a series of talking heads. But Lando was intent on presenting something far more dramatic. Thus, he set up a phony medical clinic on Chicago's North Side, opened the doors for customers. It wasn't long before representatives from various labs came to solicit business.

"To document these visits, we installed [a] one-way mirror behind the desk of the clinic and stationed our cameras behind it," explains Mike.[3] Under Illinois law, they were allowed to photograph the event but not to record audio of what was being discussed. So Mike positioned himself within earshot of the deal-making, hidden in a nearby closet to act as witness to the proceedings. Of eleven labs that came calling, an alarming nine of them offered bribes and kickbacks to secure business contracts—and Mike heard them all. At the pivotal moment, he would leap out of his closet and confront the suspects on camera—the quintessential "gotcha!" moment for which *60 Minutes* would soon become famous. One such exchange was al-most comical in the way the flustered lab representative became aware of the trap and tried desperately to backpedal his way out of it:

MIKE:(emerging into view) I want to interrupt you, if I can. I'm recording this for broadcast, and I just heard you say that you will give back 25 percent in a kickback, 25 percent in a rebate. Is that correct?

LAB REP: Well—wait a minute. You look familiar to me.

MIKE: Yeah. Tell me something: how much in the way of kick-backs and rebates do you get involved with and why?

LAB REP: I—I don't give—I don't give kickbacks.

MIKE: You just—I heard you right in here. You offered 25 per-cent in a rebate to these two gentlemen, to this new clinic.

LAB REP: Well, I—I didn't mean it that way. I think I better not say anything now.

It was riveting television—the fearless investigator catching a crimi-nal in the act—and far more engaging than a scripted cop show from the 1970s like *Baretta*, because this was actually happening. Real people, real stakes. Executive Producer Don Hewitt's dream of packaging news in an entertaining format was finally coming to fruition.

"The Clinic on Morse Avenue" became one of the most celebrated col-laborations between Mike and Barry Lando. There were, of course, the in-evitable naysayers—purists within the journalistic community who cried "Entrapment!" But Lando would defend himself by pointing out that the people posing as clinic staff had taken pains never to solicit any form of payment; they had instead waited for the lab representatives to make offers.

Another piece produced by Mike and Lando caused even more contro-versy. This story involving identity fraud had the *60 Minutes* team demon-strating how easy it was to obtain false papers and then using them to commit a felony. As Mike explains: "Lando and I were able to cajole a researcher on our staff named Lucy Spiegel to set about acquiring a set of phony credentials. Then we followed her step by step with a camera crew as she proceeded to construct a false identity."[4]

Spiegel began her quest at the Municipal Building in Washington, D.C., where she applied for a replacement birth certificate using the name of a child who had died two decades earlier. What made the scheme particularly cunning was that Mike and a camera crew "just happened to be there" at the same time that Spiegel was filling out her paperwork. Lando had made an appointment to interview John Crandall, the head of the office, who was unaware of Lucy Spiegel's connection to *60 Minutes*. So it was the opposite of a hidden camera investigation, for the *60 Minutes* team had declared quite openly to Crandall that they were filming a story about identity fraud. The cameraman cannily chose a position for the interview in the front part of the office. From here he could zoom into Spiegel in the background as she obtained her fake papers, while Mike drew Crandall's attention to the young woman about to get her new birth certificate:

> MIKE: And if she were an imposter—I'm sure she's not, but if she were an imposter—she could use it for fraudulent purposes?
> CRANDALL: Yes, she certainly could.
> MIKE: To rip off whatever she wanted to rip off?
> CRANDALL: I think I better go ask her if she's going to.

It could not have unfolded more perfectly. Crandall walked over to Spiegel and asked her in a playful tone, "You're not going to use that for fraudulent purposes, are you?" To which she replied indignantly, "Of course not!"

But Spiegel was lying, of course. Using her bogus birth certificate, the intrepid *60 Minutes* researcher proceeded to obtain a fraudulent driver's license, social security card and U.S. passport—with Mike and the camera crew following her at every step. Then began the felonies.

Spiegel used her documents to apply for food stamps and open a bank account, from which she proceeded to write a series of bad checks, buying camera equipment and even a plane ticket to flee the country. Mike confronted the camera salesman and airline ticket agent immediately after the purchases, asking them pointedly whether they thought the customer was legitimate. Neither had any doubt, which was deeply ironic, for the audience knew that Lucy Spiegel had, in fact, just fleeced them.

It was another television milestone—the first time a crime had been committed on camera by a network news employee. And there was inevitable fallout: after watching the show, one man was able to create ten aliases, steal $10 million and flee to Central America. Lando would also have regrets about some of the collateral damage *60 Minutes* may have inflicted by willfully conning those salespeople: "We probably cost some innocent people their jobs . . . by putting them on national television and making them look foolish."[5]

"But back then," writes media critic David Blum, "Lando embraced the latitude *60 Minutes* gave him to get the story, and Wallace . . . well, Wallace just loved the camera, and he knew precisely how to use it for maximum effect. His pointed post-scam interviews put his instincts as a showman on full display, and once the story aired, the response only fueled his desire to flaunt his on-air persona."[6]

While delighting in the role of the investigator, Mike continued to do profiles and more straightforward interviews—though, in his piece on Johnny Carson, the media-shy comedian would make an ironic joke of his unworthiness to sit opposite Wallace: "I'm not running a boiler-room operation. I have no phony real estate scam. I'm not taking any kickbacks. I did steal a ring from Woolworths once when I was twelve years old, and I think that's why you're here." In a subsequent Friars Club roast, Carson would call Mike "the proctologist of interviewers."

No topic was off limits for Mike and his team of producers. In another watershed broadcast, they actually took on *themselves*—an investigation into corruption within the media, specifically the widespread practice of accepting gifts in exchange for favorable coverage. Many of their colleagues—

including Walter Cronkite, the "most trusted man in America"—had been guilty of such transgressions. Mike and Lando seemed to relish pointing cameras at their own network, when they filmed a TV critic from the *Pittsburgh-Post Gazette* on a press junket in New York as he opened an envelope of cash to cover "incidentals"—a gift from CBS.

Not to be outdone, producer Marion Goldin soon jumped on the investigative bandwagon, designing a journalistic sting of her own that became Don Hewitt's favorite segment. It involved a cancer clinic at Murrieta Hot Springs, California run by a pudgy man with a greasy comb-back named R. J. Rudd. By then, *60 Minutes* was getting over a thousand letters a week, and had received a surprising number of complaints about this clinic, which claimed to offer a "miracle" cure for cancer. R. J. Rudd seemed to be preying upon the terminally ill, and Goldin convinced Mike to con the con man.

Like the "Fake ID" segment, it would involve a two-pronged proposition, combining an undercover operation with a cards-up approach that would entail Mike and his crew arriving on the scene to film the interview parts of the story. The undercover team consisted of soundman James Camery playing the part of "The Colonel," a wealthy retiree purportedly suffering from leukemia, along with a small retinue that included his "nephew" (cameraman Greg Cook) and "secretary" (producer Marion Goldin), all of whom arrived at the clinic in a Rolls Royce.

Upon signing in, they informed the staff that the Colonel's "nephew" was a professional photographer who intended, conveniently, to film his uncle's experience at the spa—reducing the need for subterfuge even in the undercover operation.

The "miracle" cure offered at Murrieta consisted of a three-day fast during which the Colonel ingested only distilled water and lemon juice, followed by a vegetable diet augmented with vitamin and mineral supplements. The patient's urine was taken twice a day and analyzed by the staff, who praised the Colonel for making remarkable progress, even though he never actually fasted. The *60 Minutes* team even randomly substituted urine samples from Goldin and the cameraman without detection, proving there was no actual lab work being performed at Murrieta. Meanwhile, R. J. Rudd began to press the Colonel for an investment in the clinic, an offer he made to all his wealthy patrons.

Then Mike arrived with a second crew to interview Rudd and other staff members. When asked about his credentials, Rudd claimed to be an ordained Baptist minister with two doctorates in economics and philosophy—both, it turned out, from bogus mail-order institutions. The undercover team, moreover, had smuggled out a sampling of the costly health products that the clinic sold to its patients as part of their treatment, and in analyses by an independent lab these tonics and elixirs proved as worthless as Rudd's diplomas. Yet the charlatan seemed unfazed by the confrontation, even when "The Colonel" revealed himself to be a part of the *60 Minutes* investigation. Even when Mike called him a con man to his face, accusing him on camera of preying on the elderly, Rudd maintained his innocence to the end.

As a result of the *60 Minutes* broadcast, however, the State of California closed down the Murrieta clinic, which had amassed some $37 million in debt, and convicted R. J. Rudd of conspiracy and fraud. (Indictments and jail time would become an increasingly common outcome for the unfortunate subjects of a *60 Minutes* investigation.) Enthusiastic viewer response convinced Goldin to do a follow-up piece on one of the mail-order diploma mills that had issued R. J. Rudd his phony doctorates: California Pacifica University, run by an exuberant swindler named Ernest Sinclair.

Sinclair was on the phone when Mike and his crew barged into his low-rent office above a wig shop in Hollywood. His reaction to Mike and his microphone was becoming all too typical:

> SINCLAIR (on phone): Hey, wait a minute. Hey! *60 Minutes* is here. Can you believe it?
> MIKE: How are you?
> SINCLAIR: *60 Minutes* here?! Hold the phone.
> MIKE: Nice to see you.

SINCLAIR (to the person on the phone): I'm trying to tell you his name. Let's see, there's Dan. No, this—hey, this is my favorite. Gosh! What's your—what's your last name?

MIKE: Wallace. Mike Wallace.

It was Mike's "James Bond" moment where, smooth and confident, he reveals his identity to the soon-to-be opponent. Though Sinclair was thrilled to be in the presence of his favorite *60 Minutes* correspondent, he, too, would soon be indicted on charges of mail fraud following the broadcast.

"Ingratiating to the end," notes Mike in amusement, "Sinclair wrote later from prison to inform me that he intended, finally, to go straight and to thank me for helping him see the light."[7]

Swindlers and scam artists increasingly became the subjects of some of the most popular segments on *60 Minutes*, which prompted Don Hewitt to wonder, "Why would someone who is obviously a crook go on *60 Minutes*?"

Morley Safer's answer: "A crook doesn't feel like he's really made it as a crook until we've told his story on *60 Minutes*."

Mike's observation: "*60 Minutes* itself hadn't really made it with America's television audience until we started telling stories about crooks, con men and scoundrels."[8]

By the end of the 1977–78 season, *60 Minutes* had risen to become the number six show on television, eclipsing the wildly popular *Charlie's Angels* and *Starsky & Hutch*, which prompted *Time* magazine to print a tongue-in-cheek rhetorical quiz, as follows:

Would more television viewers prefer a program in which:

a. Three beautiful young women solve crimes unencumbered by bras

b. Two handsome young cops solve crimes unencumbered by civil liberties, or

c. Three not-so-young and not-so-handsome reporters solve crimes encumbered by a camera crew?

Like its fellow primetime shows, there was a dramatic, even quasi-fictional component to the *60 Minutes* formula—its trio of superhero journalists were evolving into carefully crafted archetypal caricatures of who they really were. At the top of his game, Wallace had solidified his reputation for being something of a human lie detector, a highly skilled investigator capable of uncovering fraud and deceit wherever it lurked. But in the years to come, Mike would let his growing celebrity go to his head—and, like a tragic hero, he would start believing in his own invincibility.

Chapter Seventeen

Sickeningly Happy?

I hate to sound sickeningly happy but I confess that I am," Mike told a journalist during the 1970s heyday of *60 Minutes*. "My kids are healthy, I'm devoted to my wife, I like the work I do, my health is fairly good."

"I feel a little guilty about all of that," he added. "But it didn't come easily. The process of growing was long and difficult for me, and I got there in a strange and devious way. But I'm there now and I like it."[1]

A perfect time, thought Mike's book agent Bill Adler, to pen a memoir. He pitched his client on the idea, but Mike had his doubts. Ever the perfectionist, Mike avoided getting involved in anything to which he couldn't devote himself fully, and the current demands on his time were brutal. Adler told Mike he had another client who could act as a ghostwriter. Mike cringed at the thought, but agreed to meet with him—an unassuming sports columnist named Neil Offen, who had written several books on baseball.

"Mike wasn't sure," explains Offen. "He wanted to do it himself but he didn't have the time or the organizational predisposition to do it."[2]

They agreed to meet for dinner. "Mike still had some trepidation," remembers Offen. "As someone who wrote, he was reluctant to acknowledge that he needed extra support, extra help."

But the two hit it off, and Bill Adler promptly sold the book idea to

Michael Korda, editor-in-chief of Simon & Schuster. Neil Offen went to work collecting background information and talking to many of Mike's associates. Then, when it came time to interview the subject himself, Mike magnanimously invited Offen and his wife to spend a few weeks at his summer rental on Martha's Vineyard. Offen found Mike to be extremely pleasant and cordial, a thoroughly genial host. But as they sat down to begin the interview process, it became apparent that Mike had a certain type of book in mind that did not involve a great deal of revelations about personal matters.

"Mike was not terribly reflective on his own life," said Offen. "He was much more interested in speaking about what he did rather than what he thought.

"For a book to work, you need a lot of ability to reflect. You have to think 'What does all this mean, how does it affect the cosmos?' And that was always difficult with Mike. He was very much a doer and not a thinker."

Offen was stymied. As a ghostwriter, it was imperative that he get inside the head of his subject. "Maybe he's not a reflecting kind of guy," thought Offen. "Maybe he's someone who goes from one thing to the other and doesn't take time to step back and look at what it all means."

Not that Mike was withholding information. He readily recounted details of his multiple marriages and checkered career, and even delved into the most painful chapter of his biography: the death of his son. It was a moment that caused Offen to drop his pen.

"When I first heard the story and the description of the story, which is extraordinarily painful and riveting at the same time, I said to myself: 'Wow!' "

He knew that he had found a window into the heart of his character. "It gave an insight into him that most people did not know. I thought it explained his drive . . . it was incredibly dramatic. I really thought that was the prism through which his whole career could be seen."

Yet Wallace was reluctant to go into great detail about the terrible loss, even though as a journalist he knew Peter was the key to the story—it's certainly where he would have set his own sights as an interviewer. But Mike wasn't quite ready to go there as an *interviewee*.

Says Offen, "I really, really tried to push to get more of that from him, and he pushed back."

Mike had recently returned to Greece for a story about the military junta—and it had, on some level, affected him. In the decade since Peter's death, he had worn only black ties as a gesture of mourning—but it was a private acknowledgement of his inner pain, one that few people were even aware of. For the outside world, Mike made sure that his still-vulnerable heart was well protected.

As *The New York Times* put it: "The public Mike Wallace is a masterful creation, one that has matured and grown in size over the years, and he works hard—choosing the right stories, framing questions in advance, structuring pieces in the editing room—to make sure it retains its razor sharp edge."

The tough guy façade that he had cultivated so painstakingly as an interviewer was an attempt to bunker himself from outside inquisition, which is why he rebuffed the personal questions from Neil Offen. Mike was still sensitive to the fact that he had only begun his newsman career in earnest at midlife—age forty-five to be precise, when he shed all the other "frivolous" roles that he felt undermined his journalistic credibility. This personal metamorphosis, moreover, was deeply tied to the emotions of losing his son. So he parried the probes by Neil Offen, or anyone else for that matter, lest they awaken the profound sadness whose debilitating power Mike had already felt.

At home, Lorraine was going through her own trials. The *60 Minutes* years had not been easy on her, particularly as Mike's mystique began to take him over. Though Lorraine possessed refined, even aristocratic social graces, she was never suited, nor did she expect, to be a media wife. And yet it was Lorraine who arranged for the intimate dinner parties with *New York Times* publisher Punch Sulzberger, *Time* magazine's Henry Grunwald, Abe Rosenthal and other members of the New York media elite. Though Lorraine was far more at home at the country house in Sneden's Landing, these evenings allowed her to showcase their East Side town house. And it certainly helped her husband's credentials to be dining with journalistic power brokers. But most nights, whether in Manhattan or across the Hudson, Lorraine found herself alone—drinking and abusing tranquilizers.[3]

"I was there in Tel Aviv interviewing Golda Meir," Mike wrote in 1971. "On a telephone call back to the United States . . . I was reminded by my wife that I'd spent approximately nine of the last twenty weeks away from home, flying back just enough it seemed to put my pieces on the air on *60 Minutes*, then flying out again."

The words were part of an article on "The Television Reporter" that Mike wrote for an anthology to be entitled *A TV Viewer's Guide to the News*, which was to illustrate the difference between print and television journalism. Mike's article, which was never published, continued:

. . . perhaps it would be useful to include here an item little written about but much discussed in the fraternity—the home life of the television correspondent. It is one of the hazards of his craft that his family life suffers from neglect, more one must imagine than in most professions. For the correspondent is a wanderer, if not by nature, then perforce . . . And since his name turns up on television screens in all these far off places, he becomes an object of some curiosity to the local ladies, to whom his trench coat beckons as a badge of mystery, which they'd like to plumb. Such attention can be flattering, if hazardous, to the stability of home and hearth.

As *60 Minutes* hit the top of the charts on television and its correspondents attained celebrity status, certain of them indeed succumbed to the temptation of life on the road. To some, it became almost sport—a woman in every port, so to speak, or motel. But not Mike—he never had the makings of a serial philanderer. In fact, he was always a romantic at heart, almost old-fashioned in his courtships. Mike would become smitten and remain loyal to one woman at a time. The one wartime affair in the Pacific was hardly casual—Mike briefly considered staying in Australia to see it through, which is what happened in the tryst with Buff Cobb, whom he married. Then came Lorraine, who Mike considered the love of his life. He was fiercely devoted to her, always intensely protective of Lorraine, even more so as she began to lose her stability and withdraw. Lorraine, like Mike, was prone to severe depression. Harry Reasoner would say about Lorraine, "Every year, a few more cards slip from the deck."[4]

Indeed, while Lorraine's increasing fragility sometimes made Mike feel that he was walking on egg shells, he would do anything for her. In 1976, at Lorraine's behest, Mike became a shopkeeper. Together, they opened a retail establishment in her beloved Haiti—an emporium named Ambiance that sold everything from kitchenware to furniture, artwork, clothing and more. It was a family affair. Lorraine's daughter, Pauline, who had solid retail credentials (she worked at Design Research, the precursor to stores like Crate & Barrel and Design Within Reach), was enlisted to be the main buyer. Lorraine's brother, an artist and architect, was contracted to renovate a house in Port-au-Prince that would serve as the storefront. A cousin, Nancy Chenet, who resided in Haiti, would act as manager. The establishment, as portrayed in *The New York Times,* was:

> *. . . one of those Victorian gems with courtyards in front and back, louvered French doors all around, shaded by mango trees and breadfruits, with turrets covered in bougainvillea, and all around the sound of dogs barking and cocks crowing in the middle of the day, and in the distance, the bells of the Cathedral tolling on the hour.*[5]

The author of that lyrical depiction was none other than Mike, himself—in an uncharacteristically sensual and poetic mood. It was a side that few people saw, but one that thrilled Lorraine, who was already hatching plans for their retirement, a time when they could move back to her island paradise.

But retirement was the furthest thing from her husband's mind. This was a man who couldn't bear to slow down. He was a poster child for what Deepak Chopra has called a trap of the Western mind—becoming a human *doing,* rather than a human being.

As prolific as Mike had been in the past, the '70s marks an almost superhuman level of output. In addition to his ever-increasing investigative pieces, Mike was now churning out some of his most memorable profiles on such luminaries as Maria Callas, Norman Mailer, Gore Vidal, Vladimir Horowitz and Roman Polanski.

The interview with Norman Mailer was the third time Mike and the author had gone head to head. Their first two bouts, in 1957 and 1960, had plenty of posturing and fireworks. In this 1973 encounter, Mike accused Mailer of playing loose with the facts in his biography of Marilyn Monroe.

"Monroe, Mailer, and the Fast Buck," as the segment was entitled, infuriated the novelist, who in a fit of braggadocio told reporters that the next time he ran into Mike he was going to work him over, concentrating his blows to the body because Mike's "face is already so ugly that there's no point in doing any damage to it."[6]

In Mike's encounter with Roman Polanski, he likewise tried to elicit some sparks when he asked the exiled director about his alleged drug use and debauched lifestyle with Sharon Tate prior to her brutal murder at the hands of the Charles Manson gang. There was a poignancy to Polanski's reply:

> . . . if I tell you that we lived quietly, that we had quiet evenings and lis-
> tened to music, that—that Sharon was a lovely cook, it will all seem like ali-
> biing, and it will serve no purpose, because the very fact that you have to ask
> this question puts me—puts me already in a bad light. Because if you ask
> someone a question, "Is it true that you had intercourse with a zebra in the
> middle of Trafalgar Square?" it puts him in a bad light, whether he—even if
> he says, "Are you completely crazy?" or "Are you joking?" Whatever he will
> say, there will be in the memory of the people this question—that he was
> asked whether he had intercourse with a zebra.

It was a variation of the criticism that Mike was receiving increas-ingly for his "ambush interviews"—an oft-used component of *60 Minutes* investigative pieces. In print journalism, if the subject of an investigation refuses to respond to allegations, the reporter simply writes: "Mr. X declined to comment." In the *60 Minutes* formula, however, subjects would be stalked by a camera crew and chased down outside their residence or office, while Mike shoved a microphone in their face as they attempted, inevitably flustered, to obscure themselves. And by choosing to broadcast this image, *60 Minutes* would taint the subject with the appearance of guilt in a way that carried far more weight than the relatively benign printing of "no comment." This signature technique was certainly controversial, but it provided viewers with the high entertainment value that they had come to expect from *60 Minutes*, which continued, as it climbed in popularity, to raise audience expectations.

"I feel the need to keep topping myself and I deplore it," admitted Mike in an interview with *People* magazine. "I suppose I've established a pattern for myself that is difficult to break."[7]

A *New York Times* piece on *60 Minutes* said, "Charges have recently increased that it sometimes engages in overkill, going after gnatlike stories with journalistic bazookas."[8]

To some, *60 Minutes* was starting to become a runaway train. In order to stay on top of the ratings, they needed bigger scoops and more aggressive tactics, which had the inevitable side effect of focusing media attention back at them. *60 Minutes* itself became the story and Mike Wallace was its main character. But Mike steadfastly refused to allow *himself* to be subjected to a "Mike Wallace-style" interview.

"As an interview subject himself, Mike Wallace is guarded," reported *The New York Times* in 1979. "During one recent session, he snapped off the reporter's tape recorder every time the conversation edged into what he deemed sensitive territory."[9]

What was Mike trying to hide? A growing disconnect, for one, between the outer Mike Wallace—the fearless investigative reporter, the journalistic juggernaut, the iconic newsman that Americans by the millions were cheering on—and the inner Mike, a man who was still insecure and increasingly weary.

Quoted in a piece for *American Film* in 1977, Mike said, "I'm 58 now, I have waves of being tired. It's been eight years of jet lag, strange hotel beds, a variety of waters and diets, the pressure of coming back and forth.

There was a time I enjoyed immensely taking a bag and walking down an airport ramp. But after the first five years it got a little old. About a year ago, I wanted to quit. Except where do you go? There isn't a job in television that's as good."[10]

As Bill Leonard explained it, "Mike Wallace had a habit of pursuing his job to the point of physical and mental exhaustion and then complaining that he was overworked."[11]

"The traveling we do, jeez, it's just unreal," Mike remarked in early 1979. "I work too hard for a sixty-year-old man. I'm a little concerned right now. Maybe because it's the end of the season and to a certain degree it's physical tiredness. But for the past six months, I haven't felt as fresh. I'm getting a little more cynical, a little more . . . I know this is a good story but so what."[12]

It was around this time that Mike read a draft of his autobiography as ghostwritten by Neil Offen, who, not surprisingly, had chosen to lead with the death of Peter Wallace. It's not how Mike wanted to tell his story; he would have been more comfortable starting with one of his famous interviews.

"What came out just wasn't me," he told *US* magazine. "I realized that if I was going to do it, I'd have to do it myself."[13]

So Mike took out pencil and paper and jotted down some 15,000 words during his summer vacation, intent on setting the record straight on the question: Who is Mike Wallace?

"I guess I would like to believe that there's more than one string to my bow. That's why I'm writing this. The media tends to typecast you as always being a tough guy. And to a certain extent, you become captive to that personality."[14]

He would never complete his own version of the manuscript, however. Several years later, he would team up with a second collaborator, and they would produce a memoir that focused largely on his achievements, rather than what made him tick. But the ticking they ignored was, in fact, a time bomb—for, three months after that book's release, Mike would attempt suicide.

Chapter Eighteen

A Life Beyond Reproach

The Middle East was a minefield—particularly for Mike. Within
days of his interview at a secret location in Beirut with Kamal
Nasser, a close lieutenant to Yasser Arafat, the PLO operative was
assassinated by an Israeli hit squad. The year was 1973, which marked the
twenty-fifth anniversary of the founding of Israel, and tensions in the region were high. The prior summer eleven Israeli athletes had been gunned
down by Palestinian terrorists at the Munich Olympics; by the fall, Arabs
would launch their surprise attack against Israel on Yom Kippur, the holiest day in Judaism.

Kamal Nasser's assassination occurred on April 10, 1973, when undercover commandos from Israel's elite Special Forces burst into the bedroom
where the Palestinian was asleep and shot him in the head. The Israeli
team reportedly included future Israeli prime minister Ehud Barak, then
twenty-nine and dressed in drag by way of disguise.

Mike was the last Western journalist to have seen Nasser alive, and
some members of the PLO suspected Mike of having leaked his whereabouts to the Israelis. The suspicions had been fueled by the fact that, directly after his encounter with Nasser, Mike had traveled to Tel Aviv to

conduct an interview with Aharon Yariv, the former head of Israeli Intelligence. The accusations of Mike's complicity were without merit, of course,
but it cast him in a bad light among certain members of the PLO, who
counseled Mike to steer clear of Lebanon if he valued his life. The warning troubled him on several levels.

Throughout his journalistic career, he had taken great pains to stake
out neutral territory between two opposing viewpoints. In domestic politics, he had managed to command the respect of both Republicans and
Democrats. His coverage of the civil rights struggle in the 1960s had gained
him the trust of even the most militant crusaders against white oppression
such as Malcolm X. Here in the Middle East, Mike was likewise determined to balance his reporting and present both sides of the conflict. But
the Middle East was a powder keg and, despite Mike's ginger attempts to
walk a straight line, a few missteps would earn him the ire of many.

In 1972, Mike had interviewed Libyan strongman Moammar Gadhafi, who would make headlines the following year when he nationalized
U.S. oil interests in his country and declared, "The time has come for us to
deal America a strong slap on its cool, arrogant face." Gadhafi was among
the leaders in the oil embargo against the United States that followed the
Yom Kippur war, causing the gas shortages that forced people to stay at
home and, according to Mike, bolstered the ratings of *60 Minutes*.

At the time, access to countries like Libya and Saudi Arabia was severely restricted for American journalists, but Mike visited them all and
interviewed nearly every figure of importance in the Middle East—an exhaustive list that included Golda Meir, Moshe Dayan, Menachem Begin,
Yasser Arafat, Anwar Sadat, Benjamin Netanyahu, the Shah of Iran, Ayatollah Khomeini, Iranian president Mahmoud Ahmadinejad, to name a
few. His coverage of the region, however, would subject Mike to some of
the most blistering criticism of his career—for, though he struggled to
strike a balance, Mike would be perceived in a number of instances as coming down too hard on the Israelis and too soft on their enemies.

In several encounters with Menachem Begin, for example, the Israeli
prime minister became livid at Mike for having the temerity to compare

Begin's revolutionary tactics in the 1940s to those used more recently by PLO leader Yasser Arafat and Black September, the terrorist group responsible for the massacre in Munich. Mike did not think the comparison was all that far-fetched. In the years before the formation of Israel, Begin had been commander of a radical guerilla group committed to the violent overthrow of British rule in Palestine. They were responsible for a 1946 bomb blast in the King David hotel in Jerusalem that killed ninety people and injured scores more.

Menachem Begin, however, took serious umbrage at Mike's line of questioning, calling a halt to their interview in 1977 and berating Mike off-camera for his impudence. The Israeli defense minister walked onto the scene and joked that his prime minister was engaged in a "fist fight" with an American journalist, which Mike took as a compliment. Returning to his hotel, Mike bragged about the encounter to some fellow reporters at the bar, and the next thing he knew, the incident was all over the Israeli press. But this was nothing compared to the firestorm that he generated in a piece about Syria, entitled "Israel's Toughest Enemy."

The report, described by *The Christian Science Monitor* as "The most controversial segment in the eight-year history of '60 Minutes,'" characterized, among other things, the life of the tiny Jewish minority living in Syria, thought by Westerners to be oppressed and mistreated in a pervasive atmosphere of anti-Semitism. But Mike's reporting discovered that things were not nearly as bad as he had imagined. He found that Jews in Syria led thriving lives with few restrictions on their freedom.

"Life for Syria's Jews is better than it was in years past," declared Mike in the broadcast, a simple statement that brought down the wrath of Jewish leaders across America. Mike's office was flooded with mail from angry viewers demanding "Was Mike Wallace trying to deny that he is Jewish?" or accusing him of being a "self-hating Jew." It was a very painful episode.

As Mike admits, "There have been times over the years when I have openly courted controversy and confrontation . . . to pursue stories that I felt would have some impact and stir up a useful fuss of one kind or another. But . . . that was not my intention when I took on the Syrian assignment."[1]

Mike became the target of the American Jewish Congress, which demanded a closed door meeting with him. The AJC representatives secretly recorded, then released a fourteen-page transcript of their talk to the media, along with a letter condemning the reporting as being one-sided, "flatly wrong, astonishing and completely insupportable." Mike stood by his story and even returned to Syria six months later to do a follow-up piece with similar conclusions. But the "self-hating Jew" label would continue to follow him for decades to come.

In 1990, just two months after Saddam Hussein's invasion of Kuwait, Mike and Barry Lando would do a piece set in Jerusalem that resulted in what Don Hewitt describes as "the low point of my more than fifty years at CBS."[2]

It was the third year of the so-called *Intifada*, in which Palestinian youths had taken to the streets to protest Israel's annexation of the West Bank and occupation of East Jerusalem. The geography of Jerusalem, a city revered by all three of the world's monotheistic religions, is bound to cause strife. The Western Wall, Judaism's most hallowed shrine, sits directly below the Temple Mount, a thirty-five-acre compound that contains the Dome of the Rock and Al-Aqsa Mosque, two of the holiest sites in Islam. On October 8, 1990, a tragic incident occurred at the intersection of these different faiths, when Israeli police clashed with rock-throwing Palestinians.

The story, as reported by all major media outlets in the U.S., including CBS News, was that, while Jewish worshippers were praying quietly at the Western Wall, Palestinians began bombarding them with sizable rocks from above. The Israeli police were forced to storm the Temple Mount, where they fired upon the Palestinian demonstrators, killing twenty and wounding some 150 more. The use of deadly force was deemed necessary by the Israelis, but it seemed somewhat excessive to the U.N. Security Council, which condemned it—one of the only votes in which the U.S. has sided against Israel. The resolution called for an independent investigation of the event by U.N. monitors, but Israel refused to comply.

Barry Lando decided to conduct his own investigation. By going through the original tapes from eight CBS cameras that covered the event, as well as raw footage from the other networks and Israeli TV, Lando constructed a very different picture of what happened that day.

"It was a fascinating study of video journalism, how seeing something doesn't mean that it actually happened, and how easy it is to distort and actually lie about what goes on simply by moving pictures around," recalls Lando.[3]

When Mike arrived upon the scene to interview the eyewitnesses, he could hardly believe what he was hearing. The Israeli response, he determined, had been extremely disproportionate to the provocation. And once riled up, the Israelis fired indiscriminately at civilians, including doctors and nurses. One nurse was hit while tending to the wounded *inside* an ambulance. It was, according to most people interviewed by the *60 Minutes* team, a massacre. After the piece went on the air, the public outcry exceeded that of the Syrian story. Mike received hate mail from every Jewish organization in America and was vilified in the Israeli press.

Although many of Mike's and Lando's findings would be corroborated six months later in independent investigations by Human Rights Watch and others, the accusation of betraying his Jewish heritage would continue to haunt Mike until well into his eighties. And it was hardly the only stigma against him. Throughout his tenure at *60 Minutes* Mike would be dogged by some more disturbing labels, these against his person.

A round the time that Neil Offen met with Mike to begin the process of ghostwriting his book, publisher Simon & Schuster had another autobiography in the works, to be written by fellow CBS newscaster Sally Quinn. Blond and voluptuous, Quinn had come to CBS from the *Washington Post*, where she wrote a snappy column for the "Style" section while having an affair with managing editor Ben Bradlee, whom she would later marry. Though Quinn had no prior television experience, CBS had hired her in

1973 as part of an ill-fated attempt to neutralize Barbara Walters, then a rising talent at NBC.

Quinn's book, *We're Going to Make You a Star*, was to be an exposé of the many shenanigans that occurred behind the scenes at CBS News. And, as its publication neared, Don Hewitt was becoming increasingly upset, for Quinn's manuscript described a series of unwanted sexual advances and harassment by Hewitt while the two were doing a story in London.

Hewitt was notorious for such behavior. A female producer at CBS had told Quinn, "Everybody knows that Hewitt makes passes at women with aspirations in TV. But nobody talks about it. If you're smart you'll keep your mouth shut."[4]

Mike had heard about the contents of Quinn's manuscript at a dinner party in Washington. Worried that he, by association, would be tarnished too, Mike placed an agitated phone call to Marion Goldin.

"You're on the road with me," said Mike to the lone female producer on his staff. "You know this sort of thing doesn't happen."

Goldin's steely response: "If you think I'm going to be a character witness for you, you've got another think coming."[5]

Mike was hardly innocent when it came to matters of sexual harassment, though his behavior was more provocateur than Lothario. He would sneak up behind women and snap their bra straps or smack them on the rear. No one was immune to Mike's antics, be it a female receptionist or the wife of a colleague. In one case, Mike caused such a stir that he was forced to write a formal letter of apology. It involved the wife of CBS legend Eric Sevareid, Suzanne St. Pierre, a prim and peevish woman from New England who worked as a sometime producer for CBS News.

"She walked by my desk," recalls Barbara Dury, then working as a secretary to Wallace, "and Mike was standing right there and he hit her on the ass with the newspaper. She stiffened up and was horrified. He had to ultimately apologize to her and it turned into a bit of an international incident."[6]

The reason the incident went "international" was that Mike, having found an easy mark, could not let up—he was like a bulldog. Sometime later at a formal dinner, according to Dury, Mike was seated at a table with St. Pierre and just couldn't resist making some lewd comment about her "snatch." The remark, outrageous in and of itself, became scandalous because also seated at the table was St. Pierre's husband. Eric Sevareid made his displeasure at Mike's antics be known to the higher-ups at CBS and demanded a formal apology. Thus, Mike was forced to write his letter of contrition, a note that took the better part of a day to compose and dispatch.

The fact is that Mike, like the unruly child from Brookline, remained a compulsive prankster, a jokester, a needler—especially when it came to sexual matters. For example, he would call his secretary, Barbara Dury, breathing heavily into the phone, and whisper, "What are you wearing?" He would routinely ask staffers, both male and female, direct questions about their sex lives. "Did you get lucky last night?" began the typical inquiry. Then Mike might press for details about what had transpired in their bedrooms. His preoccupation with things of a sexual nature has been described by staff members as "juvenile." Others have called it a bizarre power trip.

"It was part of his humor," says Marion Goldin, "part of his shtick."[7]

At the time, Mike convinced himself that the behavior was relatively harmless—a test of character, of sorts. He didn't cross the line like Hewitt, who had been accused of pinning a woman against a wall and kissing her against her will.[8] Mike was simply trying to get a rise out of people— went his reasoning, and, if they couldn't handle his ribbing, they probably shouldn't be working at *60 Minutes*. Mike's bra-snapping behavior would continue well into his seventies.

Then, in 1991, a scathing exposé of the chauvinistic atmosphere at *60 Minutes* was published in *Rolling Stone* magazine. Reporter Mark Hertsgaard wrote:

Mike Wallace's abuse of underlings is legendary. Again and again, colleagues chose the word bully *to describe his lacerating treatment of subordinates.... Wallace is accused of repeatedly making lewd comments about women's physiques and bedroom abilities, pinching their bottoms and both snapping and unhooking their bra straps.*[9]

As damning as it was, this was nothing compared to what Hertsgaard wrote about Don Hewitt, who did his best to keep the story from publication. Though he failed to kill the piece entirely, Hewitt managed to get *Rolling Stone* publisher Jann Wenner to delay it by a year and water it down considerably, according to Hertsgaard. When the article was finally published, Mike, showing a little more remorse than his boss, admitted to the behavior and promised that it would cease.

But the sexual antics were just one component of what made working for Mike an exhausting proposition. Hypercompetitive to the point of compulsion, he would work his teams like a slave driver, often playing them off against one another to work harder.

Marion Goldin remembers a time when her husband was rushed to the emergency room with heart issues. When Goldin, who had been working out of the New York office, rushed back to Washington to be with her spouse, Mike called her "self-indulgent" for deserting the story they were working on.

It was one of the many times that Goldin considered quitting. Mike, according to Goldin, was "capable of intentional cruelty." He had a Jekyll and Hyde personality—sometimes magnanimous and charming, other times almost sadistic. He was famous for dressing people down in public like a drill sergeant—particularly new employees—often reducing them to tears over minor infractions.

"His use of the word 'cunt' disgusted me then," says Goldin, "and disgusts me now."[10]

Many of Mike's producers developed a love-hate relationship with him. On the one hand, he could be utterly intolerable; on the other, he was the best interviewer in the business, his stories always led the broadcast and therefore received the most attention. But working for him was a pact with the devil.

Mike remembers a time when one of his producers, Norman Gorin, was hospitalized. "I sent him a cactus, and on the get-well card I wrote: 'From your prickly friend' . . . A few days later, he came back with a riposte. 'Nice try,' his thank-you note read, 'but adding a suffix doesn't change a thing.' "[11]

According to Barry Lando, Mike's volatility increased in the late 1970s as *60 Minutes* rocketed to become the number one show on television and then had to fight to keep that crown. "Success can be a tough taskmaster," former CBS News president Fred Friendly told *The New York Times* in 1979, referring to *60 Minutes*. "They're a good show, but now they're in the ratings business. They think that if they slipped out of the top 10, they'd be in trouble. So there is some kind of impulse that makes them always go for the target, always play that game of fox and hare."

"It may do something for Fred Friendly's ego to rap me," bristled Don Hewitt in response. "It does nothing to my ego to reply." Then, after a pause, he added: "Please quote me on that."

"There is a tendency to caricature themselves," said CBS News president Dick Salant, "to do confrontations just for the sake of confrontations. That tendency has to be watched very, very carefully." Especially if your name is Mike Wallace.

"He plays the game of arrogance, arrogance and attack," commented Italian journalist Oriana Fallaci, whom many have likened to a female Mike Wallace. Remarking on the time that Mike did a profile on her, Fallaci said, "In my case we had two interview sessions. He was not happy with the first because I was more arrogant than he was. In order to correct this disproportion of arrogance, he was forced to cross the ocean and start all over again."

In 1981, with mounting criticisms of its tactics, *60 Minutes* decided to assemble a panel of its most vocal critics and give them a forum to air their grievances. During the broadcast, media critic Jeff Greenfield turned to Mike and asked, "How would you like it done to you? How would you like somebody to point a camera at you that you didn't know was there, to confront you with embarrassing material, perhaps about a life you once led or something you once did?"

Mike's deadpan response: "I wouldn't like it, which is why I live a life beyond reproach." It got a laugh, as expected.

Though Mike had his share of skeletons, he worked tirelessly to control his public image, particularly the way he appeared on screen. "I was very surprised to note," said novelist Jerzy Kosinski, whom Mike interviewed for a piece on fugitive director Roman Polanski, "that they seemed to care as much about the questions as the answers. I noticed it after the interview was over, when they turned the camera around to film Mike reasking the questions. The process is very studied and very precise: he assumed an expression that was at once that of a man who already knows and a boy who wants to find out, a fascinating mixture of the inquisitive and the inquisitional."

Was it all just an act? Had Wallace—overworked and jetlagged, cranking out stories by the dozens—inadvertently morphed back into an actor who now played the part of "Mike Wallace," an iconic archetype created by the collective projections of his 30 million fans? And, if so, who then was the real Mike Wallace?

"I think Mike's core was so deeply hidden and protected," says Barry Lando. "I certainly didn't get to it. I don't know if anyone ever did."

Despite their thirty years of work together on some of the most celebrated pieces in the *60 Minutes* canon, Lando wonders whether their friendship was truly genuine.

"I was never really sure how personally interested he was in me . . . he asked personal questions about my wife, my kids, and he seemed to be interested in the answers, but I never really knew at the very bottom of it all, and the very bottom of himself, how sincere that interest was—and I doubt that he could have told me himself.

"There was a certain lack of confidence. A lot of people come on very strong, very self-confident—in fact, that self-confidence is hiding an underlying lack of self-confidence. That was true with Mike. That was true for a lot of people on television because they live by their image. There's not any kind of store of value that they've accrued. It's simply how they go from week to week and month to month, so it's a very fleeting kind of fame and power. They constantly need to be reassured. Mike was constantly examining, prodding stories to see if the story was really there.

"Sometimes talking to him was like an onion where you peel away and you keep peeling away but there's never really any core there, you just keep peeling away and it's just onion."

Mike had bunkered himself sufficiently by now to fool his closest associates and even himself. But the suffering and self-doubt were still there. And they would not remain hidden indefinitely.

Chapter Nineteen

Mike Wallace Is Here

When dawn broke across the gilded minarets, a bearded muezzin chanted the call to prayer and pigeons took to flight as throngs of sleepy worshippers crossed the square to enter the Fatima al-Masumeh Shrine. Their rugs would face southwest in this mosque for it was in the Iranian holy city of Qom, about a thousand miles northeast of Mecca. And their prayers would be charged with fervor on this day, November 18, 1979—exactly two weeks after Iranian students had overrun the U.S. Embassy in Tehran and seized sixty-six American hostages.

In a few hours, a jeep would roll into town carrying a CBS camera crew, Barry Lando and Mike Wallace. They would be escorted to the headquarters of Ayatollah Ruhollah Khomeini, where Mike, his face brimming with unabashed glee, would waltz past his competitors, Peter Jennings of ABC, John Hart of NBC and Robert MacNeil of PBS, who had been waiting in frustration in the anteroom. Mike would scoop them to snag the first interview with the Supreme Leader of Iran since the hostage crisis had broken out and gripped America.

"What a joy!" Mike has said of the moment.[1]

It was something of a miracle that it ever came to be. Lando had had serious doubts that the Ayatollah would agree to the interview, given Mike's several audiences with his archrival, Shah Mohammed Reza Pahlavi, whom Khomeini had recently deposed. Mike and His Majesty seemed to have hit if off; he had found it easy to converse with the Shah.

"He wanted to be on TV," recalls Mike. "He was comfortable with being asked any question as long as you preceded it with 'Your Majesty.'"[2]

Things were altogether different with Ayatollah Khomeini. First of all, the cleric had demanded that all questions be submitted in advance, which was in violation of CBS News standards. But Bill Leonard, who had been promoted to president of the news division, authorized an exception in this case, given the importance of the interview. On November 16, Barry Lando got word that their questions had been approved and he was ordered to come immediately for an interview with the Ayatollah. Mike was 7000 miles away in San Francisco on another story, which he dropped instantly to fly to Iran, knowing that his competitors at the other networks would not be far behind. Mike figured he could grab the red-eye to London and pick up a connecting flight to Tehran. But there was one problem—he didn't have his passport.

Three factors conspired to produce the extraordinary rule-bending that ensued, enabling the San Francisco Airport authorities to allow Mike to board his flight to London: 1) that he was Mike Wallace, Number One newsman in America; 2) that he was on his way to interview America's Number One Nemesis; and 3) that Mike's secretary had agreed to catch a plane to London and meet him in the international transit lounge at Heathrow Airport, passport in hand. Thus, Mike made it to Qom for his historic interview.

But, though he had scooped his competitors, Mike was hardly welcomed by the Ayatollah. "I put out my hand and he swept past me, sat down and waited for the questions."

All had been preapproved, so the Ayatollah droned his scripted responses, all the while staring off coldly, without ever even glancing in Mike's direction. So, Mike being Mike, he decided finally to throw out the rules and ask an unauthorized question.

"What are they going to do? Take me hostage?" he thought.[3] Never in

his forty years of broadcasting had Mike done an interview in which the
subject had failed to look him in the eye—often in fear, or at the very least
perturbed—and Mike was certainly not going to let this fish get away. So
he cleared his throat and began:

"Imam, President Sadat of Egypt, a devoutly religious man, a Muslim,
says that what you are doing now is—quote—'a disgrace to Islam.' And he
calls you, Imam—forgive me, his words, not mine—'a lunatic.'"

Mike was proud of himself. It was a zinger, but one that had been mas-
terfully feathered with the requisite softeners to make it more palatable—
the repeated use of "Imam" (equivalent to using "Your Majesty" with the
Shah), preceding the jab with "forgive me" and putting the provocative
words in the mouth of someone else (Anwar Sadat), which was a trick that
Mike employed with some regularity in his questions. But, despite all of
Mike's calculated modifiers, the question was met with stony silence. The
Farsi translator stared at Mike in shock with an expression that said, "If you
expect me to translate that question then it is *you*, sir, who are the lunatic."

But Mike demanded that the translator relay the question to the Ayatollah, insisting that he had heard Sadat use those very words on American television. The translation went ahead—and then, finally, came the
eye contact.

"Khomeini looked straight at me," brims Mike, "and I thought I detected a faint glint of curiosity in his eyes."[4]

After eyeing the "infidel" for a moment, the Ayatollah declared that it
was Sadat who was the disgrace to Islam, adding, "I demand that the Egyptian people try to overthrow him, just as we did with the Shah." And, in fact,
by 1981 Anwar Sadat was assassinated by Egyptian fundamentalists.

Mike, meanwhile, would continue to file stories on Iran, including
several during the hostage crisis that lasted 444 days. One piece, "The
Iran File," turned the lens on America and its own culpability in the
standoff—an indictment of how the CIA had aided the Shah and trained
his secret police in torture and interrogation methods. This was the segment that had President Carter calling Bill Leonard and begging him
not to air it. But, here too, Mike had held his ground. Whether he faced a

supreme Islamic leader or a sitting U.S. President, Mike was not one to back down, certainly not at this stage of his exalted career. He would very soon, in fact, be hitting his peak.

THE FOUR MOST TERRIFYING WORDS IN THE ENGLISH LANGUAGE, ran the 1983 headline: MIKE WALLACE IS HERE.

It was, actually, a paid advertisement by the Coors Brewing Company, which had become the subject of a *60 Minutes* investigation. Mike had flown out to Colorado to investigate allegations about discriminatory hiring practices and mistreatment of workers at Coors. In the course of reporting the piece Wallace largely debunked the allegations, attributing them to labor union leaders who had been frustrated by their inability to organize Coors employees. Thus, having survived the scrutiny of *60 Minutes*, company CEO Joe Coors proudly created a full-page ad that ran in newspapers across the country, inviting people to tune in for the piece and declaring:

> *We didn't sponsor it. We had no say in what they said about us. But we think what Mike and his people found out about Coors is of interest to anyone who likes good beer.*

In reacting to the four-word slogan, Mike would say: "It's asinine, but it's flattering."[5]

The Washingtonian magazine had recently run an article with the headline: IF MIKE WALLACE CALLS, HANG UP. Indeed, some businessmen would go to extreme lengths to avoid an encounter with Mike. When he did a story entitled "Welfare for the Rich" about excessive corporate fringe benefits, Mike and his crew staked out a small airport outside New Orleans to catch executives flying in on their private jets to see the Super Bowl. But no sooner had the planes landed then they turned around and flew off like frightened ducks, having gotten wind of who was waiting for them.

"We had a book with all the tail numbers of the various private jets used by corporations around the country," recalled Mike. "So we knew when the Rockwell plane or the CBS plane or whatever was coming in. It was fascinating to watch these company planes come in and suddenly hear over their radios that we were waiting for them on the ground with our cameras, and then zoom off into the wild blue yonder."[6]

As author Gary Paul Gates has written: "By the early 1980s, many business executives had become so apprehensive about a face-to-face encounter with Wallace or some other aggressive television interviewer that they enrolled in special courses set up to help them cope with that ordeal." Around the shop at *60 Minutes* it became known as "Mike Fright"—a condition that many staffers had themselves experienced. Wallace was sufficiently amused by the phenomenon that he actually did a story on the media coaches who help you to overcome "Mike Fright."

Mike *was here*, all right—center stage in the national consciousness. But there was a profound irony to this milestone, for, just as he was fulfilling everything he had set out to accomplish, it came time for him to exit the limelight.

On May 18, 1983, Mike turned sixty-five, the mandatory retirement age for everyone who worked for CBS. It was a long-standing corporate policy affecting all employees, regardless of their stature—no exceptions. Even Walter Cronkite had been forced to turn over the reins of the nightly news to Dan Rather in 1981.

The prospect of having her husband at home elated Lorraine, who was more needy than ever—but for Mike it was tantamount to death. As Barry Lando puts it: "He knew that if he didn't do what he was doing, he would cease to exist."[7] Signing off the airwaves, moreover, could not come at a worse time for Mike, who was still reeling from a humiliating incident that had people across America calling him a racist.

The accusations involved an interview that he had conducted in 1982 with Richard Carlson, a vice president of a small savings and loan company called San Diego Federal. Mike and his team were out to expose some predatory lending practices that targeted minorities. The alleged scam worked as follows: the Trane Company, a manufacturer of air conditioners, had been selling residential units to low-income black and Latino communities in San Diego. The expensive systems required financing, which is where San Diego Federal came into the picture, underwriting thousands of such deals. But the agreements were lien-sale contracts that used the underlying house as collateral, so individuals in default wound up losing their homes—all for a lousy air-conditioning system. With limited reading skills, many of the scam's victims had missed the fine print, and that was the injustice that Mike wanted to redress through his story.

San Diego Federal's Richard Carlson agreed to talk to Mike, but, being a former journalist himself, he took a precaution. Carlson hired his own crew to film the interview along with the CBS cameraman, to ensure his remarks would not be distorted through deceptive editing techniques—a criticism that had been leveled repeatedly at *60 Minutes*. Mike agreed to the stipulation, provided that when CBS stopped filming, so too would the second crew. Midway through the interview, the CBS camera had to reload, so Mike took the opportunity to say something to Carlson off the record. He grabbed a copy of one of the lien-sale contracts and began to fumble his way through the complex legalese.

"They're hard to read," admitted Carlson.

"You bet your ass they're hard to read," Mike remarked, adding with a laugh, "if you're reading them over the watermelon or the tacos!"[8]

It was a tactic, of course. Like a chameleon, Mike was slipping into a little bigotry to disarm his subject and make him relax his guard—to probe, to fish, to invite him into territory that might otherwise have seemed blasphemous. Mike had used the ruse to brilliant effect in 1976, when interviewing Phil Barasch, an accountant who had engaged in tax fraud. Leaning in conspiratorially, Mike had said, "I mean, look, between you and me . . . you do it, everybody does it." The ploy allowed the accountant momentarily to forget that their conversation was being recorded—so he agreed with Mike and admitted to cooking his books, which were promptly subpoenaed by a federal grand jury following the broadcast of the program.

Mike's "watermelons and tacos" slur was made with similar intent. But this time, he failed to elicit a confession. What's worse, the whole gambit backfired, for, while Mike had taken care to do it while the CBS camera

was not rolling, unbeknownst to him the second crew hired by the savings
and loan had continued to roll and had captured Mike's remarks on tape.
Interviewee Richard Carlson found it deeply ironic: "Here's the master of
the ambush—the guy who quite literally represents the public interest in
this country, the final arbiter of truth and justice, if you will—and who
would think that a small savings and loan company in California would
catch Mike Wallace."[9]

Several weeks after the interview, the incident was leaked to *The Wall
Street Journal.* Mike was livid and launched into damage control, first
calling the local cameraman, then trying to strike a deal with San Diego
Federal, according to a *Los Angeles Times* report.

"I know this is not a good thing to ask in this era of erased tapes,"
pleaded Mike to San Diego Federal, "[but] I would be extremely grateful
if you could excise them for me. I know this sounds lame but I want you
to erase the parts of the tape this [*The Wall Street Journal*] guy is trying
to make a federal case out of."[10] Mike was worried that the glib remarks,
taken out of context, would make him "look mean, graceless and bigoted,
and I'd like to believe I'm none of those things."[11] In fact, throughout his
career, Mike had prided himself on being a friend to minorities and a champion of the underdog. He had conducted well-regarded interviews with
Martin Luther King, Malcolm X, Louis Farrakhan and other leaders in
the civil rights struggle.

Mike was deeply regretful about what had happened at San Diego
Federal, and issued a formal apology. But the backlash from the incident
would haunt him for years. Later that year, he had been scheduled to deliver the "Ivy Day Speech" at the University of Pennsylvania, but student
leaders called for his replacement after learning about the racist remark
he had made. Five years later, the same thing happened at his own alma
mater, the University of Michigan, where Mike was invited to speak at
the commencement and receive an honorary degree. Several black student groups expressed outrage, citing the fact that Nelson Mandela would
be receiving an honorary degree on the same stage. Mike found it hard to
believe that the issue was still plaguing him.

"I plead guilty in my sixty-eight years from time to time of having told ethnic jokes, obscene jokes . . . it's been my style," he told the *Michigan Daily* in 1987. "The strange thing about all of this is that before this broke, I was writing this speech and I intended and still intend to talk about this very subject—intolerance, bigotry and racism."[12]

Later, in a town hall interview, when questioned about being a racist by a student, Mike fired back: "Not now, nor ever have I been a bigot. And a body of work of over thirty-five years I believe attests to that."

The university authorities stood by him and Mike delivered his speech, which tackled, among other things, the subject of racism:

It is the mean stuff that worries me, the behind-the-hand stuff, the self-aggrandizing put-downs, that begin to creep in and infect the dialogue little by little that take on a life of its own. The stereotypes harden and they hurt. The last thing that any of us who is decent wants to do, is hurt another person and certainly not because of circumstances of origin or color.

But at least a dozen students in the crowd refused to accept Mike's declaration, standing and turning their backs on him in a highly visible gesture of protest, which was very hurtful to Mike.

Controversy would never leave his side, even when he refused to retire—or perhaps because of it. In fact, the price that Mike would pay for his obstinacy was far greater than he could ever have imagined.

Chapter Twenty

Three Strikes

T he marriage was dead the moment he walked through the door. Lorraine had been waiting for him, watching the clock. Mike was late, as usual. Always late. And that didn't bode well, given the issue at hand. Mike did not make eye contact as he removed his coat. When he turned finally, Mike announced that he would not, in fact, be retiring. It was the final straw. Lorraine said she was leaving him.

For years, Lorraine had been begging Mike to cut back on his hours, not because he couldn't handle his workload—he was as healthy and vital as ever. Lorraine was the one who couldn't handle it, particularly Mike's long absences and overseas travel. While Mike's career continued its dramatic ascent, Lorraine felt herself withering—losing her beauty, inspiration and purpose. Depressed and unstable, she needed Mike at home.

Every CBS employee who turned sixty-five had been forced to retire, even Walter Cronkite who left his anchor chair in 1981—and Lorraine fully expected Mike to follow suit, which would mean they could spend more time together in Martha's Vineyard or at their Haitian villa. But CBS had made some rare exceptions to its retirement edict—exactly two, to be precise—and Mike had secretly been lobbying to become the third to get a contract extension beyond sixty-five.

The first to skirt the retirement rule was none other than Founding Chairman William S. Paley, who managed to stay on for nearly two additional decades beyond 1966, the year he should have retired. The other was CBS News President Bill Leonard, who had been instrumental in replacing Walter Cronkite with Dan Rather in 1981, the same year that Leonard himself turned sixty-five. So CBS made Leonard exception number two, allowing him to stay on another year to smooth the sensitive transition between anchors. (Cronkite did not disappear altogether it turns out but managed to retain an Emeritus status as a senior CBS newsman.)

With Paley, Leonard and Cronkite's Emeritus exception, Mike figured he had plenty of precedent to squeeze a few more years out of CBS. They gave him five. And that's when Lorraine decided to pack her bags.

"Where are you going to go?" asked Mike quietly.

"Fiji," she responded.

Mike couldn't believe it. Lorraine was going to live 8000 miles away on a remote island with her wayward son, Tony, with whom Mike had never seen eye to eye. Their temperaments were so radically different, it proved hard to have both of them under one roof. So Tony, who was fifteen at the time of Mike's betrothal to Lorraine, was quickly shipped off to boarding school, then went on to attend Bowdoin College.

Both Tony and his sister ended up marrying early, like their mother. Pauline wed Ivy Leaguer John MacDonald Snyder in 1967, but their marriage, like Lorraine's first, was destined to be short-lived. The same went for Tony, who also married that year into extreme wealth to Anne "Terry" Pierce, daughter of Standard Oil heiress Rebekah Harkness. The union was not only doomed, but would be marked by tragedy, when a daughter, born with a serious brain malformation, died at aged ten. Tony and Terry moved to Hawaii, where they lived an isolated life on Kauai. After the breakup of his marriage, Tony chose an even more remote place to call home in Fiji. He eventually married a Fijian and had two children, earning a modest income farming kava and other crops.

When Lorraine announced in 1984 that she was walking away from a twenty-nine-year marriage to live an alternative lifestyle in Fiji with

Tony, it crushed Mike. Profoundly saddened, he went alone that summer to Martha's Vineyard, feeling utterly despondent about his three failed marriages—Norma, Buff, and now Lorraine. He had been deeply attached to Lorraine. She had seen him through his darkest hour, and he, hers—the loss of her father, the loss of his son, the loss of her grandchild. Together, they had built a life. She had supported him through a whirlwind professional transformation, from a man who would have been laughed out of a newsroom to the most famous broadcast journalist in the country. But that triumph had its price.

Lost in the shadow of her husband's success, Lorraine had become acutely depressed, and it had begun to rub off on Mike. As clinicians now know, depression is as contagious within a household as a virus. By the summer of 1984, a pall of gloom had started to hit Mike, too. He found himself thinking a lot about Peter, whose death was still haunting him, even twenty years later. The recollections had been awakened by the fact that Mike was finally preparing for the publication of his long-gestating memoir—this version co-written with Gary Paul Gates, and ready for a fall release by William Morrow and Company.

While not opening the book with the death of Peter, which was what previous biographer Neil Offen had proposed, Gates did include the sad event, as well as the many missteps of Mike's early career and marriages. He had to update the final chapter, in fact, to account for the dissolution of Mike's third marriage. It was extremely exposing. And that was just the beginning of a period of intense scrutiny that would soon descend upon Mike. A series of escalating events would conspire to place him in the most glaring spotlight imaginable: at the defense table in a public courtroom, surrounded by a media circus. Mike had been served papers in the biggest lawsuit of his career.

At issue was a CBS News special entitled *The Uncounted Enemy: A Vietnam Deception*, which had aired in 1982. The ninety-minute documentary, narrated by Wallace and produced by George Crile, alleged that General William Westmoreland, Commander of U.S. troops in Vietnam, had altered intelligence reports and deliberately understated the strength of Vietcong insurgents during the late sixties in order to maintain U.S. troop morale and domestic support for the war—a decision that proved disastrous. American forces were caught unprepared when the Vietcong launched a country-wide surprise attack on Vietnam's biggest holiday, the Tet New Year's celebration of 1968. In a well-coordinated strike, some 50,000 communist insurgents hit more than 100 towns and cities. They managed, briefly, to take over Saigon's main radio station and even storm the U.S. Embassy, where they shot five marines.

When the dust finally settled on the Tet Offensive, 2,500 American soldiers lay dead. At home, many turned against the war, and turned their backs on Lyndon Johnson, whose popularity had been sinking steadily. Despite the national humiliation of Vietnam, General Westmoreland managed somehow to keep his reputation more or less intact. That is, until *60 Minutes* came knocking on his door.

Like many before him, Westmoreland felt as though he'd been ambushed by Mike, deliberately "tight-framed" in shots that made him appear anxious, licking his lips, mopping sweat from his brow. In 1983, he filed a $120 million lawsuit against Wallace, Crile and CBS. And Westmoreland's case seemed to have merit. In pretrial depositions, evidence emerged that Crile had taken certain liberties in coaching subjects and reshooting key interviews. What made Mike incredibly uneasy about all of this was that he was being held responsible for these decisions, even though he had nothing whatsoever to do with them. *The Uncounted Enemy* was not a *60 Minutes* piece; it was a network special produced and reported by George Crile, to which Mike had simply lent his voice and interviewing skills.

In fact, the trial was apt to shatter unequivocally the myth of Mike as the fearless investigative reporter who leaves no stone unturned in his ceaseless pursuit of the truth. It would reveal instead what Mike to some measure had become—an actor reading a prepared script and asking questions written by others, albeit doing it brilliantly.

The Westmoreland trial would not begin until the fall, but before that Mike had to contend with another stressor: the release of his biography and the upcoming book tour, where he would have to talk about the authorship of a memoir that was entirely ghostwritten by someone else (with whom Mike shared credit). Mike, who needed support and companionship, dreaded the prospect of being alone in an empty beach house, so he invited a trusted, close friend to share the Martha's Vineyard house with him—someone who understood loss deeply. It was Mary, the widow of his former partner, Ted Yates, who had been shot accidentally in Jerusalem in 1967.

Neither Mike nor Mary expected they would become romantically involved. Mike needed a friend more than anything, and so did Mary, the single mother of two teenagers and a young adult, all of them precocious and a little wild since the untimely death of their father. Mary, a talented journalist in her own right, was still drop-dead gorgeous and many suitors had lined up to woo her, including Frank Sinatra, among others. But none had made the cut. Mary's focus was on her three boys, who were not yet teens when they lost their father.

"The boys were no fair shakes for suitors," admits Angus Yates, the youngest son. "We were all pretty fierce and probably scared most of them off."[1]

"The story between my father and my mother was a classic love story," continues Angus. "They were a dynamic couple and no one even came close until my father's former partner twenty years later."

Mary was an extraordinary woman. She had grown up in Lacrosse, Wisconsin, when it was still a very small farming community—a good girl from a good Midwestern family. But Mary also had a wild side that couldn't wait to get out. After graduating from the University of Wisconsin, she wound up touring Europe as a model for Italian designer Emilio Pucci, who appreciated Mary's quintessentially American features. Pucci would soon become a darling among iconic American women, famously creating the dress in which Marilyn Monroe was buried.

Mary's modeling career then took her to New York, where she entered the world of broadcasting. As a result of her perfect skin and complexion, her first job in television was as a "Test Pattern Girl." This was the era when Orthicon picture tubes had just been introduced and needed careful calibration in order for the multiple TV cameras on a particular set to match up. Studio technicians used both a calibration chart and a live model—in this case, Mary. But she was far too bright to be a glorified mannequin and soon moved to the other side of the camera on the production team of the *Tex & Jinx Show*, where she met Ted Yates. They dated for exactly one week, falling madly in love and promptly getting married. Their first child was born two years later, and the others followed at two-year intervals. Life was good for the Yates clan, until the day an Israeli sniper pulled his trigger by mistake.

Since that tragic moment, every member of the household had suffered from some form of anxiety or depression. As the boys hit adolescence, they were becoming too much for Mary to handle. So when Mike extended the invitation for the whole family to spend the summer of 1984 at Martha's Vineyard, she jumped at it.

"And that was a big deal," says Angus. "I mean none of us were prudes here but everyone went 'Woah!', including her kids. Because she had never done that. Ever. Here's Mary Yates, spending time at Wallace's house on the Vineyard."

As Mike explained it in his 2005 memoir: "The more time we spent together, the more we came to realize that our long friendship was blossoming into something deeper."

At this fragile juncture in his life, Mike needed someone he could trust. After another failed marriage and the waves of accompanying self-doubt that were greatly exacerbated by the potentially career-ending lawsuit, Mike felt like he simply couldn't handle it alone.

Mary needed him as much as he needed her. Her sons lacked a father, and she, a mate. But Mary didn't realize that Mike, in 1984, was hardly able to be an equal partner. He was barely hanging on.

Chapter Twenty-one

The Trial of His Life

In late August 1984, Mike Wallace found himself flying eastward over the Pacific Ocean. The cobalt water that stretched from horizon to horizon appeared cold and daunting. This trip to Fiji had been an effort to patch things up with Lorraine, but it had failed miserably. Instead, the two had agreed to file divorce papers and discussed the dissolution of their assets. While Mike had been down this path before, it was different this time—in a marriage of nearly three decades, the couple had built a life together, bought property, created businesses. They were deeply intertwined and the divorce would be messy and painful.

Landing in Los Angeles, he was met by producer Lowell Bergman, who'd recently joined *60 Minutes* after an impressive run at ABC. An accomplished investigative journalist, Bergman had been chasing an explosive story involving Nevada senator Paul Laxalt, chairman of the Republican Party and President Reagan's closest personal friend. Just four days prior, Laxalt had placed the president's name in nomination at the Republican Convention. He was at the helm of Reagan's reelection effort, widely expected to yield a landslide victory.

The Bergman/Wallace *60 Minutes* piece, however, could change that. It charged that Laxalt (and Reagan by association) had extensive ties to the mob. Bergman was surprised that Mike had agreed to do the story in the first place, given his close ties to the Reagans. Mike had known Nancy Reagan for decades, having worked with her mother back in his Chicago radio days. Meeting Nancy as a student at Smith College, Mike described her as "a prim and proper young lady who often wore white gloves and Peter Pan collars."[1]

But personal ties rarely bought immunity from a *60 Minutes* sting. And Mike, as a respite from his personal woes, needed something he could sink his teeth into. He and Bergman flew together to Las Vegas to interview a former FBI agent named Joe Yablonsky, who had investigated the mob for two decades and had strong opinions about Laxalt. Indeed, the interview was explosive. Yablonsky called the senator the worst kind of politician you can imagine, a tool of organized crime. Lowell Bergman couldn't believe what they were hearing.

"It just unfolded in front of our eyes, on camera," he said. Charge after blistering charge against one of the most powerful Republicans in America, a man joined at the hip to the sitting president. Wallace and Bergman boarded the next plane to New York, videotapes in hand. Bergman was on an adrenaline high as he arrived at the CBS News building on West 57th Street and marched the cassettes into a bay where the editor was waiting to shape the material into the opening story of the fall season.

The pressure was on at the news division. Everyone felt it, from the anchors to the security guards. *60 Minutes* had been in a heated battle with *Dallas*, another CBS show, for first place in the annual Nielsen ratings. They had been neck and neck since 1979, with two wins for *60 Minutes* and three for *Dallas*. The competition was fierce. "Number One Show on TV" conferred some serious bragging rights, not to mention hundreds of millions of dollars in revenue. Don Hewitt made no secret of wanting the trophy for 1984, and Bergman had assured him that *60 Minutes* would come out swinging with a sizzling season opener.

Mike, however, found it difficult to get caught up in the excitement over the Laxalt piece—he was feeling overwhelmed. The Westmoreland trial was due to start in one month's time. Then there was the divorce.

On instructions from his lawyer, Mike placed his East 74th Street town house—the home that Mike and Lorraine had shared for twenty-eight years—on the market. It would now be sold as part of the settlement. So he had to pack his bags and move out, inflicting another trauma on his increasingly disoriented psyche. Then there was the book tour.

Close Encounters, Mike's memoir, was now on the shelves and in need of promotion, lest it disappear like so many other journalists' autobiographies and become a humiliation. The reviews had been lukewarm. "Interesting but frustratingly impersonal," wrote Lee Margulies in the *Los Angeles Times*. Jesse Kornbluth of *The New York Times* called it "uneven, overlong and incomplete."

Needless to say, having to promote a book could not have come at a worse time for Mike. When he addressed an eager brunch crowd gathered at the Plaza Hotel for the sixth annual New York Is Book Country fair, his sagging spirits made their way into his speech.

"I can't understand why anyone would write a book," began Mike. "It's damn hard work done in solitude." He recounted the various fits and starts he had made over six years "of self-doubt, alternating with self-pity" before he threw in the towel and enlisted the help of a coauthor. Mike finished the lackluster speech to a smattering of applause and bolted toward the exit. He couldn't help himself. He was beginning to lose his rudder. It would only get worse as fall turned to winter.

On September 14, 1984, he made an appearance on *The Phil Donahue Show*, during which Donahue asked him what viewers could expect in the upcoming episodes of *60 Minutes*. In a moment of hubris, Mike mentioned that his season opener on Senator Paul Laxalt "could very well alter the outcome of the presidential election."

That simple boast would have major repercussions. "He couldn't keep his fucking mouth shut," laments Lowell Bergman. "There's a rule in journalism . . . you don't talk about stories before they run."[2]

When Laxalt learned of the intended broadcast (scheduled for September 23, 1984) he pulled out the big guns. The CBS brass at Black Rock received repeated calls from senior White House officials and other Republican powerbrokers. On the Wednesday before the airdate, CBS received a letter from the senator's New York attorney, Seymour Shainswit, reportedly threatening the network with "libel missiles that can inflict very substantial damages."[3] Without naming an actual figure, Shainswit suggested the size of the lawsuit would be "massive."

That same week, Laxalt had filed a $250 million suit against the *Sacramento Bee*, which had printed an article alleging that he had skimmed millions of dollars in the 1970s from a casino he owned. The article had run on November 1, 1983, nearly a year earlier, but Laxalt hadn't taken any legal action at the time. A small regional paper posed no threat to him. National exposure on *60 Minutes* was quite another matter.

If the timing of the lawsuit was meant to intimidate, it certainly worked. Just days before the broadcast, CBS shelved its exposé. The incident left Mike feeling numb. Though he had already been on the air promoting the show, he hardly put up a fight when Don Hewitt made the decision to scrap it. Bergman was livid. "I seriously questioned whether I could continue working for CBS," recounts Bergman,[4] who stands by his story. Ultimately, though, he chose not to quit until ten years later, when a similar scenario would repeat itself in another Bergman/Wallace collaboration about tobacco whistle-blower Jeffrey Wigand.

Whereas the media would jump all over "The Insider" scandal in 1995—including a feature piece in *Vanity Fair*, which became the basis for an Oscar-nominated film—the cancellation of the Laxalt story somehow slipped below their radar. This dramatic decision to scrap a major *60 Minutes* exposé—the season opener, no less—went largely unreported by the press, save for a single article that appeared the following year in *The Village Voice*. Throughout the fall, however, Mike remained concerned that the decision to pull the plug on the Laxalt piece would be leaked and damage his reputation, which was already taking a pounding. Laxalt, for his part, was countersued by the *Sacramento Bee* and ultimately recovered some $650,000 in attorneys' fees after both suits were settled.

On Tuesday, October 9, 1984—not three weeks after the threatened lawsuit by Paul Laxalt—the Westmoreland trial began at the Federal

Courthouse in New York's Foley Square. Westmoreland's cocky attorney, Dan Burt, declared, "We are about to see the dismantling of a major news organization."[5] It made front-page news across the country. *Newsweek* magazine dubbed it "the Libel Trial of the Century." CNN, desperate to provide gavel-to-gavel coverage, had gone so far as to petition the U.S. Supreme Court for the right to broadcast the trial, a motion that was ultimately denied.

With no cameras allowed in the courtroom, outside, the media pressed in from all sides. A phalanx of photographers lurked on the courthouse steps, their motor drives whirring. Mobile television vans ringed Foley Square, dishes raised and ready to transmit any development as it broke. The media circus, said one reporter, was like "a hydra-headed, multi-eyed beast of prey, bristling with antenna-like microphones on long poles."[6] They assaulted Mike daily as he emerged from his limousine, subjecting him to the types of ambush interviews that he himself had made famous.

A well-known general suing a major news division for libel was big news. But there were two such lawsuits at this time—two generals, two trials, running concurrently in the same courthouse. On the first floor, below Room 318 where Wallace and Westmoreland would be squaring off, Israeli General Ariel Sharon had launched a similar lawsuit against *Time* magazine, which had portrayed him as secretly condoning the massacre of Palestinian civilians in Lebanon. Both generals accused the media of deliberately misrepresenting them. They were in the fight of their lives, all-out battles to restore their honor.

As he sat in the courtroom listening to opening statements, Mike became increasingly anxious about the trial's outcome. Four years of Reagan's presidency had emboldened the Right and fueled charges of a left-wing bias in the media. Many believed that CBS News was the nexus of liberal news coverage, at the forefront of a conspiracy to undermine conservative values in America. In its exhaustive discovery, the Westmoreland team produced what it considered to be the smoking-gun memo: a note from George Crile to Mike, written when the story was nearly in its final form. "It looks beautiful," penned the zealous producer. "Now all you have to do is break General Westmoreland and we'll have the whole thing aced."[7]

It appeared from the memo that Crile and Wallace had been conspiring to slant the story in a way that would support their preestablished views about the Army and the U.S. government distributing misinformation on Vietnam. What made matters worse for the defense was an unexpected judicial ruling in a neighboring room of the Manhattan federal courthouse in yet another libel case. Astonishingly, this story likewise featured a prominent Vietnam War hero whose reputation had been torn asunder after an ambush interview—by none other than *Mike Wallace.*

It was the $45 million lawsuit by Colonel Anthony Herbert, now in its tenth year and counting. Since the airing of the story in 1973, the case had been mired in pretrial motions, one of which had landed in the Supreme Court in 1979. The court's landmark decision—that a litigant has the right to inquire as to the "state of mind" and editorial process of the reporters accused of defaming him—became a major victory for Colonel Herbert, setting a precedent which would affect all future libel suits against the press, including *Westmoreland v. CBS.*

After more years of discovery and depositions, U.S. District Judge Charles Haight had denied a last-ditch effort by CBS lawyers to have the Herbert case dismissed, and it was finally returned to federal court for trial on Friday, October 12, 1984. It happened to be the same week and in the same courthouse that saw the start of the Westmoreland case, an uncanny coincidence that added even more stress to an already overwhelmed Mike. The potential at stake now stood at $165 million, his portion of which would ruin him financially and likely leave his reputation in tatters.

Mike, returning to his apartment that weekend, felt the weight of impending doom. Everything in his life seemed to be unraveling. It was all dark and foreboding, save for one ray of hope: Mary Yates, who had now moved in with him to help him through the ordeal.

Says her son Angus, "This is the kind of business [where] people don't often do that. If you're famous and successful you're loved. If you're getting creamed and demolished, you learn very quickly who your friends are . . . and one of them was my mother."[8]

With infinite patience and compassion, Mary helped Mike get out of bed and get dressed and fed him breakfast as the trial dragged on and on into winter and became increasingly tortuous. He couldn't bear hearing witness after witness impugn him and his credibility as a journalist.

"I didn't realize what was happening," he recalled in an interview years later with Larry King, "but to sit in a cold and drafty federal courtroom being called thief, liar, cheat, et cetera—because the plaintiff had first crack at me . . ." To Katie Couric, in another interview in 2005, he said, "To sit there and hear yourself in a courtroom called 'thief,' 'cheat,' 'liar . . .' " To *Time* magazine: "When you're called a liar, a cheat and a fraud . . ."

Mike has given dozens of interviews on the subject and his answer is always the same, the wording largely identical. Yet the people calling him names were not so much inside the courtroom, but *outside*. Segments of the news-watching public had turned against Mike in this volatile trial. The pile of hate mail that arrived at CBS News in 1984 was higher than it had ever been; the tone of the letters more and more vitriolic. One note to Mike called him "A paid shill with no morals, a sniveling lap-dog press whore/hypocrite of the first order." The letter went on to say, "hundreds have experienced first-hand your deceptive two-faced approach with 'creative' editing which reversed the true essence of the actual interview."[9] Calling upon him to resign, the writer concluded that Mike was "a liar and cheat and low-life scoundrel who will NOT be missed by any halfway informed or perceptive American."

This missive was fairly typical of the mail that was dumped daily on Mike's desk. Liar, cheat, whore, sellout. The words began to haunt him. Everywhere he turned, he saw accusatory fingers pointing at him. The lines between newsroom and courtroom had blurred. And soon the voices were internalized. *You're a self-serving liar,* went a whisper in his head. *A fraud. Not a real reporter. Never were. And now the world will know.*

Mike had started truly to doubt himself, and with the doubt came shame. "I began to believe," Mike admitted in a recent interview, "that maybe I *was* guilty."[10]

Chapter Twenty-two

A Call for Help

S hortly after the November 1984 election that gave Ronald Reagan his second decisive victory, Mike received a call from his producer Barry Lando, also a co-defendant in the Herbert case. Lando proposed doing a story on the deadly famine in Ethiopia, but he had little hope that Mike would say yes. "Mike hated Third World stories, particularly ones about Africa," explained Lando. "I pitched him Ethiopia, thinking there was no way he was going to do it."[1]

But—lo and behold—Mike petitioned the court for a leave of absence and jumped on the next plane to Addis Ababa, where Lando was waiting for him. They took a puddle-jumper, followed by a bone-rattling jeep ride on an unpaved road to a remote refugee camp. "I was amazed that you agreed to do this," Lando remarked to Mike, who rolled his eyes, gazing at the clouds of dust that blew relentlessly across the barren grassland.

Lando soon realized that Mike was "looking for any excuse to get away from the Westmoreland trial."

Arriving at the refugee camp that Lando had scouted, they came upon a scene of unspeakable misery. This was one of the most devastating famines in history, one that would leave over a million people dead and lead the international pop music community to come together in January 1985 to record the fund-raising anthem "We Are The World."

A Catholic lay worker escorted the two men through the overcrowded camp, where hundreds of corpses lay untouched in the sand, flies buzzing to scavenge the last drops of moisture from their eyes. "It was a very desperate scene," Lando recalls grimly. Mike maintained an utterly professional composure, however. He was actually happy to be there—to be *anywhere* but Manhattan.

"In spite of the horrors we saw," he said in a 1984 *New York Times* interview, "it was a respite."

"The Westmoreland trial was harrowing for him," explains Lando. "Mike suffered tremendously. He was very overwrought and very concerned about Westmoreland, much less the Herbert trial." When Mike returned, reluctantly, to New York he found he had managed to miss the entire testimony of William Westmoreland. Next to be cross-examined was his producer, George Crile, who gave a powerful testimony for the defense. As the days progressed, however, Mike found himself slumping despondently farther and farther into his leather chair.

"The accusations ate at me," Mike remembered. "Doubts started to haunt me. Did I do something wrong? It was as if all my experience in radio and TV news didn't count for anything anymore. What if I really am dishonest as a reporter? Dishonest as a person?"[2]

The Westmoreland team landed what seemed to be a knockout punch on the day when jurors were shown outtakes from an interview in which Crile appeared to be coaching his subject, George Allen, a CIA analyst who specialized in Vietnam. Allen had written a book that argued that the failures of the war lay squarely on the shoulders of leaders in Washington, D.C., who, in their frantic search for victory over Communism, ignored professional experts offering opinions and information contrary to what the White House wanted to hear. The CBS interview with Allen was to be the lynchpin of the piece—a "smoking gun" that Westmoreland would be hard pressed to refute. But Crile wasn't satisfied with the first interview he did with Allen (before Mike became involved in the piece), and he chose to reshoot it. It was this second interview that was being screened for the jurors in Room 318 of the Manhattan federal courthouse.

"Where am I?" asks George Allen in the film clip. "What do you want me to say, George? I'm sorry, George, I don't know what you want me to say. I don't know what you're expecting me to say . . ."

In his courtroom chair, and clearly uncomfortable, Mike tried to make eye contact with Westmoreland, who was sitting ramrod straight at the plaintiff's table. The general didn't return his gaze. He glanced, instead, at the jury. Then Westmoreland, the picture of dignity in his gray flannel suit with a Vietnam service ribbon pinned to his lapel, turned to his wife Kitsy, who looked up in a brief but encouraging smile before returning nervously to her needlepoint. Throughout this ordeal, Kitsy Westmoreland had sat faithfully at her husband's side, sewing quietly in the third row of the courthouse. As Mike noticed the look between them, he felt dead inside. It was happening more and more frequently. Day by day, Mike was losing his bearings—slipping inexorably into a darkness that would soon envelop him.

One month later, on a blustery day in late December 1984, a steady rain fell on the leafless trees of Central Park. A gray sky loomed over the wind-swept expanse as an ambulance blasted toward Lennox Hill Hospital. Inside lay a comatose Mike Wallace. He had taken an overdose of sleeping pills on the day before New Year's Eve.

Mary had discovered Mike's limp body at 3 A.M. along with a suicide note.[3] She couldn't wake him and was terrified. In a panic, Mary summoned their private doctor rather than calling 911—worried, as a former journalist, about the need to contain the story. By way of ridding the scene of damaging evidence, Mary threw out the remaining pills and even ripped up the suicide note, which, befitting Mike, was rather impersonal—relating to financial matters rather than his feelings.

The doctor could not resuscitate him on the spot and called for an ambulance, which was able to get Mike to the ER in time to pump his stomach. After the fact, people close to Mike have speculated that the episode was a cry for help, rather than a bona fide attempt to end his life—that Mike was far too narcissistic for that. But certainly the crisis was real, and called for substantial damage control.

"Nervous exhaustion," was the phrase CBS used to explain Mike's ten-day hospital stay. Mary knew full well that he was clinically depressed, but that diagnosis was still taboo in 1984. Mike's personal physician remained adamant about projecting an image of strength.

"You don't need help," he said. "You're a tough guy. Everybody knows that. You'll bounce back in no time."[4]

It was bad for Mike's image to say he was depressed,[5] the doctor warned.

"I was ashamed of acknowledging the fact ..." confessed Mike. "You don't use that word."[6]

Mary forced Mike to get a second opinion from Dr. Marvin Kaplan, a psychiatrist she had consulted for her own grief over her husband's death seventeen years earlier. Mike was too numb to refuse. Ironically, or perhaps fittingly, Dr. Kaplan didn't watch television. Mike, to him, was just another patient. "You are suffering from a depression," he stated impassively. "We can treat it."[7]

Mike started seeing him with some regularity. After Dr. Kaplan prescribed Ludiomil, an early antidepressant that was crude but effective, Mike began to feel relief. It took a while for the trust to develop between Mike and his doctor. Then Dr. Kaplan figured out what was terrifying Mike.

"You know something, Mr. Wallace," he said. "What you're worried about ... is that you're going to have to get ready to answer the kind of questions that you like to ask."

Mike stared at him in realization. He had hit the nail on the head. They had reached the critical moment. Paradoxically, one way out of depression is to look squarely at the worst-case scenario.

"You have to get ready to lose," intoned Dr. Kaplan. "Because if you lose, you think your life is gone."

Mike swallowed, taking it in.

"Well," continued Dr. Kaplan, "we're going to try in these sessions to get you ready for that."

Mike was scheduled to testify in early February 1985 as a witness for the defense, which had started to regain some ground after the prosecution's strong start. As power litigator David Boies mounted his case, the charges against Mike and CBS began to crumble. District Judge Pierre Leval, in numerous sidebars, found himself repeating to Westmoreland's team the specific evidence needed to prove libel against a public figure. "The fairness of the broadcast is not at issue," he explained in a ruling to exclude CBS's own investigation of the affair. "A broadcast may be slanted, one-sided and even appear unfair, as long as the broadcasters never recklessly or maliciously included material they knew to be false."

It's a tough standard to prove. Dan Burt, lead counsel for Westmoreland, was beginning to sweat. It didn't help matters that he, like Mike, had just seen the collapse of his third marriage, and missed his children terribly. He had mixed feelings, in fact, when a source secretly offered him a copy of Mike's file from Lennox Hill Hospital, which listed attempted suicide as the reason for admission, not "nervous exhaustion" as the CBS spin machine had been insisting. Burt leaked the information to at least one reporter, though he wasn't sure whether it would help or hurt their increasingly flimsy case. The Westmorelands, for their part, continued to show grace under pressure. One of the first bunches of flowers Mike received in his hospital room bore a simple card signed by the general and Kitsy. Mike was touched by the olive-branch gesture, since the Westmorelands were acutely aware that the trial's momentum had shifted in favor of the defense. But Mike remained deeply worried. Several times a week, he took a taxi to Dr. Kaplan's midtown office during the courtroom lunch break. Despite the Ludiomil pills, he couldn't shake the sense of looming catastrophe.

The medication had troublesome side effects, including a trembling of the hands and a bad case of dry-mouth that required near constant hydration. He was increasingly panicked about these side effects: "I could just see myself sitting on the [witness] stand five yards from the jury with a glass in my hand . . . and my hand shaking . . . and the jury saying: 'Any guy whose hand is shaking that way is obviously guilty.' "[8]

The Westmoreland team, meanwhile, was dealt a major blow on January 24, 1985, when the jury downstairs decided against Ariel Sharon in his lawsuit against *Time*. Though they found that the publication had indeed defamed the Israeli general, the panel concluded it had not done so with malice, and thus granted no damages. It was a sobering reminder of the difficulty of proving libel against a public figure.

Westmoreland's attorney, Dan Burt, grew increasingly nervous and began screaming at everyone around him, including his client. "I let it go in one ear and out the other, as if it was unreal," said Westmoreland in an interview for the book *Vietnam on Trial*. Everyone on the prosecution team knew that their ship was sinking fast, including Westmoreland, who recalled, "I had to keep telling myself, 'There's nothing you can do about it.' "

On February 1, 1985, Kitsy Westmoreland, who'd been trying hard to maintain an even keel, suddenly collapsed, her blood pressure spiking to 220. The general rushed her to the emergency room at Lennox Hill, the very hospital that had recently treated Mike. Mary and Mike, however, did not send flowers and were unaware of the snowballing disarray in the Westmoreland camp. All Mike knew was that the trial could turn on a dime if he were to blow it on the witness stand, which remained a distinct possibility given his fragile stand of mind. As the days ticked down until Mike's scheduled testimony, Mary feared a suicidal relapse and would not leave his side. Mike had regressed to a state of complete despondence. "I was copeless," Mike admitted. "Not just hopeless, but copeless."[9]

"I didn't want to get out of bed. I lost my appetite and no longer had any interest in doing things . . . I could barely summon up the energy to get out of bed each morning."[10] As a defendant in the trial, Mike was still required to report daily to the courtroom. Mary had to feed him, dress him, and put him to bed—and get him up.

"The days in this condition were like decades in my mind," lamented Wallace in his 2005 memoir. It felt endless. The ogling stares of the jury.

The secret lunchtime taxi rides to Dr. Kaplan, who would mock-grill him in preparation for his imminent testimony.

"So essentially the whole idea of you as a reporter is a lie," the psychiatrist might ask.

"No," Mike would stammer.

"It's a façade," Dr. Kaplan would insist. "You're nothing more than a mouthpiece. Your producers do all the real reporting, and then hand you a list of questions. Don't you regard that as irresponsible, even outright deceptive?"

"It's the nature of TV news," Mike would defend himself. "The correspondent doesn't have time to do the field work."

"So what happens? You read prepared questions? You follow a script?"

"The script is simply a template. I digress from it all the time!"

"Indeed," the psychiatrist might raise an eyebrow. "How many times did you digress from the script with William Westmoreland?"

And Mike would slump disconsolately into the sofa, embarrassed at how easily he'd been duped. The question about whether Mike Wallace read from a prepared script in his interviews for *60 Minutes* was a hot-button issue, one that went to the core of his fears about his upcoming testimony. On some level, he remained insecure about his credentials as a reporter.

When he took the stand, the public would become acutely aware that Mike, despite his numerous Emmys, Peabodys and countless other accolades, was not, strictly speaking, a journalist. The *real* reporting was done by his behind-the-scenes staff numbering several dozen—teams of producers, researchers, fact-checkers, assistants, editors, camera persons, undercover operatives and more. CBS and other networks worked hard to maintain the illusion that their correspondent was "the reporter." But this charade would crumble when Mike was grilled in testimony that would be seen the world over.

As fantasies go, the correspondent-as-reporter myth was fairly innocuous, like the artifice of professional wrestling perhaps, accepted as television convention by viewers who don't particularly care one way or the

other. But now it would be laid bare for all to see in excruciating detail.
The public would understand that Mike was what he'd always been: a performer. Perhaps one with no equal, but a performer nonetheless.

When asked to sum up the gift of Mike Wallace, many of his professional associates concur. "He's an actor," says Barry Lando.[11] Like all great
actors, Mike listens attentively and provokes unexpected, often electrifying
responses by immersing himself completely and fearlessly in the moment—
whether sharing the stage with a tyrant or a diva. No one doubts Mike Wallace's talent. Except perhaps Mike Wallace.

It wasn't simply that he was afraid of losing the trial. He was afraid of
being exposed. Since Peter's death in 1962, Mike had worked tirelessly to
overhaul his image. Early in his career, there had been no denying it: he was
a showman, a pitchman with a flair for the dramatic, someone who clearly
had not realized his full potential. Now, decades later, he was facing glaring
reminders of the man he had left behind. After twenty-eight years, another
failed marriage. Compounding that, he was in the trial of his life—one that
attacked the essence of his credibility and reputation as a reporter. He had
been sued before in some fairly high-profile cases, but this was the first instance in which Mike would have to testify in his own defense.

Scheduled to take the stand on February 19, he was just days away
from having to answer questions for a week or more, not only under oath,
but under the merciless glare of the media. The tables had turned—there
was simply no escape.

But Mike never made it to the witness stand. On February 17, 1985,
to the shock of the media and all who were watching the trial, William
Westmoreland abruptly and unceremoniously withdrew his lawsuit. The
general's team concluded that it did not have a case and wanted to avoid
the embarrassment of a jury verdict. After two and a half years of litigation, a half-million pages of legal documents, dozens of witnesses and 300
hours of testimony, it was suddenly all over.[12]

WESTY RAISES THE WHITE FLAG, trumpeted the *New York Post*. The CBS
brass popped open the champagne, having maintained a perfect record of
never losing a libel suit.

Wallace, for his part, was stunned. The Herbert case would likewise be withdrawn—but that, too, proved a hollow victory for Mike, who felt as though he'd just gone to hell and back. For weeks now, he'd been sitting on the leather couch in Dr. Kaplan's office, painstakingly rehearsing his testimony, rehashing the questions that would invariably arise, trying to maintain his composure while suffering the side effects of a crude medication that left him with an unquenchable thirst and shaking hands. He'd been saved from death by his soon-to-be-wife, had his stomach pumped, dodged questions from nosy reporters. And now . . . it was over?[13]

After the courtroom commotion died down, Mike got whisked away by Dan Rather and Don Hewitt for a private celebration at the 21 Club. Mike sat through the lunch in a daze. His outward smiles could not calm the inner turmoil. Hewitt and Rather slapped him on the back as they ordered a second round of drinks. Mike went through the motions. Within months, he would, once again, be on the brink of suicide.

Chapter Twenty-three

Tabloid Satori

Though Mike Wallace would be on the air for two more decades at *60 Minutes*, he never quite bounced back from the nadir of the Westmoreland trial. In the coming years, he would watch loved ones and colleagues die around him, some by their own hand. He would see close friends struggle—not always successfully—against crippling depression. He would see newsgathering techniques pioneered by *60 Minutes* become the mainstay of tabloid television, used to great and shocking effect by members of his own family. Like it or not, Mike had become the patriarch of a media dynasty, with little control over the next generation. Some would disappoint him, some would surprise him. One of Mary Yates's sons would turn his investigative skills inward to explore the human psyche. It was he who finally got Mike to discuss on camera the very thing about which he was most guarded: his depression.

The winter of 1984 had been the most grueling season of Mike's life. He urgently needed to put the whole episode behind him and erase every trace of its memory. That included jettisoning the antidepressant, with its unpleasant side effects. Now that the trial was over, he declared to his doctor that he was done medicating himself. Dr. Kaplan warned him that he needed to stick with the drug for at least six months. But Mike, in his hubris, didn't heed that advice, and went cold turkey.

A few months later, Mike found himself playing tennis on Martha's Vineyard. Still combative on the court even at age sixty-six, Mike raced back to save a lob, lost his footing and landed on his wrist, which bent at an excruciating angle and cracked. He soon found himself in a cast and once again feeling quite helpless. Not having the use of his left hand, he couldn't get dressed without assistance, much less go to the bathroom. It was another humiliation, another stark reminder of his own fragility, one more crisis that sent him spiraling into a second bout with clinical depression—this one even worse than the first.

"I'd look out the window at all the people on the streets of New York. So much energy out there, so much going on, and all I wanted to do was turn my back on it," Mike remembers. "I didn't care about anything except how miserable I felt and how I might end this pain."[1]

In his anguish, Mike, agnostic though he was, turned to prayer. "Maybe the only constant, the only part of my day-to-day life that hadn't changed . . . was what I said before I fell into bed at night. The *Shema*, one of the oldest and most important prayers of the Jewish faith. *Shema Yisrael Adonai Eloheinu Adonai Echad*, I would recite each night, as I had every night since I learned those words growing up in Brookline, Massachusetts. *Hear, O Israel, the Lord our God, the Lord is One*."[2]

But it brought little relief to the insomnia, which got progressively worse. Every aspect of his existence seemed to compound the despair and "dark thoughts." And although Mary was his closest ally in this ordeal, Mike found himself lashing out at her—which was hurtful and confusing to Mary, even though she had already seen Mike in the throes of depression.

"No matter how hard I try, nothing I do is right," Mary said at the time. "It's never enough, and everything always seems to be my fault."[3]

The problem was that Mike was still too proud (or scared) to disclose his state of mind. The only people who knew about the depression were

Mary, his son Chris, stepdaughter Pauline, and Doctor Kaplan, who had forced him to get back on the medication. And there were two close friends whose support was instrumental in Mike's eventual recovery: syndicated columnist Art Buchwald and author William Styron, both of whom spent summers on Martha's Vineyard and had themselves suffered from clinical depression.

Of the three, Buchwald had been most deeply affected by the condition. Shortly after his birth, Buchwald's mother had been institutionalized following a mental breakdown, and she remained there for thirty-five years. Buchwald, himself, was hospitalized in 1963, during his first depressive episode. Styron, a lifelong sufferer as well, entered into an excruciatingly desolate period in 1985, which became the basis of his bestselling memoir *Darkness Visible*, an unflinching account of how the disease took complete hold of his existence. By disclosing his state of mind to these trusted friends, Mike came to realize that he was not alone in his disease. The trio bonded over their shared misery, proclaiming themselves the "Blues Brothers."

When the drugs finally took effect and Mike's battered psyche returned to a state of relative normality, two things became patently clear: that clinical depression was a lifelong medical condition—extremely dangerous and never to be taken lightly—and that he literally could not have survived without Mary. They now had the profound bond of having seen each other through their lowest moment. Mike had been a good friend to Mary when she lost Ted, and she, in turn, had rescued him from death. What's more, Mary, unlike Mike's former wives, was herself a journalist. She had already been married to a hyperambitious reporter, so she understood fundamentally what drove these men, and she felt neither threatened nor neglected by their obsessive immersion into their calling.

So Mike proposed and Mary accepted; they were wed in 1986 under an apple tree on Martha's Vineyard. As in Mike's marriage to Lorraine, he inherited a stable of new stepchildren—Eames, Ted, Jr. (Teddy) and Angus—whom Mike called the "Three Vikings" because of their large build and red hair. Mary's sons were adults at the time of the marriage and all three had media aspirations, so Mike ended up being more of a mentor to them than a stepfather.

"He would have been a real difficult father because his personality is one of inquisition rather than canned advice," recalls youngest son, Angus. "Canned advice is great to have but it's not very challenging. Mike was really always brilliantly challenging and would provoke thoughts rather than dictate direction."[4]

So when Angus went to Mike for career guidance, he got the third degree. What do you think about this? Why haven't you done that? Vicious inquiry, rather than preaching.

"Typically, in a situation like that a young person is given buckets full of 'OK, son, here's what I did and here's what you oughta do.' Mike didn't do that," said Angus. "Whenever we talked about the business or my personal aspirations or ambitions it was always through a kind of probing conversation of what I was thinking, which looking back on that, was really useful, really challenging . . . nothing was easy with him."

Angus ended up getting a job at CBS, where he worked for Charlie Rose on *Nightwatch* and covered hard news and politics on the *Evening News* for Dan Rather. He went on to become senior Washington producer with *The Christian Science Monitor* TV news program, before being tapped by Discovery Network as worldwide Director of Special Projects.

Angus's brothers did not experience quite such smooth sailing. Middle child Teddy was sadly destined for a life of suffering as a result of a terrible accident that occurred on New Year's Eve, 1979.

"They were out on a small country road," remembers Angus, "driving around on a Saturday on a vacation day, and the car got away from my older brother."

Eames was at the wheel with Teddy riding shotgun in the passenger seat, and a friend in the back. Driving way too fast on a small hardtop in Maryland, Eames came screaming up to a one-lane bridge, couldn't make the sharp turn and ricocheted off the embankment. Eames, miraculously, got away without a scratch; Ted, Jr. was not so fortunate.

"He should not have lived," says Angus. "He suffered head injuries, was in a coma, broke both his legs, shattered much of his body, lost his peripheral vision, had migraine headaches and over time those injuries just grew."[5]

Mike did everything in his power over the years to help the boy get the medical attention he required. But no amount of doctors could furnish any lasting relief. Over the next decade, Teddy's problems would worsen until they became unbearable.

Meanwhile, consumed by guilt, Eames began his own career in television news. He had gotten his start at *NBC Nightly News* in 1977 as a copy boy and assistant to David Brinkley, a job facilitated by his late father's distinguished association with the network. Eames then went on to do the rounds at ABC, CNN and the *MacNeil/Lehrer NewsHour*—all brief stints without any real traction—before finding a true mentor in Burt Kearns, one of the godfathers of trash TV, who had helped to fulfill Rupert Murdoch's ambition of creating the television equivalent of his tawdry but highly lucrative portfolio of tabloid newspapers.

Kearns had broken into television news at New York's Channel 5, the very same station where Mike and Ted Yates had launched their groundbreaking *Night Beat*. He was also moonlighting at CBS News, where he wrote copy, like Angus Yates had, for *Nightwatch* and the *CBS Morning News*, having replaced a writer who had committed suicide.

But Kearns lasted less than two months on the job before leaving in disgust. As he explains it: "There was something about CBS that didn't smell right—something cultish in the way the employees saw themselves upholding some sacred tradition, carrying out some grand mission to spread the CBS orthodoxy."[6]

What Kearns wanted was the antithesis of CBS; with the nihilism of punk rock, he wanted to demolish the whole smug institution of network news. Thus, he would become managing editor of *A Current Affair*, which was launched as a lurid late-night alternative to Ted Koppel's highbrow *Nightline*. The tell-all format of *A Current Affair* proved so profitable that Rupert Murdoch soon moved the program into primetime on Fox Television. So enticing was this new magazine show that it would soon attract to its staff Don Hewitt's own daughter.

It was not long before Eames Yates joined the fray as Burt Kearns's partner in crime, to help create another tabloid show: *Hard Copy*, whose mandate, according to Kearns, was to "throw the tabloid TV rules out the window and reinvent the form as a hard-hitting investigative, MTV version of *60 Minutes*."[7] Who better to have as your New York bureau chief than the stepson of Mike Wallace?

As Kearns affectionately describes the man: "Eames Hamilton Yates was a large, red-faced rambling ranch of a man; the big, fat, thirty-something black sheep of several first-class families and traditions . . . He was in and out of jobs, in and out of rehab, in and out of whoever'd let him do the old in and out, a heavy drinking, heavy smoking, heavy duty heavy boy."[8]

Just like Lorraine's son, Tony, Mary's eldest child had also married into Rhode Island royalty—a doomed union to Dallas Pell, daughter of Senator Claiborne Pell. "Thanks to his lineage, Eames was dropped into television at the top of the slide," says Kearns. But Eames chose to slide down past the cushy network niches to land in the sandpit at *Hard Copy*, dubbed by *Los Angeles Times* critic Howard Rosenberg as "the most repulsive show on television." It is here that Eames Hamilton Yates succeeded beyond everyone's expectations. Eames, according to Kearns, became the show's "secret weapon."

Like Mike, Eames fashioned a caricature of himself, a cartoon version of his already large personality, which became his on-air persona. But it was the antithesis of Mike Wallace.

"Eames didn't sound like a reporter. He didn't have a trained 'TV voice,'" explains Kearns. "He squeaked and cracked like an ordinary Joe whose job was on the line with every story . . . To the *Hard Copy* viewer, he was the lovable, slightly lost buffoon whose bosses forced him to venture into strange towns to uncover the seamiest sex and crime scandals that no one wanted to talk about . . . He was always getting punched out or thrown out . . . The audience was always on his side."

Eames would cover a murder in a nudist colony, wondering, "Where did he hide the weapon?" He confronted an octogenarian judge accused of molesting his secretary of thirty years—showing up with his crew like a would-be Mike Wallace, only to have the geezer deck him on camera. He would investigate the abusive circus freak, whose battered family hired a hit man to rub him out. The stories were irresistible.

As Kearns sums it up, by the time *Hard Copy* ended its whirlwind fourth season in 1993 as the trashiest of trash TV, Eames had "attained a sense of personal achievement that had always eluded him before among the giants and strivers in his family. At last, he stood tall, as their equal. Eames had achieved a level of tabloid satori."[9]

While Eames Yates and Kearns had been fomenting their tabloid revolution, the establishment forces at CBS seemed to have fallen asleep at the wheel. In 1988, for the first time in its history, the network finished in third position, trailing both NBC and ABC in annual ratings tabulations. *60 Minutes* in its twentieth season remained the top show on CBS, but had ceded its championship crown as the most-watched show on television, dropping to #8. According to critics, Hewitt and his correspondents had become part of the establishment and lost their edge.

As correspondent Harry Reasoner remarked: "I think it's quite probably peaked . . . half our viewers are younger than the youngest correspondent . . . many of us [are] getting on, and it sometimes produces bad decisions."[10]

Reasoner had returned to *60 Minutes* in 1978 following an eight-year stint at ABC. The 1980s also saw the addition of two other correspondents: Ed Bradlee and Diane Sawyer, who had star power that rivaled Mike's, which became quite threatening to him.

But while his professional status was arguably declining, 1988 was a personal watershed for Mike. On December 10, he appeared as a guest on an NBC talk show, *Later with Bob Costas,* which was broadcast at 1:30 A.M. Costas began by asking him questions about *60 Minutes,* but then Mike had an epiphany—he realized that significant numbers of the late-night audience might be insomniacs who, like he, suffered from depression. Thus, Mike decided impulsively to disclose his condition on the airwaves.

"I just felt a responsibility to do that and let depressed people know that there's no reason for shame," said Mike. "It's a medical illness no different from any other . . . and there are ways to get treated just as I was."[11]

Considering Mike's concerns about protecting his tough-guy image, he took a big chance by coming out on the Costas interview show. It was a breakthrough moment—he had finally mustered the courage to step up as an interviewee and reveal the darkest part of himself. There was also a personal benefit to what he had done.

"It lifted an extraordinary burden," he explained. "Since that time I have talked about it fairly openly for the reason that it can be helpful for other people to say, 'Well look, here's a guy who was at the bottom of the heap, miserable, and look, he has it back. He's . . . surviving.' "[12]

Of the many who stood up and took notice of this moment, none were more impressed than the Yates clan: the "Three Vikings" and their mother, Mary, now Mike's wife.

Eames Yates, in particular, was deeply affected by Mike's example. In the decade to come, he would find his own apotheosis by taking his work to a new level. Just as his father had developed an almost mythic reputation for fearlessness in pursuit of war stories, Eames would turn his attention to the battlefields within. As a documentarian for HBO, Eames would examine the ills that ravage our psyches—anxiety, depression, addiction and suicide. For subjects, he would have to look no further than his own family.

Chapter Twenty-four

Oh, Shit. He's Dead!

T he 1990s began with a scare. As Mike and Don Hewitt settled into their seats of an MGM Grand plane bound for New York on March 12, 1991, Hewitt was swaggering even more than usual, having just been inducted into the Television Academy's Hall of Fame. But the color suddenly drained from his face as "Mike got up to get something from the compartment over his seat, and collapsed. Actually, he didn't collapse; he went down like a tree in a forest and lay there in the aisle of the plane, motionless."[1]

Hewitt readily admits that the first thought that went through his mind was: "Oh, shit, he's dead. Now we're never going to [beat] *Cheers!*"

Mike was rushed off the plane to a hospital, where doctors outfitted him with a pacemaker and he bounced back from the incident with seemingly more energy than before. But others in the aging stable of *60 Minutes* stars were not quite so resilient. Harry Reasoner, who had lung cancer, had undergone two operations and, by 1991, was no longer able to function as a correspondent. *60 Minutes* aired a tribute show for Reasoner in May and threw him a retirement party at the Russian Tea Room, a gathering notable for its lack of warmth. Granted, the *60 Minutes* giants were a competitive lot, given to jibes and ribbing, and not particularly known for their sentimentality, but some staffers were appalled by the absence of sincerity in the sendoff.

"They treated him like shit," recalls producer Jeffrey Fager, who would one day replace Don Hewitt as *60 Minutes'* show-runner. "Nobody got up and gave a good toast . . . It was really odd for those of us who were young producers then to watch it happen. Mike got up and said something snide. Don got up and said something snide. Morley got up and said, 'Never a noble moment.' We all came back and thought, My God. Harry could barely walk. He died a month later . . . He had abused himself. He'd been smoking too much, he'd been drinking too much. And because of that they had no respect for him."[2]

Reasoner's demise was a stark reminder of their own looming mortality. Don Hewitt was pushing seventy, while Morley Safer, at a relatively spry fifty-nine, still chain-smoked Rothman Specials. Mike, now with his pacemaker, finally gave up cigarettes for good after years of trying. But Mike had another serious health issue to contend with: his state of mind.

Indeed, when he turned seventy-five in 1993, it coincided with the twenty-fifth anniversary of *60 Minutes*, and those dual milestones hit Mike like a freight train—powerful enough to send him into his third bout with clinical depression.

"Suddenly I was going through it again. Boom!—it came out of nowhere. I felt like I couldn't beat this one."[3]

After years of relative balance, Mike was off medications, and this episode, like the others in 1984 and 1985, caught him unprepared. He returned immediately to Marvin Kaplan, who this time put him on Zoloft, one of the SSRI medications that had recently been developed. But Dr. Kaplan warned that it might take up to six weeks before the Zoloft fully kicked in. Those weeks proved harrowing, and particularly hard on Mary.

"You become very alone," she explained, "because you don't want to go out with the girls at lunch and say my husband is just awful; he won't talk to me; he won't eat; he's mad; he loses his temper. So you become isolated too. And I think it's a very good idea [for] somebody's who's living with a depressed person to go and get some help themselves."[4]

Like Mary, producer Lowell Bergman was well-acquainted with Mike's dark side. On their very first story together, Bergman had been subjected to a full dose of the legendary Wallace temper, when, in a public parking lot, Mike screamed at Bergman like a drill sergeant, dressing him down relentlessly over a relatively minor infraction while bystanders watched, mouths agape.

"He just delivered the most vicious monologue in the loudest I've ever heard his baritone voice . . . 'I don't know why we ever hired you, why I agreed to work with you' . . . everything you could think of that you wouldn't want the guy who hired you to say on the first day of work, three inches from your nose at a hundred decibels."[5]

This is one of the reasons that Bergman insisted on getting a clause in his contract that allowed him to live in Berkeley while working for *60 Minutes*. Barry Lando, too, had moved his base of operations to Paris at this point. Both producers realized that they could work far more serenely if removed from the madness of West 57th Street.

"Mike can be incredibly difficult, no question about it," says Bergman. "But on the other hand, from a professional point of view, he not only invented it but there really isn't anybody better than he is. The problem is, he knows it sometimes."[6]

After a few years apart in what Bergman calls a "divorce, of sorts," he and Mike were again working together in the 1990s. And Bergman had landed a "get" (a highly desirable interview) but it involved significant risk. As Mike describes it, "I had an opportunity to go to Beirut to interview the head of Hezbollah, Sheik Fadlallah—I talked to the CIA and they said, 'Well, look, this could be very dangerous and something bad could really happen if you do this interview.' "[7]

Palestinian militants had likewise warned Mike to stay clear of Beirut, ever since PLO leader Kamal Nasser was assassinated in 1973, following Mike's interview with him. In the ensuing decades, well over 100,000 civilians had been killed in the ongoing Lebanese civil war—and Mike and Bergman, as Jews, were prime targets. Some 240 U.S. servicemen had been slaughtered in a single bombing in 1983 that was allegedly orchestrated by Sheik Muhammad Husayn Fadlallah, the very man whom Mike was hoping to interview. Yet despite all the warnings and warning signs, Mike took the assignment willingly, for he was in a state of utter despair. He had been on Zoloft for five weeks and still hadn't felt the slightest relief.

"As far as I was concerned, if something happened during that trip, that was a good way to die," he said. "I was quite serious about that. I didn't care right then if I lived or died."[8]

It was the same spirit with which had he agreed to go cover the famine in Ethiopia while suffering through the torturous Westmoreland trial. He had little to lose. "I was up in the hotel in Beirut, looking down into a destroyed part of the city and just hoping, waiting for the Zoloft to take hold."[9]

Mike's mood was as bleak as the bombed-out landscape. But then, by the miracle of modern medicine, he awoke the following morning to a brand-new day. The hellish internal torment was gone—and Mike was able to do his interview, as planned, without a hitch.

Bergman saw no evidence of Mike's depression—not in Beirut, nor earlier for that matter. He is one of the few people close to Mike who wonders how serious it really was.

"I don't know what depression means, personally. If you tell me that someone is walking around moping, not getting out of bed in the morning . . . I didn't see that. I never saw him not get out of bed in the morning. I was on the road with him. If you're telling me that depression is that he may have had suicidal feelings, probably. I've had suicidal feelings . . . I understand the stresses of the business from a reputation point of view."[10]

Call it depression or stress, there was certainly more emotional turmoil ahead for Mike and Bergman. In 1995, they embarked on another story that would cause major commotion at CBS and considerable embarrassment to Mike, whose gaffes this time would be laid out for all to see in a *Vanity Fair* exposé that eventually inspired an Oscar-nominated film. It was *The Insider* scandal, involving tobacco whistle-blower Jeffrey Wigand, the former vice president of Research & Development for cigarette manufacturer Brown & Williamson.

After a long courtship by Bergman, Wigand had finally agreed to an interview with Mike, in which he lambasted his former employers, claiming that they had deliberately introduced dangerous chemicals such as ammonia into cigarettes to increase their nicotine delivery and, hence, addictiveness. The story was huge. Wigand was the first high-ranking former tobacco executive to come forward with damning evidence. Less than a year earlier, seven CEOs from the big tobacco companies, including Brown & Williamson, had raised their palms and sworn before members of Congress that they did not believe nicotine to be addictive. Wigand, in his interview, said that they were flat-out lying, a charge that could make them guilty of perjury.

The problem was that the terms of his severance package included a gag order that expressly forbade Wigand from talking to the media—and the tobacco giants were notoriously litigious. ABC had recently settled two lawsuits instigated by Philip Morris and R. J. Reynolds, which forced the network to issue an on-air apology and withdraw all claims that the companies purposefully boosted the nicotine levels of their cigarettes.

There was a further complication at CBS. The current CEO of the network, Larry Tisch, who had taken over from William Paley, happened himself to be in the tobacco business by virtue of his controlling interest in Loews Corporation, which owned Lorillard—makers of Kent, True and Newport cigarettes. This posed a clear conflict of interest. As Mike explains, "One of the tobacco executives who had sworn under oath that he believed nicotine was not addictive was Andrew Tisch, the CEO of Lorillard and the son of CBS Chairman Laurence Tisch."[11]

What's more, Lorillard, at the time, had been in secret negotiations to purchase six cigarette brands from Brown & Williamson, where Wigand had worked. And, to top it all off, Tisch was in the midst of negotiations to sell CBS to Westinghouse for $5.4 billion. Even the threat of litigation might have quashed the deal.

Thus, for the first time in the twenty-seven-year history of 60 Minutes, Don Hewitt was ordered by CBS corporate officers to kill a story. Lowell Bergman hit the roof, and so did Mike. After months of hand-wringing,

Hewitt proposed a compromise: airing a reworked cut of the tobacco story that could include some leaked documents that Bergman had compiled, but *not* the key interview with Jeffrey Wigand. Mike agreed to Hewitt's plan with one qualification: "The only way I could go along with the sanitized version was if I could close the program with some on-camera remarks that would be critical of the suppression that management had imposed upon us."[12]

Thus, in November 1995, *60 Minutes* aired a watered-down version of the tobacco story, complete with Mike's disclaimers against CBS management. Shortly thereafter, *The New York Times* ran a critical editorial entitled "Self-Censorship at CBS," and, days later, the New York *Daily News* named Jeffrey Wigand as "The Insider"—a fact presumably leaked from a source inside *60 Minutes*. The next domino fell when *The Wall Street Journal* printed a confidential deposition by Wigand for an unrelated case in Mississippi that included the same allegations he had made in the interview with Mike. Thus, *60 Minutes* had been scooped and embarrassed—and Lowell Bergman resigned in disgust.

In the wake of the *WSJ* story, CBS had no reason to withhold broadcasting the original cut of the tobacco story with Wigand's damning interview; it did so in February 1996, but clearly *60 Minutes*' thunder had been stolen. Later that spring *Vanity Fair* ran a lengthy exposé of the affair, which portrayed Mike and Don Hewitt as having caved in to corporate pressure without a fight.

But Mike indignantly defended his actions in the case: "I was upset about it and made it apparent that I was upset about it . . . [So] I negotiated [a deal] with the people at CBS, which permitted me to say that for the first time in the history of *60 Minutes*, for the first time in the history of CBS News, as I know it, I was told *not* to do something."[13]

Many were highly critical of what had happened at *60 Minutes*, however, including Walter Cronkite, who said, "The management of *60 Minutes* has the power there, quite clearly, to say, 'I'm sorry. We're doing this because we must do it. This is a journalistic imperative. We have this story and we're going with it. We've got to take whatever the legal chances are on it.' Well, they didn't. They felt it was necessary to buckle under the legal pressures and that must send a message to every station across the country where they might have any ambitions to do investigative reporting, 'Hey, look, if *60 Minutes* can't stand the pressure, then none of us ought to get in the kitchen at all.' I mean, it's just—it's just a hopeless cause."[14]

The incident crushed the morale at *60 Minutes* and caused a major rift between Mike and Don Hewitt, which continued, and even escalated, when the drama was turned into a movie starring Russell Crowe and Al Pacino. But this was just one of several episodes that began to lower Mike's standing in the public's eye.

Whether through sloppiness, recklessness, being cavalier or just plain unlucky, scandals would accompany Mike through the bonus years he had bought himself after what should have been his forced retirement. If, before the Westmoreland trial, he had seemed invincible, the years that followed showed Mike as an ordinary mortal—prone to errors, misjudgments and defensiveness. But it was in owning his own mortality that Mike would become truly heroic.

Chapter Twenty-five

Journalistic Malpractice

Controversy over Mike Wallace's ideology as a reporter had begun a decade prior, when he appeared as a panelist on a PBS series called *Ethics in America* in 1987. The episode, "Under Orders, Under Fire," was a riveting debate about the ethical dilemmas faced by soldiers and reporters during wartime, moderated by Charles Ogletree, a professor at Harvard Law School. For the purposes of the discussion, Professor Ogletree created a hypothetical war between the fictitious nations of "South Kosan" and "North Kosan." Ogletree then posed a series of challenging moral dilemmas to his panel, made up of Mike, ABC News anchor Peter Jennings, members of congress and the clergy, as well as several high-ranking military officers, including General William Childs Westmoreland, still smarting from his recent lawsuit against CBS.

Professor Ogletree proposed a scenario to Peter Jennings, asking him to imagine that he was imbedded as a journalist with an enemy unit of North Kosanese fighters. What if this well-armed unit unexpectedly crossed paths with a small group of American and South Kosanese soldiers, and set up an ambush which would allow them to slaughter the Americans and Southerners? What would Jennings do? Would he tell his cameraman to "Roll tape!" as the North Kosanese opened fire?

Jennings sat silently for about fifteen seconds, then declared, "If I were with a North Kosanese unit that came upon Americans, I think that I personally would do what I could to warn the Americans."

"Even if it means losing the story?" Ogletree asked.

Jennings nodded. "That's purely personal," he added, "and other reporters might have a different reaction."

That was Mike's cue. He declared he was "astonished" at Jennings's answer, then turned to his colleague and proceeded to lecture him. "You're a reporter . . . I'm a little bit at a loss to understand why . . . you would not have covered that story."

Ogletree prodded Mike. Didn't Jennings have some higher duty, either patriotic or human, to do something other than just roll film as soldiers were being shot?

"No," Wallace fired back. "You don't have a higher duty. No. No. You're a reporter!"

Jennings backtracked suddenly, saying Wallace was right and admitting, "I chickened out." Everyone in the room stared at the two journalists in horror.

Professor Ogeltree turned to General Westmoreland for his reaction. Careful to maintain his composure, the general stated tersely, "Well, it's rather repugnant to me and I think it would be rather repugnant to the American listening public to see, on film in the United States, the ambush of an American platoon. The conclusion to be drawn is that the network is in cahoots with the enemy."

Most appalled among the men in uniform was Marine Colonel George M. Connell. If the tables were turned and the journalists were wounded, the colonel declared unequivocally that U.S. Marines would not hesitate to risk their lives to drag the newsmen to safety, rather than leaving them to die on the battlefield.

"And that is what makes me so contemptuous of them," he concluded, eyeing Mike and Jennings in disgust. "Marines will die going to get . . . a couple of journalists."

The room fell into dead silence. Then a young congressman ventured an opinion—it was Newt Gingrich, some years before he assumed the role of House Speaker. He said that one thing had become clear from this discussion: "The military has done a vastly better job of systematically thinking through the ethics of behavior in a violent environment than the journalists have."[1]

Indeed, attacks on Mike's ethical standards would multiply in the years to come, particularly in his partnership with Bob Anderson, a new producer on his team. In 1994, Mike and Anderson were taken to task by the media and the president of CBS News for a violation of journalistic ethics in which they used "very, very poor judgment" in filming a segment for *60 Minutes*. It was particularly ironic, for the story itself focused on journalistic practices.

In August, *Connecticut* magazine had run an article in which Bill Meyer 3rd, a resident of West Hartford, explained how he had helped his terminally ill father commit suicide. After its publication, local law enforcement decided to reopen its investigation into the death and approached the reporter who had written the article, freelance journalist Karon Haller. When Haller willingly surrendered her notes and tape recordings to the police, they were able to charge Meyer with second-degree manslaughter, which could carry a sentence of ten years' imprisonment. Mike was interested in what compelled Karon Haller to turn over her notes to the police—a request that many journalists, like Mike himself, would refuse as a matter of principle.

Assisting in a suicide is a crime in all fifty states, though it is rarely prosecuted because the evidence usually dies with the victim. In this case, Meyer had spelled out his involvement to Haller, who printed the details in her article—and then cooperated with police investigators. It was a very touchy story. Karon Haller agreed to talk to *60 Minutes*, but made it absolutely clear that she would not do so on camera. Explains Mike, "She was worried about close-ups and that maybe I would badger her."[2] Haller, a journalist herself and well aware of Mike's reputation and tactics, had set forth clear guidelines for her cooperation—conditions that were agreed upon by Mike and his producer, Bob Anderson. But when Haller entered Mike's office on November 3, she noticed something slightly odd: "I thought it was strange that he would have makeup on his hands and face and it was only 10:30 in the morning."[3]

Mike and Haller proceeded to discuss the assisted suicide case at some length in his office. All the while, unbeknownst to Haller, the encounter was secretly videotaped by a hidden camera that was concealed in the drapes of Mike's office, its lens the size of a button. A second miniature camera faced Mike, which explains why he was in makeup. Both angles were patched to monitors in the office next door, belonging to Morley Safer, who was absent at the time.

This entire set-up appeared to be in violation of CBS News standards, which required that any use of hidden cameras be approved by senior executives in the division. Don Hewitt, who was also kept out of the loop, was flabbergasted. "What the hell were you doing with a hidden camera on a journalist?" he asked Bob Anderson, who assured his boss that they were never planning to use the footage without Haller's permission. They just wanted "to let her see that she'd be darned good on camera," and convince her after the fact to allow the interview to be broadcast.[4]

Mike likewise defended the decision. "The pictures were perfect. The sound was perfect." And, without all the crew and production paraphernalia, they were able to get a "good, relaxed" interview—but he also admitted, somewhat sheepishly, "[CBS News President Eric] Ober is very upset, and I don't blame him."[5]

When Anderson finally called Haller to inform her of what they had done, she was outraged. "I thought I was working alongside them. I didn't think they were going to zero in on me."

She said the pair tried to "assuage" her by saying, "Oh, but Karon, you look great and you're so articulate on camera." A furious Haller refused to cooperate. With respect to Mike, she chose her words carefully: "Maybe I should remind him that doing these things is bad for his image." CBS executives apparently agreed; News Vice President Joe Peyronnin delivered an official reprimand to both Mike and Anderson, saying that, while he believed the team's explanation for their actions, "This nonetheless is a violation of our standards, and in my view it was unethical to do this without her knowing it."[6]

Once again, someone inside *60 Minutes* leaked the story, and the *Washington Post* ran a front-page indictment of the affair, causing ripples throughout the media. Charles Monagan, editor of *Connecticut* magazine, which had printed Haller's original story, said, "Here's Mike Wallace asking her tough questions about journalistic practices, and meanwhile they're secretly taping her. It's just the height of arrogance. If the word gets out, who's ever going to respect them again? . . . I wouldn't even expect this from a tabloid show."

The piece never aired. Some years later, Mike admitted that the decision to surreptitiously film an interview with a fellow journalist who had expressly stated her objection to going on camera was dead wrong. "That was a big mistake, and I'm ashamed of it. I made a speech at Harvard later, and I proposed an annual malpractice award for egregious sins against the standards and principles of journalism. I said that I should be the first recipient."[7]

Yet despite his confession of journalistic "malpractice," the following year Mike and Bob Anderson became enmeshed in another case of questionable journalism. This story *also* involved a suicide—the 1993 death of Deputy White House Counsel Vincent Foster, a former law partner of Hillary Clinton and close confidant of the president and first lady. Foster's body was discovered on July 20, 1993 in Fort Marcy Park, the victim of an apparent suicide, six months to the day after Bill Clinton took office.

Though a number of different investigations all concluded that Vincent Foster had indeed taken his own life, there seemed to be some discrepancies in the forensic evidence. Foster's shoes, for example, were free of soil, which seemed unlikely had he walked across the park to kill himself. The scene also seemed lacking in the volume of blood that would normally result from a gunshot wound to the head.

It was enough to pique the interest of *Pittsburgh Tribune-Review* reporter Chris Ruddy, who conducted his own investigation and wrote an article calling the events "one of the biggest cover-ups in American history." Instrumental in this cover-up, according to Ruddy, was the U.S. Park Police that had jurisdiction over the crime scene. Park Police Officer Kevin Forn-shill, who discovered the body and was criticized by Ruddy, decided to sue him for libel. That's when *60 Minutes* became involved.

Anderson persuaded Mike to repeat the set-up he had used twenty years prior in the Colonel Herbert story: to interview journalist Chris Ruddy in one room, while Park Police Officer Fornshill waited in the wings with his attorney Philip Stinson. "We just want to nail Ruddy," an associate pro-ducer had told Stinson.[8]

But, this time, the plan backfired—because Mike strayed from the scripted plan of attack, according to acclaimed investigative journalist Dan Moldea. In *A Washington Tragedy*, his book about the Vincent Foster case, Moldea wrote, "After Ruddy arrived and the interview began . . . something unexpected happened: Wallace started buying into what Ruddy was saying about the problems with the Foster case. For over two hours, Fornshill and Stinson listened with stunned disbelief as Ruddy appeared to be persuading Wallace, who, according to Stinson, seemed 'confused and unprepared.' "[9]

When it came time to break for lunch, Ruddy left the set and Fornshill and Stinson were given the all-clear to come out of the room where they were hiding. "It's not going well," lamented Anderson allegedly. "The sto-ry's dead. I can't believe this: Mike is blowing it!"

He asked Fornshill and Stinson to spend their lunch break in Mike's office to "deprogram" him, and drill him on several solid talking points that could debunk Ruddy. When the interview resumed in the afternoon, Mike was indeed more aggressive, but part of him remained unconvinced—and, ultimately, Fornshill and Stinson were never summoned from their hiding place to confront Ruddy on camera. As far as Anderson was con-cerned, it looked like the only way to salvage the piece at this point was to "fix" it in the editing room. Indeed, they hacked up the interview, often cutting Ruddy in midsentence, making Mike seem far more aggressive than he had been in the room, and showing him snickering and even cackling in reaction shots. Dan Moldea, in his book, called Mike's performance dis-crediting Ruddy "unprofessional, heavy-handed and vindictive."

Critics went into overdrive in the wake of the broadcast, particularly the right-wing press. One week after the piece was aired, the Western Journalism Center took out a full-page ad in *The New York Times* defending Chris Ruddy and accusing Wallace of complicity in the cover-up.

Then, Mike got a taste of his own medicine. Earlier that week, Ruddy had recounted the whole saga on another program, *The Other Side of the Story*, hosted by Reed Irvine of Accuracy in Media. Later, Irvine telephoned Mike to get *his* side of the story. According to Irvine, the bulk of the forensic evidence indicated that Foster's body was moved and placed at the crime scene—a fact that he pointed out to Mike. The phone call, which Irvine recorded and which reveals Mike floundering, was included in a video that was posted on the Internet for all to see:

> IRVINE: There's no forensic evidence that he died in the park, contrary to what you said.
>
> MIKE: Well . . .
>
> IRVINE: Can you name one piece of forensic evidence that proves that he died . . .
>
> MIKE: Reed, all I want . . .
>
> IRVINE: One piece, one, tell me one piece of forensic evidence that proves that he died in the park.
>
> MIKE: I will, I tell you what.
>
> IRVINE: One, one . . .
>
> MIKE: I, I, I will . . .
>
> IRVINE: One, just one.
>
> MIKE: You know what?
>
> IRVINE: Name one.
>
> MIKE: I— (nervous laughter)
>
> IRVINE: One, just one lousy piece. I mean, you studied, you said you examined all these, all the questions.
>
> MIKE: Yep.
>
> IRVINE: So you must—and you said all the forensic evidence points to this, one piece of forensic evidence that proves he died in the park.

MIKE: Reed . . .

IRVINE: One!

MIKE: No matter . . .

IRVINE: Can you name one?

MIKE: Just a moment.

IRVINE: Yeah?

MIKE: You know perfectly well, Reed, that no matter what evidence, forensic or otherwise, that I— (hesitates)

IRVINE: Mike, try me. Name me one.

MIKE: All right, I'll, I, I tell you what I'll do. I won't do it on the telephone, I'll put it on paper.[10]

Irvine has said that he never received a written follow-up from Mike, who was clearly flustered by the phone call and seemingly not versed in the facts of his story. He could not have felt particularly good about the encounter. But Mike stood by the story, which was rebroadcast six months later, and Mike's introduction began: "A few right-wing groups still contend, despite evidence to the contrary, still believe that Vince Foster did not commit suicide . . . that he was murdered."

That same year, suicide would touch Mike personally, when he received a deeply disturbing call from Fiji. It was Tony, with news about his mother Lorraine, who despite living on this island paradise, had become increasingly morose in the decade without Mike.

On one particularly painful day in 1994, Lorraine walked into a river in the South Seas and drowned herself. She was seventy-three years old. Neither her daughter Pauline nor brother James flew to Fiji to attend the funeral. Both had grown estranged from Tony, whom they blamed for Lorraine's death.[11]

As much of a blow as Lorraine's death was, it would not be the last time in the decade Mike would be touched by suicide—both personally and professionally.

In November 1998, Mike did a segment on Jack Kevorkian that was controversial on multiple levels. The piece featured an interview with Dr. Kevorkian along with a disturbing tape that he had provided to *60 Minutes*— showing the doctor ending the life of one of his patients. While Kevorkian had been acquitted in three prior incidents involving assisted suicide, this case was different in that the doctor, rather than assisting from the sidelines, administered the lethal injection himself—all of which was clearly shown on the tape, a fact that would serve finally to incriminate Kevorkian for manslaughter. Airing the lurid video—a network first—provided *60 Minutes* with a significant ratings boost during the critical November "Sweeps Week," where the Nielsen Media Research company compiles data that directly affects a network's advertising revenue.

CBS was taken to task for the timing of the broadcast, which appeared to have the hallmarks of a publicity stunt. There was a particular irony in a question posed by Mike during the interview with Dr. Kevorkian:

MIKE: You were engaged in a political, medical, macabre publicity venture, right?

KEVORKIAN: Probably.

MIKE: And in watching these tapes, I get the feeling there's something almost ghoulish in your desire to see the deed done.

KEVORKIAN: Well, that could be. I can't argue with that. Maybe it is ghoulish, I don't know—it appears that way to you. I can't criticize you for that. But the main point is the last part of your statement—that the deed be done.

One week after the broadcast, Mike was attacked for his part in the "deed," when he appeared as a guest on the PBS *NewsHour* in a segment which also included Ned McGrath, a spokesman for the Archdiocese of Detroit, where the so-called "mercy killing" took place.

Mr. McGrath accused *60 Minutes* of being duped by Dr. Kevorkian in an effort to chase ratings: "They went from reporting the news to repeating the political agenda of Jack Kevorkian ... using Jack Kevorkian, his documents, his videotapes, anything else that he supplies, as a reliable and credible source of information, is journalistically naïve."[12]

After a few spirited exchanges, Mike allowed that "We're used by Jack Kevorkian. We are used by Jack Kevorkian, yes. We've also been used by Martin Luther King and Jerry Falwell and presidential candidates . . ."

Then moderator Terence Smith pointed out, "CBS announced this evening that it would, in fact, release the tape to the police. Now, Mike Wallace, you're not normally so accommodating with your outtakes, the portions not broadcast. What's different in this case?"

Ironically, it was the very issue for which Mike had criticized journalist Karon Haller when she handed over her interview tape in the assisted suicide story in Connecticut. In both Haller's case and the *60 Minutes* story, the released tapes would help police secure convictions. But Mike defended himself, stating that the tape, in fact, belonged to Dr. Kevorkian, who consented to its release, for he was willing to serve jail time to make his point—which he did, serving eight years in a state penitentiary.

Upon Dr. Kevorkian's discharge in 2007, he would face Mike in a follow-up interview. In it, the doctor said he would continue to crusade on behalf of the practice that he insisted was entirely humane—there are times where the degree of suffering is so great that suicide can be the only rational option. Indeed, Mike experienced this within his own family.

In 1999, Mary's middle son, Ted Yates Jr., drove alone to the family cabin in Montana. He had been in chronic pain for two decades, since the terrible car crash with his brother, Eames. Countless doctors, procedures and prescriptions had failed to provide Teddy with any lasting relief. He was at the end of his rope. So he aimed a shotgun at his head—and pulled the trigger.

Shifting Sands

T he news of my younger brother's death from suicide devastated me," declared Eames Yates. "There was little I could do at the time but go through the zombie-like motions of dealing with my family, our friends and getting my brother's body in the ground. That was just the beginning of my grief and anger."[1]

Eames, along with his youngest brother Angus, had discovered the body and stoically took on the task of cleaning up the blood before their mother arrived. Questions began to flood his mind: "How could someone I had loved so much hurt me so badly? Why did he do this to his family and friends? What could I have done to prevent his selfish and hurtful act?"[2] Eames clearly felt betrayed on some level but also must have been consumed with remorse, for he had been behind the wheel of the car that fateful night.[3]

"Because of my anger and grief, I decided to make a film that would take an unflinching and deliberate look at the ugliness I experienced," said Yates, who was working at HBO at the time, producing documentaries for *America Undercover*, a remarkable and courageous departure from the tabloid television he had previously been doing. His film, *Suicide*, became perhaps the most poignant and personal episode of that gritty series. Yates called it: "a personal exploration into the raw pain and anguish that suicide leaves behind."

It was not Eames's first foray into the frailties of the human psyche. Several years prior, he had approached Mike about participating in a film about depression, also for HBO. Mike took some time to consider it. While he was already "out" about his depression, having appeared in 1988 on *Later with Bob Costas,* that moment had been a spontaneous admission on a talk show. What Eames was proposing for HBO was a program devoted exclusively to the subject of depression, and Mike's appearance would surely be used in its advertising and promotion. It would make Mike a spokesman for the disease.

There was also the delicate matter of control. Mike's image, in this documentary, would be entrusted to Eames, and he took a dim view of the kind of tabloid journalism that Yates had cut his teeth on. Indeed, when Burt Kearns wrote *Tabloid Baby,* a tell-all memoir of his wild days with Eames and others in the seedy world of trash television, he had asked Mike for a blurb for the book jacket. Mike called it "[The] sad, funny, undeniably authentic . . . tale of what befell too much of mainstream television over the past couple of decades as the bad drove out the good."

One of the reasons that Mike Wallace had been so controlling in his career was the simple fact that in certain instances where he had ceded editorial control it had landed him in hot water—as with the Westmoreland special, the content of which had been largely dictated by George Crile. If Mike agreed to appear in the depression documentary, he would likewise be at the mercy of Eames Yates.

But Eames, in midlife now, had had an epiphany—not unlike what happened to Mike in 1963, after the death of Peter, when he gave up his less serious television jobs to focus exclusively on the news. Eames was similarly beginning to find his own compass. "I'm finally starting to figure it out. Documentary films happen because you're invited in as a guest. It's due to the kindness of strangers that you're allowed to make your living. These are tragic people, and you've got to treat them with nothing but respect. You have to be polite. You have to listen. The less of you that's in the film, the better."[4]

Thus, after some consideration, Mike agreed to appear in Eames' documentary. In his mid seventies, Mike was coming to a new insight, a realization that his life had attained a particular purpose now—a mission that could perhaps transcend his myriad accomplishments as a journalist.

"There's nothing to be ashamed of about depression," Mike would insist in public forums. "Find a good psychiatrist . . . it's an illness, like any other, not like any other but it's an illness."[5]

Meanwhile, Mike's fellow "Blues Brother," William Styron, had already come forward in his own medium, publishing a harrowing and haunting memoir of depression in *Vanity Fair* in 1989 and expanding it the following year into a book. Art Buchwald, too, had done his share of speaking and writing about his own battles with the disease, including an appearance on *Larry King Live* that provoked an unprecedented response. The same was true of Styron's writings on the subject. As the author explained: "The overwhelming reaction made me feel that inadvertently I had helped unlock a closet from which many souls were eager to come out and proclaim that they, too, had experienced the feelings I had described. It is the only time in my life I have felt it worthwhile to have invaded my own privacy, and to make that privacy public."[6]

Mike took inspiration from Styron's courageous example. Thus, despite his decades of bravado, despite all that Mike had invested in his onscreen image as the fearless investigator, the television torpedo who could penetrate even the thickest and most impenetrable façade, the interrogator who riled Norman Mailer, got Streisand to cry and Khomeini to blink, who extracted confessions from criminals and tell-alls from tyrants . . . despite everything he had created for himself up to this point, Mike realized it was time for Oz to step out from behind the curtain. It was his turn to reverse the lens of inquisition onto himself—and to become an example.

"Take a look at me," Mike would use himself as an example to those contemplating suicide, ". . . because I was saved, I had twenty more years of very productive life. And this is the lesson that I take from it, I was out of my mind. I was a little crazy."[7] Mike became a spokesman for getting proper care and treatment.

How perfect that his own stepson, Eames Yates, was offering him the opportunity—and in Mike's own milieu of investigative television, no less. Wallace not only agreed to give his testimonial, he convinced Bill Styron to appear on the program, as well. The hour-long documentary, *Dead Blue: Surviving Depression*, powerful and deeply inspiring, received an Emmy nomination in 1998 for outstanding nonfiction special. Its airing launched a new phase in Mike Wallace's life, for, finally, he had let himself be seen.

Eames would go on to produce more explorations into crippling afflictions within our minds, including *Crank: Made in America*, about the hellish world of methamphetamine addiction, and *Panic*, featuring Kim Basinger and football legend Earl Campbell discussing their battle against paralyzing anxiety disorders—a piece that finally won Yates an Emmy.

Styron, Buchwald and Mike, meanwhile, began to venture out in public as the musketeers of melancholia, speaking together on panels or making joint media appearances. As Angus Yates explains: "They used to call them the three amigos because they were all really famous, really successful and they were all dying on the inside, and they teamed up and made a conscious decision before it was cool [to do so] to be really open about it. They relied on each other and presented themselves to the world tirelessly to put their stories out there, which was very brave."[8]

"The conventional wisdom was that depression was a dark, dirty, internal private secret that successful people didn't want to project at all because it was counter to their success. And those guys turned that on its head. . . . It was huge."

In one such program, *Gray Matters: Depression and the Brain*, produced by Public Radio International, Mike served as announcer and moderator, telling us the sobering statistics:

Depression has been described as the cancer of the 21st century. It hits one out of every five people around the world at least once during a lifetime. Over any six-month period it is estimated that between 5 and 7 percent of the world's population will be suffering from a serious depression.

A new study by the World Health Organization estimates that by the year 2020, depression will be the second most burdensome illness in the world. The economic and social costs of that are staggering.

Then, Mike, along with Buchwald and Styron, put a human face on the disease with forthright testimonials of how they had been deeply affected by it. Mike also explained the critical importance of friendships and the support of loved ones, stating that he would never have made it without the companionship of Buchwald: "Arty called me night after night. It was so reassuring to know that what I was feeling was normal for a depressed person, to talk to someone who has been through it and come through the other side."[9]

Mike gave profound credit to Mary, whom he had married on Martha's Vineyard. His relationship to the island deepened, too, in this period. He decided, in fact, that it was the place where he wished to be buried.

Author John Hersey, like Bill Styron, a longtime resident of Martha's Vineyard, had discovered a little private cemetery tucked away in the woods of the area known as West Chop. As Art Buchwald explained, "They were selling plots for $500 with the condition that you couldn't sell them for a profit. We called everybody, all our friends—Styron and everyone. We said you've got a place to die. John Hersey is there, my wife is there and that's where I'm going."[10]

Mike and Mary followed suit, and then Buchwald used that fact to shame Mike into finally buying a home on the island, as well. For decades Mike had been renting his summer house. "You have to have Cronkite's money to buy on the Vineyard," Mike used to quip.[11] Well, the fact was that Mike now had Cronkite's money, so Art Buchwald persuaded him to bite the bullet and buy, lest his tombstone read: "Here lies Mike Wallace. He was always a renter."[12]

So Mike and Mary bought a place on outer Main Street in Vineyard

Haven, dubbed "Writers' Row" because its residents included William Styron, John Hersey and Art Buchwald—Pulitzer Prize winners, all of them.
And as he settled into the role of a true islander, Mike found himself relaxing into life at a deeper level. Take the descriptive language he used in
an article entitled "A Haven on the Vineyard" that he penned for the local
newspaper:

> *Something extraordinary happens to me every time I leave my "real"
> life in New York City and arrive at home in Vineyard Haven. All the magic
> of my schoolboy excursions to the Vineyard comes flooding back, all the early
> memories. For some inexplicable reason whenever I get here and settle in for
> a while the world outside slowly evaporates and the simple pleasures of island
> routine take over. The Vineyard is the only place I know where somehow I
> feel utterly and totally relaxed ... the simple fact [is] that the Vineyard repre-
> sents some of the happiest times of my life.*[13]

Meanwhile, back in New York, things were changing at CBS. Leslie
Moonves had assumed the role of president and CEO of the corporation,
following the Tisch regime, and Mike was realizing that, just as priori-
ties were shifting in his personal life, so too were changes afoot at the
network.

"It's an utterly, utterly different business today. Les Moonves is not
Bill Paley. Les Moonves was able to turn the network around as far as the
ratings are concerned, and some of what he has done has been first-rate,
but some of what he's done ..." Mike stopped himself midsentence, then
stated simply: "Bill Paley valued his news division. It was what distinguished his network from the others."[14]

By 1995, CBS was owned by Westinghouse, and like any other Fortune
500 corporation, decisions boiled down to the bottom line. Its *60 Minutes*
flagship would be reeling from *The Insider* scandal for the remainder of
the decade, and even the "Mike Wallace" brand had been compromised—
tarnished in the eyes of some. People were commenting on Mike's psyche
across the Internet like Arts blogger Eve Berliner who wrote: "Beneath the

brash, unnerving persona, the master of the jugular who has raised intimidation to an art form, lies a more hidden man, a man of scars and storms
and deep black melancholies."[15]

60 Minutes began facing a series of broadside attacks—from rival networks, but also from within CBS. In an effort to draw in younger viewers,
CBS programming executives had created *West 57th Street*, an alternative
newsmagazine to be staffed by new faces. Run by Andrew Lack, who had
been a producer for Dan Rather, *West 57th Street* had taken over the floor
below the *60 Minutes* offices. Speaking of his vision of the program to *The
New York Times*, Lack had declared, "It's geared to reflect my interests and
the interests of my colleagues whose ages start in their twenties and go
through their mid-fifties."[16] It was, by design, half the age range of the
60 Minutes staff. Both Don Hewitt and Dan Rather, now ensconced in
Cronkite's chair at the *CBS Evening News*, had campaigned hard to kill
the show, which they saw as encroaching on their domains. Eventually,
they prevailed, with Hewitt luring Meredith Vieira and Steve Kroft, the
top correspondents from the now-cancelled *West 57th Street*, into the *60
Minutes* fold.

Beyond internal competition within CBS, *60 Minutes* was also under
assault by the other networks. In 1996, NBC decided to go head-to-head
with its rival by programming its own newsmagazine, *Dateline*, in the
same timeslot as *60 Minutes*. NBC even tried to recruit Mike's son, Chris,
who was working at ABC at the time, as a correspondent for the show. He
considered it for a time, before deciding to remain at ABC. "I would have
loved to help *Dateline* knock off *60 Minutes*," said the forty-nine-year-old
Chris Wallace, "but in the end ABC is home."[17]

Looking to update its offerings, CBS itself tried to fashion a vehicle
with which to woo Chris Wallace. In 1997, over vociferous protests from
Don Hewitt, Mike and many of the other *60 Minutes* correspondents, Leslie Moonves approved the creation of *60 Minutes II* and entered into secret
talks to hire Chris Wallace, who bore a superficial resemblance to his father.
But negotiations between the network and the younger Wallace ultimately
broke down when ABC refused to release him from his contract. Chris

Wallace ultimately found his home at a news division that would alter the landscape of broadcast journalism, drawing viewers away from the networks into the universe of cable TV.

And while Mike would enter the new millennium with plenty of fight left in him, it was not long before the staggering mileage on his sixty-year career would begin to take its toll.

Chapter Twenty-seven

The Old Man Has Lost It

In the sweep of his career, Mike Wallace had witnessed firsthand nearly every milestone in the development of broadcast journalism. He had cut his teeth in radio, where unedited news was read directly off the wires. Then writers were hired and the broadcasts became more elaborate. With the advent of television, the news was enhanced with visuals, made even more vivid by the subsequent introduction of color. Mike and those around him were at the forefront of all these innovations; indeed, Mike pioneered techniques like hidden cameras and ambush interviews that became widely used across many areas of broadcasting.

Now, as the millennium turned, Mike—already in his eighties—would watch, both proudly and reluctantly, as the torch passed to the next generation. But he wasn't going without a fight, even if this meant duking it out publicly with his own son, Chris.

The ideological landscape in twenty-first-century newsrooms was vastly different than the one in which Mike had built his career. In 1996, *The Wall Street Journal* had published an op-ed piece declaring that CBS News showed a consistent liberal bias in its coverage of political issues.

While not new—accusations of a left-wing slant in mainstream media had been floated since the Nixon administration—the views echoed a sentiment that had become increasingly widespread. Conservatives were particularly up in arms about what they saw as unfavorable coverage of their candidate in the 1992 elections, in which incumbent president George H. Bush lost his office to Bill Clinton.

No one understood this mounting bitterness more than Rupert Murdoch, who, that same year, launched the Fox News Channel with its promise of "fair and balanced" coverage. Fox News soon became the most dominant cable news station in the country—and provided a new stage for conservative views. It was here that, after the national tragedy of 9/11, Chris Wallace found his true calling.

After Chris joined Fox News in 2003, the relationship between Mike and his son, already fairly strained, became even more constricted—but it was not strictly an ideological disagreement. Wallace family politics have always been somewhat slippery. Though often perceived as a staunch liberal, Mike has admitted to voting twice for Republicans and once for a conservative. Chris, for his part, has been a registered Democrat for decades, for the simple reason, he claims, that being a Democrat is the only feasible way to participate in the political process in heavily Democratic Washington, D.C. But that hardly makes him a friend to Washington liberals.

Chris would become famous in 2006 for his aggressive interview with Bill Clinton—the first and last time the former president has been interviewed by Fox News—in which an incensed, finger-wagging Clinton lost his composure and fumed, "So you did Fox's bidding on this show. You did your nice little conservative hit job on me."[1]

But Chris's abrasiveness was not limited to Democrats. As Chief White House Correspondent for NBC in the 1980s, he had the temerity to call Ronald Reagan a liar to his face. It was during a charged 1987 news conference, in which President Reagan admitted to dealing arms for hostages. Chris stood up and asked the president flatly why he had denied that Israel was involved with the arms sales to Iran "when you knew that wasn't true." A vintage Wallace moment.

Indeed, Mike had watched his son make a series of sensible and strategic decisions in his career. After graduating from Harvard, Chris had gotten his start in print journalism at *The Boston Globe*, with encouragement from both Mike and stepfather Bill Leonard—and it gave him a solid foundation in writing. After the 1972 elections, Chris made his move to television at the CBS Chicago affiliate, WBBM. From there, he went to the networks, clocking in fourteen years at both NBC and ABC before moving on to Fox News, where he began anchoring *Fox News Sunday.*

Mike proudly admitted of Chris: "He demonstrates week in and week out that he's better at anchoring a news show than I ever was."[2] And it appeared as though there was a real détente between the two. But then, in 2005, Mike and Chris had a very public falling out—and not over ideology or network rivalry. It was personal, and precipitated by the release of books that each had written.

Mike and Chris shared a book agent, Bill Adler, who had recently approached them both to write books. To Mike, he said it was time for a new memoir. So much had occurred in the two decades since his 1984 book, *Close Encounters*, whose narrative had ended frustratingly in the most volatile year of Mike's life: the end of his twenty-eight-year marriage to Lorraine, the onset of the Westmoreland trial and all of its fallout. Since that time, Mike had faced multiple episodes of clinical depression and gone public about his battles with the disease. He had also conducted important reporting on the first Gulf War and the 9/11 attacks. And there were the inevitable controversies that Mike seemed to stir up every couple of years— Jeffrey Wigand, Karon Haller, the "North Kosan" incident and so on. It was high time, said Bill Adler, to put these in a new biography.

Mike agreed and they naturally summoned Gary Paul Gates, with whom Mike had worked on *Close Encounters*, to lend a hand. Given everything that Mike had been through since his first memoir, he wanted this book to be written in the first person, and to delve more deeply into his private life, so he did not particularly like the idea of sharing credit this time. Gary Paul Gates, a bestselling author, was appalled and wrote an angry letter to Hyperion, the book's publisher, in which he refused unequivocally to ghostwrite without credit. After some haggling, Hyperion agreed to offer the credit "MIKE WALLACE with GARY PAUL GATES," but Mike's name would be set in a considerably larger typeface. It was a significant demotion from their previous collaboration on *Close Encounters* ("MIKE WALLACE and GARY PAUL GATES"), where both names were the same size. Nonetheless, after some grumbling, Gates accepted the deal and got to work.

Meanwhile, Chris Wallace had reached the point in his career that he, too, should be writing a book. In Chris's words: "Bill Adler . . . called me up and said, 'Have you ever thought of writing a book?' And I said, 'Yes, but I never have had an idea.' And he kind of had some ideas, and we sort of put the idea together and then we went to . . . Rugged Land, a small publishing house with a relationship with Random House."[3]

Adler's idea was a rehash of one that he had proposed to Mike thirty years prior, which itself was a variation on the book that had won John F. Kennedy his Pulitzer Prize in 1955: *Profiles in Courage*, about valor amongst members of the Senate. Back in the early '70s, Adler had pitched Mike the idea of putting his name on a book to be called *Profiles in Journalistic Courage*, but it never came to be. So now, in 2003, he pitched a book to Chris to be named *Character: Profiles in Presidential Courage*, which would feature acts of boldness by the nation's most esteemed commanders-in-chief. Chris loved the idea.

". . . a feel-good book about American democracy," he ruminated, ". . . about presidents who don't do the poll-driven thing, who don't do the popular thing, who, you know, don't do what sometimes seems a little craven but who stand up and do what is in their core conviction, what they believe is right for America."[4]

Chris, unlike his father, had no trouble accepting help from multiple ghostwriters, all of whom were willing to work, in this case, without credit. As Chris's Harvard classmate Bob Somerby wrote in *The Daily Howler,*

"Wallace had only a glancing acquaintance with the material which appears in his book. To his credit, he routinely acknowledged that the book was more-or-less written by committee."[5]

The "committee" of writers helped get Chris's book to press one year earlier than his father's—and it was released in time to coincide with the 2004 election, when President George W. Bush was running for his second term. But the reviews were not exactly glowing. Said one:

Wallace displays a presidentialist bias, often discounting the cautions or alternatives offered by the President's critics and even seeming to dismiss out of hand advice from members of Congress, staff, and citizens. At times, what Wallace calls courage may just as easily be pigheadedness, abuse of power, or folly.[6]

The biggest criticism of the book was that it devoted its final chapter to George W. Bush, which had the appearance of a campaign ploy—elevating him prematurely into the pantheon of "great" presidents before history could judge Bush's true accomplishments.

It was this particular detail that seemed to grate on Mike, for he was touchy about the fact that his son had more access to the Bush White House than he did. In fact, Mike chose to close his own book, which was released in 2005, with the words:

I myself have never gotten a chance to interview the current president of the United States. Karl Rove wouldn't let me talk to him even when he was merely governor of Texas. So . . . I've interviewed just about every president since Abe Lincoln, including Bush the elder, number 41, but never George W., number 43.

So how about it, Mr. President, isn't it time you gave this old man a break?

Despite Mike's blatant, albeit tongue-in-cheek, appeal, he did not get any calls from the White House. At eighty-seven, Mike was truly hoping for this one last jewel in his crown before his inevitable retirement. In fact, he couldn't stop talking about it. Mike mentioned the presidential snub in several media appearances while promoting his book.

"It's a stonewall," he grumbled to *The Philadelphia Inquirer.* "I don't know why it should be personal . . . It's a strange, secretive White House."

His first television appearance to promote the memoir that fall was not on his own network, but on NBC's *Today Show.* It confused Mike. "Nobody was interested at CBS. It was quite apparent . . . CBS knew the book was coming. It's really strange. Nobody reached out."[7]

Perhaps one of the reasons for the oversight was that Hyperion, the book's publisher, was a corporate sibling of CBS competitor ABC. Ultimately, it was NBC's Katie Couric who first interviewed Mike, and her introduction began: "In the lion's den of investigative journalism, Mike Wallace is the father of the pride. He is fierce, fearless, and unrelenting. For half a century, he has taken on the most notable and notorious figures in modern history, never hesitating, in the hunt for truth."

Yet book reviewers had pointed out that the truth—at least the personal truth about Mike Wallace—was sorely lacking from his memoir. Tara McKelvey, in *The New York Times,* complained that in Mike's long and storied career "he has collected more than enough material for a first-rate memoir. Or so you would think."[8] Then she cited a moment from Mike's interview with Arthur Miller, where the playwright said that he had always worked hard to provide "some little moment of truth up on that stage that people could feel made them a little more human."

"Too bad you won't find moments like those from Wallace," bemoaned McKelvey. "At least not in this book."

Despite Mike's initial desire to write a more personal account of his life, he ultimately had fallen back on an inventory of his myriad interviews. But Couric, in her own interview with Mike, forced him to get personal. "Before he married Mary in 1986," she narrated to the audience, "Wallace admits he was married to the job."

"I was not a very good husband," said Mike on camera.

"Any regrets about that?" asked Couric.

"In retrospect, yeah," allowed Mike. "I did what I felt that I wanted to do. Fairly selfishly. I didn't know my kids as well as I should have."[9]

In November, Mike continued his television rounds with an interviewer who made him particularly nervous. As *AP Television* writer David Bauder described:

> *Before arriving at a TV studio Thursday for an interview to promote his memoir, Mike Wallace had a feeling that hundreds of people who had sat across from him with the cameras rolling would find familiar. "I was intimidated ahead of time, I have to say," he said. "Who knows what he really had in mind?"*

His interrogator was son Chris, who, despite a lifetime of relative estrangement, had invited Mike to be a guest on *Fox News Sunday*. It's notable, however, that Mike did not give Chris the "scoop"—he had already appeared on *Larry King Live* and the *Today Show*. But the event was nonetheless momentous—it was the first time father and son had appeared together on television.

Chris, possibly as nervous as Mike, must have wanted to do his father proud. But how does one impress Mike Wallace? Certainly *not* by going soft on him. So Chris began:

CHRIS: Do you understand why some people feel such disaffection for the mainstream media?

MIKE: Oh, yes. They think we're wild-eyed commies, liberals. Yes?

CHRIS: That's what they think. And how do you plead?

MIKE: I think it's damn foolishness.

CHRIS: Really?

MIKE: Look, you know as well as I, reporters are in the business because they want to be—first of all, they're patriots just as much as any conservative. Even a liberal reporter is a patriot, wants the best for this country. And people—you know, your fair and balanced friends at FOX—don't fully understand that.

They were just warming up. Chris laid into him next about why Mike so often asks questions intended to shame his subjects, such as the infamous encounter with Barbra Streisand that reduced the diva to tears:

> MIKE: These are interesting questions. Why are you asking? Because they're interesting questions. And what you do is—or what I have succeeded in doing over a period of time is to get the attention of the person that I'm interviewing . . .
>
> CHRIS: Do you never say to yourself "I'm going to embarrass him, I'm going to hurt his feelings"?
>
> MIKE: No, no. I don't have subpoena powers. They know who I am when they come on. They know the kind of questions that I ask . . .

And then Chris, in classic Wallace tradition, cut to the chase:

> CHRIS: . . . do you hate getting old?
>
> MIKE: Well, I tell you what. I had my hearing aids fixed today so that I could [properly] hear you . . . I can't see as well. I used to be able to play tennis. I now have—this has stopped me from smoking—a pacemaker, have it for about the last fifteen years. Yes, I don't like getting old.
>
> CHRIS: And you don't retire because . . .
>
> MIKE: Because I love—it is not *work*, what I do. I love what I do.

The answer that Mike had given to Katie Couric on that question, however, was far more forthright: "I wouldn't know what else to do . . . when I decided that maybe the time had come for me to quit, I got depressed. What could I do if I didn't work?"

Indeed, Morley Safer had once joked that Mike's only hobby was "pulling wings off insects." The truth was he had few outside interests. One of the things that kept this octogenarian from retiring was the sheer dread of feeling purposelessness and the terror that it would send him into a depression from which he might not emerge.

The following month, Mike was interviewed by a *Boston Globe* reporter, who began by asking the question of the day: "President George W. Bush has declined to be interviewed by you. What would you ask him if you had the chance?"

On the spur of the moment, Mike gave a response he would come to regret: "What in the world prepared you to be the commander-in-chief of the largest superpower in the world? In your background, Mr. President, you apparently were incurious. You didn't want to travel. You knew very little about the military . . . The governor of Texas doesn't have the kind of power that some governors have . . . Why do you think they nominated you? Do you think that has anything to do with the fact that the country is so [expletive] up?"[10]

When Chris Wallace read the story the following day, he shook his head in dismay. A few days later, Chris made some public comments about the matter, and soon the story was all over the press:

Only days after appearing on NBC's Dateline *and confessing that one of his greatest regrets was not being closer to his children when they were growing up, Mike Wallace has had his sanity publicly questioned by his son, Fox News correspondent Chris Wallace. All had seemed to be well between them last week, when the younger Wallace interviewed the elder, as part of his father's promotion of his new book,* Between You and Me. *But Monday, he told Boston talk-show host Howie Carr, "He's lost it, the man has lost it. What can I say?"*[11]

Chris went on to comment that "things have set in" with his father and that the family planned to have a "competency hearing" for Mike soon. Even in jest, it was a rather harsh thing to say.

True, Mike *had* been slipping of late. In 2003, he had suffered a fall while collecting his mail on Martha's Vineyard, which caused him to lose consciousness and rupture an eardrum. It was a bad enough blow to the head that the local doctor ordered Mike medevaced to Lennox Hill Hospital in Manhattan. The accident affected his vision and memory, causing him to ramble and lose his train of thought in a subsequent public appearance—which was quite dramatic for Mike, whose wits hitherto had been razor-sharp.

The following year, Mike was arrested for disorderly conduct following an altercation with two inspectors from the New York Taxi and Limousine Commission. Mike had just emerged from Luke's Bar and Grill on Manhattan's Upper East Side with take-out meat loaf, when he noticed his double-parked driver being questioned by the inspectors. Mike allegedly lunged at them in an "overly assertive and disrespectful way" and was promptly cuffed and delivered to a police station—though the charges were later dropped.[12]

It seemed that Mike was still as feisty as he'd been the last time he was arrested, thirty-six years earlier at the 1968 Democratic National Convention. The man simply refused to slow down. And retirement—well, that was out of the question. Until 2006, that is.

Mike had always said that he would throw in the towel when his toes turn up. "Well, they're just beginning to curl a trifle," he admitted in March of that year. "Which means that, as I approach my 88th birthday, it's become apparent to me that my eyes and ears, among other appurtenances, aren't quite what they used to be."[13] Thus, CBS put out a press release that Mike would be phasing out his weekly contributions to *60 Minutes* to assume the role of "Correspondent Emeritus."

But when Mike appeared on *Larry King Live* just two weeks later, he was already backpedaling:

MIKE: I'm not retiring. I'm going to be working. I'm going to be competing with you for certain individuals that you'd like to interview before I get to them.

KING: If you're not retiring, what are you?

MIKE: That's the point. That's—we were talking earlier and you said or I said to you: "How long are you going to keep doing it?" And you told me 2009?

KING: Yes, but I don't know if I'll leave.

MIKE: That's right, and I don't know that I'm going to leave either.

KING: So then this announcement amounted to what?

Larry King was mystified. And things got even livelier, when a second guest joined them on the set: Chris Wallace, in his first public appearance with Mike since Chris's barbed remarks to the press, and their second time together on TV. King asked him immediately: "Chris, what did you think of your father's decision to say good-bye?"

"I don't think he's going to say good-bye," opined Chris. ". . . six months from now, the real story will be not how *little* he's working, but how *much* he's working."

After a few exchanges, King steered the conversation over to the elephant at the table—the issue over which the two Wallaces had been feuding:

KING: Chris, your father has not met, even shaken hands with the president of the United States. Have you met him or interviewed him?

CHRIS: I have not interviewed him, although I certainly hope to. But I think this public complaining and whining is rather unattractive. You know, the fact is, he's a busy man. He decides who he wants to talk to. I have actually met the president, and several times, and been to a State of the Union briefing where he had lunch with us and discussed things. And I'm happy to pass my father's best wishes onto the president the next time I see him.

KING: You want to respond to that blast, Mike?

MIKE: That's my boy.

Finally, Larry King addressed the issue of succession:

KING: Chris, would you ever want to go on *60 Minutes* and want to replace your dad?

CHRIS: I'm very happy at FOX News, I will tell you, Larry.

KING: So the answer is, no, no, no?

CHRIS: No. Or as Dick Cheney says, no and hell no.

In fact, nobody would be replacing Mike anytime soon. As Chris predicted, six months later he was still in the saddle, undertaking a huge interview. And Mike blew it. At least according to his son.

Tough but Fair

A fter a year of intense lobbying, the president finally consented to an interview with Mike in August of 2006. But it wasn't George W. Bush—it was Bush's nemesis, Iranian president Mahmoud Ahmadinejad, a man who claimed that 9/11 was orchestrated by segments within the U.S. government, a fanatic who bragged openly about his country's ambitions to produce nuclear weapons and destroy Israel. President Bush had, in fact, singled out Iran as being part of the "Axis of Evil" in his 2002 State of the Union speech. Since then, President Ahmadinejad made sure to keep himself squarely in the public eye by repeatedly denying the Holocaust and calling for the annihilation of the "Zionist State."

Mike knew that Ahmadinejad, a calculating provocateur, could make for an interesting *60 Minutes* segment. The Emeritus Correspondent reasoned that an exclusive interview with the Iranian leader, who had been shunning the western press, was the perfect opportunity for Mike to emerge from semi-retirement.

But Mike also knew that he no longer possessed the cachet he once had. "Oh my God, I can just see it on the other end [of the call to CBS]: 'That guy doesn't realize that he's lost a certain amount of usefulness to us.' "[1]

Nonetheless, Mike instructed his producers at *60 Minutes* to chase down the interview—and, after many months, they finally got a response from Tehran. As had happened twenty-seven years prior with the Ayatollah Khomeini interview, Mike was summoned to Tehran on extremely short notice. It was August, and he had been relaxing on Martha's Vineyard with Mary and their island friends. He must have had mixed feelings as he hurriedly packed his bags. Years earlier, Mike had been similarly called to the Middle East during his vacation for a command interview with another mercurial Muslim leader, Yasser Arafat—an interview that never materialized, forcing Mike to return a week later to his summer home, deflated and thoroughly jet-lagged. Yet, despite his eighty-eight years, he could not pass up a high-profile story, so he traveled doggedly to Tehran—where President Ahmadinejad made him wait a week before finally sitting down for the interview.

It was not the triumph he had hoped for. Though CBS promoted the segment heavily and millions tuned in to watch Mike lay his legendary gloves on the controversial Iranian leader, viewers hoping for a "Mike Wallace" interview did not get one, for Mike was no longer the pugilist he used to be. President Ahmadinejad, with his permanent grin masking a canny ability to manipulate the press, walked all over Mike. It was he, not Mike, who controlled the tempo of the interview, with long-winded, self-serving answers, prompting the correspondent at one point to plead:

MIKE: Look, if you could—if you could keep your answers concise, I beg you, we'll get more questions in.

AHMADINEJAD: (Translated.) Well, one of your questions requires—all of your questions require a book-long answer. If you want me to just finish the interview, please tell me and we can wrap up right now.

MIKE: No, no, no, no, no.

AHMADINEJAD: (Translated.) Do you perhaps want me to say what you want me to say? Am I to understand—

MIKE: No. No.

AHMADINEJAD: (Translated.) If that is the case, then I ask you to please be patient. Maybe these days you don't have a lot of patience to spare. Maybe these are words that you don't like to hear, Mr. Wallace.

MIKE: Why? What words do I not like to hear?

AHMADINEJAD: (Translated.) Because I think that you're getting angry.

MIKE: I couldn't be happier for the privilege of sitting down with the President of Iran.

It was comments like these that riled the conservative blogosphere, where Mike would be roundly criticized for cozying up to a sponsor of terrorism. When Mike tried to ask the Iranian president about his ties to terrorist groups like Hezbollah, Ahmadinejad went on his own offensive:

AHMADINEJAD: (Translated.) Are you the representative of the Zionist regime? Or a journalist?

MIKE: I'm a journalist. I am a journalist!

AHMADINEJAD: (Translated.) This is not journalism, sir.

Then President Ahmadinejad launched into a polemic about how Hezbollah was a legitimate political organization. Mike, finally, tried to elicit Ahmadinejad's feelings toward the United States, which many in Iran referred to as "The Great Satan."

MIKE: What do you think of George Bush as a man and as Commander-in-Chief of the so-called free world?

AHMADINEJAD: (Translated.) Well, the "so-called" says everything.

MIKE: What do you think of George W. Bush?

AHMADINEJAD: (Translated.) What do you think I should think about the gentleman?

MIKE: Come on. Come on. You're perfectly capable of handling that question, if you have the courage to answer it.

AHMADINEJAD: (Translated.) Well, thank you very much. So you are teaching me how to be bold and courageous. That's interesting.

Mike was getting nowhere fast. In comments made after the interview, he actually dug himself even deeper into the hole he had created.

"He's an impressive fellow, this guy," Mike was quoted in the press. "He really is. He's obviously smart as hell . . . You'll find him an interesting man. I expected more of a firebrand. I don't think he has the slightest doubt about how he feels . . . about the American administration and the Zionist state. He comes across as more rational than I had expected."[2]

Conservative commentators excoriated Mike for referring to Israel as the "Zionist State." In fairness to Mike, it's easy to understand why he had misspoken—he was simply presenting the country as Ahmadinejad had referred to it. The man was pushing ninety, after all. "You're not as articulate as you used to be," he confessed.[3]

But, as the AP reported: "Wallace said he nearly fell out of his chair when Ahmadinejad told him, 'I hear this is your last interview.' " Then, apparently, Mike asked his guest, "What do you think? Is it a good idea to retire?"[4] The fact was that Mike had already retired—this interview had been a special exemption.

Indeed, many of Mike's colleagues in the media thought his retirement should have been permanent. Bret Stephens wrote a critical column in *The Wall Street Journal* entitled "Questions for Ahmadinejad (That Mike Wallace Didn't Ask)." One of the most burning involved Ahmadinejad's alleged role in the 1979 seizure of the U.S. embassy in Tehran. Several of the former hostages had identified the Iranian president as one of the student ringleaders, a position also held by persons in the State Department. But Mike did not even broach the subject.

He simply did not have the instincts he once had. Several interviewers had asked Mike in the months since his official retirement what we would want as his epitaph. "Tough But Fair," Mike had responded. His critics were now saying that he had been far too "fair" with President Ahmadine-jad and not nearly "tough" enough.

A few months after Mike left Martha's Vineyard for his interview with Ahmadinejad, the island suffered a loss with the passing of William Styron, one of the three "Blues Brothers." It was particularly sad for Mike, because the other "brother," Art Buchwald, had also been living on bor-rowed time. In February, Buchwald had had his leg amputated due to cir-culatory problems. He was suffering from kidney failure, too, but refused dialysis, and was given only a few weeks to live by his doctors. Buchwald made funeral arrangements and said his good-byes to close friends, includ-ing Mike—but somehow the humorist persevered, outliving Bill Styron and even publishing a book about his experience, *Too Soon to Say Goodbye*.

In November, when Mike and Art saw their friend Bill interred at West Chop cemetery, where they too had purchased plots, it felt as though they had lost a part of themselves. In Mike's words: "Three of us—Bill Sty-ron, he and I—suffered depression simultaneously, so we walked around in the rain together on Martha's Vineyard and consoled each other."[5]

Even in Mike's darkest hours, he knew he could count on his fellow "Blues Brothers" for support, particularly Buchwald, who checked in regu-larly. But Buchwald, too, would soon be gone—dying in January 2007, at age eighty-one, just like Styron. In an interview for Buchwald's obituary, Mike explained what a critical role his friend had played during Mike's depression.

"I traveled a lot on *60 Minutes*, and no matter where I was, every single night I got a call from Art Buchwald to listen to the same tale of woe," Mike explained. "He did the best to make life palatable, to help you be optimis-tic, to let you know he believed you would beat it."[6]

Mike had indeed beaten his depression: it had been fourteen years since his last episode. But he was beginning to fight another demon: bore-dom. Later that year, in an attempt to stay relevant, Mike made an appear-ance on the political talk show *The Colbert Report*. At eighty-eight, Mike came on stage looking remarkably trim and fit—so much so that Colbert was forced to make a joke about it: "You've been everywhere, you've done everything, you're a longtime smoker, I'm sure you went to a lot of chemical-filled landfills, you went to a lot of dangerous places and yet you lived to a ripe old age. Doesn't your life itself debunk the stories you did?"[7]

Indeed, Mike kept ticking along, doing occasional pieces for *60 Minutes* as an Emeritus Correspondent. In his 2007 interview with Republican presidential candidate Mitt Romney, Mike asked, "The rap on you, of course, is that you're too smooth, too handsome, too polished. Are you really known as Matinee Mitt?"

Not missing a beat, Romney turned the question right back on his interviewer: "That's the rap on *you*, Mike. Too smooth, too polished."

Later that year, Mike taped his second interview with Jack Kevorkian, following the doctor's eight-year jail sentence. Then, in 2008, he did another piece involving controversial injections when he sat down with baseball great Roger Clemens to discuss the player's alleged used of performance enhancing steroids.

"Will he be as effective as the Wallace of yore?" wondered *The New York Times* on the eve of the broadcast. "Is he still a journalistic bulldog who will ask the relevant questions? Will he make Clemens squirm if need be?"[8]

60 Minutes Executive Producer Jeff Fager, who had by then replaced Don Hewitt, said that he had no doubt about whether Mike remained formidable and "Wallace-esque," the *Times* reported. "Mike is strong," Fager said. "He's just a marvel. When you watch him in the interview, he's such a unique character and unique reporter. I think he does a terrific job. I feel lucky to have him on the air. He's an icon . . . who knows what else might pop up? He never wants to stop. He's Mike Wallace."

But, like it or not, Mike's pieces were becoming more about his own performance than the story he was reporting. After the Clemens interview, Mike's demeanor was deconstructed in detail by many papers, including *The New York Times*, which concluded: "Wallace will never satisfy his critics, although he asked most of the requisite questions and pushed back a few times against Clemens." Few gave Mike credit for the remarkable fact that no newsman in the history of television had conducted an interview at age ninety.

The Clemens interview, in fact, was the last. Some months later, Mike underwent triple bypass surgery, and he has been living quietly since then, "Waiting. Waiting for the end. It's inevitable. It's not about being comfortable. It's not a question of being passive. You wait to wake up the next morning. You wait to find out what's going to happen. You wait to see what's going to happen to people you love when the wait is over."[9]

In the same interview, Mike admitted: "I think I've lived too long. But I don't feel sorry for myself." His greatest regret, he said, was "Not [spending] enough time with my kids through the years."[10]

But, Mike's stepdaughter, Pauline, had nothing but praise for the larger-than-life figure with whom she grew up: "The greatest thing that happened to me in my life is having Mike Wallace as my father."[11]

Mike had even managed to make peace, it seems, with his biological son. "Chris and I—you know, we had grown apart to a certain degree," he told *The Martha's Vineyard Times.* "Now we're real pals again, maybe more than ever."[12]

Mike's life had spanned nearly a century. During the course of his career, from local radio in Michigan to the pinnacle of network news, he had conducted innumerable interviews with divas, dictators, presidents, con men, artists, terrorists—nearly every newsmaker in recent history. He had invented a new paradigm for television news, creating a signature technique that would become a standard in the industry. He had done battle on the airwaves and in the privacy of his own psyche, and had prevailed on both.

Yet, when asked when he had been the happiest, Wallace had harkened back to the most innocent time, before his marriages, before his heady career:

"Nineteen thirty-nine. Grand Rapids, Michigan. Station WOOD, twenty bucks a week."[13]

His very first job.

Acknowledgments

I wish to thank my sister, Claudia Rader, without whom this book would have never come to be. Claudia worked for Mike in the late 1980's and it was she who first introduced me to this story. Claudia also served as my copy editor and her input was instrumental in getting the manuscript into shape. Other family members lent significant assists, as well. I could not have cleared the decks and focused on this project without the encouragement and support of my stepmother, Kate Rader. My in-laws, the di Florios, were particularly supportive during a challenging period of the process.

I have tremendous gratitude to the many interviewees who shared their stories with me, particularly Barry Lando and Lowell Bergman, who agreed to go on the record even before I had a publisher. Equally magnanimous were Al Ramrus and Gary Paul Gates, who gave so generously of their time.

Other accomplished authors were kind enough to help steer this novice in the right direction. Tim O'Brien was the conduit to Lowell Bergman. Abigail Pogrebin gave me tips about navigating the waters at CBS. Stacy Schiff provided encouragement along the way, as did film producer Andrew Lazar.

I am greatly indebted to my book agent, David Kuhn and his fantastic staff, who worked tirelessly to help me polish my book proposal. Likewise, I wish to thank Tom Dunne for publishing the book, Brendan Deenan for editing the manuscript, and everyone else at St. Martin's who assisted in its launch.

Finally, there is my wife, Paola di Florio, who is my muse, my partner and my champion.

Author's Note

Like many Americans, I was aware of Mike's larger-than-life TV persona, but it wasn't until my sister went to work for him that I discovered the true extent of his sweeping story. I realized that Mike—a pioneer at every stage in the evolution of modern media and with personal calamities of Shakespearian proportions—would make a riveting subject for a biography. Though parts of this story had been told, including by Mike himself in two memoirs, it had never been examined in its totality, through the prism of a lifetime and its impact on the times.

This became my goal: to tell the story of the man behind the legend who reshaped the face of television news. I was a screenwriter, however, not a journalist, so this book, in my mind, was first conceived as a movie. But as I delved into my research, it became clear that the narrative demanded to be a book first.

My background in screenwriting led me to a cinematic style of writing; I tried to evoke vividly the setting and mood of the many dramatic events that took place in Mike's story. In certain cases, where specific information was not available, I employed a narrative convention: constructing a plausible situation with imagined dialogue that reflects the attitudes and feelings that I know to have been present at the time. These are brief framing devices at the beginning of chapters, intended to set a mood and launch the storyline.

These instances, and all the other events described in the book, are backed by comprehensive research. I conducted numerous interviews with Mike's personal associates and professional colleagues. Although Mike and Mary were receptive initially to the idea of this biography, they ultimately declined to participate, though gave me their blessing to pursue their contacts. Many people who crossed paths with Mike had authored memoirs, which proved invaluable references, as did Mike's personal papers. Throughout his life, he had been meticulous about keeping records of his speeches and correspondence—a voluminous collection totaling 170 file boxes, which Mike donated to the Bentley Research Library at the University of Michigan.

Finally, with such a public figure, there exists a wealth of interviews, recorded appearances and other material, which, along with the trove of Mike's personal documents, it was my privilege to sift through. I am honored to have been able to consolidate all these findings into the first comprehensive biography of a legendary figure who has shed light on our understanding of both the world in which we live and also on what it means to be human.

Notes

Introduction: The Two Faces of Mike Wallace

1. Bill Leonard, *In the Storm of the Eye: A Lifetime at CBS* (New York: G. P. Putnam's Sons, 1987), 207–209.
2. Mary-Jayne McKay, "60 Minutes: Milestones," CBSnews.com, http://www.cbsnews.com/stories/1999/08/20/60minutes/main59202.shtml (accessed July 18, 2011).
3. Mike Wallace, "CBS Cares: Mike Wallace. Interview," CBS.com, http://www.cbs.com/cbs_cares/topics/depression.php (accessed July 18, 2011).
4. Gary Paul Gates, *Airtime: The Inside Story of CBS News* (New York: Harper & Row, 1978), 102.

Chapter One: A Boy Named Chinky

1. Wallace is on the record numerous times as being sensitive about his looks. He answered a version of the Proust Questionnaire at age eighty-seven and answered the question *What do you dislike most about your appearance?* "My skinny bowlegs." "Proust Questionnaire: Mike Wallace," *Vanity Fair*, November 2005, http://www.vanityfair.com/culture/features/2005/11/proust_wallace200511 (accessed July 18, 2011).
2. Mike Wallace, "Mike Wallace Interview," Academy of Achievement, http://www.achievement.org/autodoc/page/wal2int-1 (accessed July 18, 2011).
3. Though I do not have evidence of this scene having taken place exactly as written, it has been constructed based on plausible events to reflect attitudes I know from my research to have been present—a narrative device used throughout this manuscript (though only cited here). See "Author's Note."
4. Mike Wallace, interviewed by John Callaway, "John Callaway Interviews," PBS, 1981.
5. Gary Paul Gates (co-author with Mike Wallace of *Close Encounters* and *Between You and Me*), interview by author.

6. A&E Home Video, *Biography—Mike Wallace: TV's Grand Inquisitor,* DVD. A&E Home Video (1998; DVD release 2006).

7. Academy of Achievement, "Mike Wallace Interview."

8. *National Enquirer,* March 17, 1987.

9. A&E Home Video, *Biography—Mike Wallace: TV's Grand Inquisitor.*

10. Mike Wallace, quoted in the *Boston Globe,* December 8, 1988.

11. *National Enquirer.*

12. Ibid.

13. Ibid.

14. Mike Wallace, Class Oration, Brookline High Schol—Murivian Yearbook (Brookline, MA), Class of 1935, 123.

Chapter Two: False Starts

1. Mike Wallace, "Memorial Service: Leo Scharfman" (Speech) Mike Wallace Papers, University of Michigan Library.

2. Ibid.

3. Mike Wallace, "University of Michigan Commencement Address" (Address, University of Michigan, May 2, 1987), http://www.umich.edu/~bhlumrec/c/commence/1987-Wallace .pdf (accessed July 18, 2011).

4. Wallace, "Memorial Service: Leo Scharfman."

5. University of Michigan, *Michigan Alumnus* 82, No. 1 (September 1975).

6. Wallace, "Memorial Service: Leo Scharfman."

7. Ibid.

8. Ibid.

9. Ibid.

10. Ibid.

11. "Tough sledding" quoted in Don Freeman, "Point of View," *The San Diego Union,* October 31, 1990, D7.

12. *LSA: University of Michigan, College of Literature, Science and the Arts* [Journal] 2, No. 1 (Fall 1978).

13. Mike Wallace Speech to CBS Radio Affiliates, 25 February 1979, Mike Wallace Papers, Box 78, University of Michigan Library.

14. Ibid.

15. Ibid.

16. Ibid.

17. Ibid.

18. Ibid.

19. Ibid.

20. Ibid.

21. Ibid.

22. "Radio: Ickes in the Groove," *Time,* September 2, 1940.

23. Wallace, Speech to CBS Radio Affiliates.

24. Mike Wallace, interview by John Callaway, *Chicago Tonight* (radio), reprinted in the *Chicago Sun-Times,* Mike Wallace Papers, University of Michigan Library.

25. Frank Swertlow, "Wallace Recalls Hectic Years Here," *Chicago Sun-Times,* May 11, 1978.

26. Nancy Seely, "Mike Wallace, Spotlight on the Nightbeat," *New York Post*, February 14, 1957, 4.

27. Swertlow, "Wallace Recalls Hectic Years Here."

28. Mike Wallace, interview by Steve McClellan, "On Switching to Straight News Reporting [Interview, Part 2]," EmmyLegends.org, http://www.youtube.com/playlist?list=PL8C51 EA7A7403AA2F (accessed July 19, 2011).

29. Ibid.

30. Mike Wallace interview, Mike Wallace Papers, Box 149, University of Michigan Library.

31. "Mike Wallace," *American Weekly*, March 9, 1958.

32. Ibid.

33. Gary Paul Gates, interview by author.

34. Mike Wallace, Letter, 28 December, 1945, Mike Wallace Papers, Box 149, University of Michigan Library.

Chapter Three: Life Imitates Art

1. Mike Wallace and Gary Paul Gates, *Close Encounters: Mike Wallace's Own Story* (New York: William Morrow, 1984), 15.

2. Ibid.

3. Robert Crichton, "Grand Inquisitor: The Mike Wallace Story," *Argosy*, May 1957.

4. George Hamilton with William Stadiem, *Don't Mind If I Do* (New York: Simon & Schuster, 2008), 163.

5. Elisabeth Cobb, *My Wayward Parent* (New York: The Bobbs-Merrill Company, 1945), 247.

6. Joel Lobenthal, *Tallulah!: The Life and Times of a Leading Lady* (New York: Regan Books, 2004), 392.

7. Irvin S. Cobb, "How to Act in 'Movies,'" *The New York Times*, July 5, 1914, X6.

8. Victor Mature wrote about Buff and his many other romances in an infamous kiss-and-tell essay entitled *What I Love About Women*, which featured such temperamental firebrands as Lana Turner, Betty Grable, Gene Tierney and dozens more. Of all his conquests, Mr. Mature declared: "Buff Cobb is the maddest character on the list."

9. Chicago Stagebill, Harris Theatre, *Private Lives*, 1947.

10. Academy of Achievement, "Mike Wallace Interview."

11. Wallace, *Close Encounters*, 16.

12. Gary Paul Gates, interview by author.

13. Ibid.

14. Mike Wallace, author's notes to *Between You and Me*, Mike Wallace Papers, Box 164, University of Michigan Library.

15. William Safire, "Of Tex and Jinx," *The New York Times*, September 15, 2003.

16. Mike Wallace, author's notes to *Between You and Me*.

17. Jack Eigen, "Jack Eigen Speaking," *Chicago Tribune*, February 15, 1957.

18. Mike Wallace, author's notes for manuscript, Mike Wallace Papers, Box 93, University of Michigan Library.

19. CBS biography of Mike Wallace (1977).

20. "William Eythe Seized; Ex-Wife Wants $2,500," *Chicago Tribune*, September 4, 1950.

21. *The New York Times*, September 4, 1950.

22. Mike Wallace, author's notes to *Between You and Me*.

23. Academy of Achievement, "Mike Wallace Interview," 2.

24. Gary Paul Gates, interview with author.

25. Val Adams, "Man and Wife Team: 'Mike and Buff' Achieve a 'Different' Format," *The New York Times*, December 2, 1951, 133.

26. Crichton, "Grand Inquisitor."

27. *USA Weekend*: Mike Wallace.

28. Ibid.

29. Robert Crichton, "Grand Inquisitor."

30. Adams, "Man and Wife Team."

31. Ibid.

32. Ibid.

33. Gary Paul Gates, interview with author.

34. WMAQ radio schedule (April 1957).

35. Adams, "Man and Wife Team."

36. Ibid.

37. Gary Paul Gates, interview with author.

38. Ibid.

39. James Lardrer, "Up Against the Wallace; After Ten Years, The Hard Edge of '60 Minutes,'" *The Washington Post*, September 18, 1977, Magazine.

40. Charles Mercer, "Mike Wallace," *The Sacramento Bee*, April 13, 1957.

41. Robert Crichton, "Grand Inquisitor."

42. Steve Johnson, "What Mike Wallace Was Like in His Younger Days," *Chicago Tribune*, November 25, 1996.

43. Robert Crichton, "Grand Inquisitor."

44. Ibid.

Chapter Four: Enter the Muse

1. Lardrer, "Up Against the Wallace."

2. Wallace, *Close Encounters*, 21.

3. "Mike Wallace," *American Weekly*.

4. Ibid.

5. Mike Wallace, interview by Paul Colford, "The Very Demanding Mr. Wallace," New York *Newsday*, October 13, 1988.

6. "Mike Wallace," *American Weekly*.

7. Mike Wallace, interview by Lorraine Wallace, *Good Housekeeping*, August, 1957.

8. James Perigord, interview by author.

9. Eulogy for Paul Perigord, Mike Wallace Papers, University of Michigan Library.

10. Mike Wallace, interview by Lorraine Wallace.

11. Associated Press, "Margaret Truman Daniel [Obituary]," Legacy.com, http://www.legacy.com/NS/Obituary.aspx?pid=102186091 [accessed July 25, 2011].

12. Letter from President Truman to Paul Hume (music critic, *The Washington Post*), 6 December 1950, Harry S. Truman Library and Museum, Independence, MO, http://www.trumanlibrary.org/trivia/letter.htm.

13. Charles Mercer, "Mike Wallace," *The Victoria Advocate*, November 3, 1955.

14. Ibid.

15. "Radio: Woman's Home Companion," *Time* magazine, November 28, 1955.

16. Ibid.

17. Al Ramrus (worked closely with Wallace as writer at WAMD in 1950s), interview by author.

Chapter Five: The Inquisitor Finds His Beat

1. "U.S. TV Aide and Photographer Are Killed in Mideast Fighting," *The New York Times*, June 7, 1967, 21.

2. Al Ramrus, interview by author.

3. Angus Yates (stepson of Mike Wallace), interview by author.

4. Al Ramrus, interview by author.

5. Mike Wallace, in his eulogy to Ted Yates, June 7, 1967, on *Personal Closeup*.

6. Wallace, *Close Encounters*, 23.

7. Mike Wallace, as quoted by Al Ramrus, interview by author.

8. Al Ramrus, interview.

9. Ibid.

10. Ibid.

11. Larry Wolters, "On Sunday: TV's Most Candid Mike," *Chicago Tribune*, April 27, 1957, F3.

12. Wallace, *Close Encounters*, 39.

13. Al Ramrus, interview.

14. *The New Yorker* cartoon; *Close Encounters*, 41.

15. Marlene Sanders (talent scout for Wallace on *Night Beat*), interview by author.

16. Ted Yates, quoted by Al Ramrus, interview by author.

17. Wallace, *Close Encounters*, 33.

18. Academy of Achievement, "Mike Wallace Interview."

19. Marlene Sanders, interview.

20. Wallace, *Close Encounters*, 31.

21. Ibid.

22. Al Morgan, quoted by Charles Mercer.

23. Jack Gould, "Tawdry Television," *The New York Times*, February 3, 1957, 93.

Chapter Six: Two Lawsuits and a Nemesis

1. "David Zurawik, "Premier Interviewer, Mike Wallace, Turns up in the Spotlight," *The Baltimore Sun*, September 26, 1990.

2. Wallace, *Close Encounters*, 42–43.

3. Mike Wallace, interview by Steve McClellan [Part 3].

4. Wallace, *Close Encounters*, 48.

5. Ibid., 49.

6. Ibid., 50.

7. Mike Wallace, interview by Larry Wolters.

8. Wallace, *Close Encounters*, 50.

9. Ibid., 51.

10. Al Ramrus, interview with author.

11. "Daly Advised CBS to Cancel Wallace," *The New York Times*, May 28, 1957, 49.

12. Al Ramrus, interview.

13. Wallace, *Close Encounters*, 52.

14. Al Ramrus, interview.

15. Wallace, *Close Encounters*, 64.

16. Ibid.

17. Wallace, *Close Encounters*, 265.

18. Wallace, *Close Encounters*, 265–266.

19. Interview, Al Ramrus.

20. Jim Heintze, "Biography of Drew Pearson," Library of American University, http://www .library.american.edu/pearson/biography.html (accessed Tuesday, July 26, 2011).

21. Simkin, John, "Drew Pearson." Spartacus Educational History Encyclopedia [U.K.], http:// www.spartacus.schoolnet.co.uk/USApearsonD.htm (accessed Tuesday, July 26, 2011).

22. Ibid.

23. Mike Wallace with Gary Paul Gates, *Between You and Me: A Memoir* (New York: Hyperion, 2005), 10–13.

24. Wallace, *Close Encounters*, 67.

25. Ibid., 72.

26. Ibid., 70.

Chapter Seven: Floundering

1. *TV Guide*, August 8, 1964.

2. Ibid.

3. Val Adams, "Wallace Future on TV in Question," *The New York Times*, July 14, 1958, 41.

4. *TV Guide*.

5. Interview, Al Ramrus.

6. E-mail sent to author by Al Ramrus.

7. Interview, Gary Paul Gates.

8. Leonard, *In The Storm of the Eye*, 75.

9. Ibid., 76.

10. Interview, Al Ramrus.

11. Wallace, *Close Encounters*, 73.

12. Mike Wallace, interview by Katie Couric, "Mike Wallace, Man of the Hour," MSNBC.com, http://www.msnbc.msn.com/id/10397477/ns/dateline_nbc/ (accessed July 24, 2011).

13. Mike Wallace, "About David L. Wolper," http://www.davidlwolper.com/about/Mike_Wallace .cfm (accessed August 15, 2011).

14. Interview, Al Ramrus.

15. "Susskind, David. U.S. Producer and Talk Show Host." Museum of Broadcast Communications, http://www.museum.tv/eotvsection.php?entrycode=susskinddav (accessed July 28, 2011).

16. Interview, Marlene Saunders.

17. Interview, Al Ramrus.

18. Interview, Marlene Saunders.

19. Mike Wallace, responses to the Proust Questionnaire, *Vanity Fair*, November 2005, http:// www.vanityfair.com/culture/features/2005/11/proust_wallace200511.

20. Steve Johnson, "What Mike Wallace Was Like in His Younger Days," *The Chicago Tribune*, November 25, 1996. Republished March 17, 2006, http://featuresblogs.chicagotribune.com/ technology_internetcritic/2006/03/what_mike_walla.html (accessed August 17, 2011).

Chapter Eight: Death & Rebirth

1. "Mike Wallace's Son Is Dead in Greece," *The New York Times*, September 1, 1962, 4.
2. Wallace, quoted in an unpublished manuscript. Mike Wallace Papers, Box 54, University of Michigan.
3. Av Westin, interview with the author.
4. Wallace, *Close Encounters*, 75.
5. Ibid., 217.
6. Wallace, unpublished interview, Mike Wallace Papers, Box 54, University of Michigan.
7. Wallace, *Close Encounters*, 79.
8. Wallace, unpublished interview, Mike Wallace Papers, Box 54, University of Michigan.
9. Ibid.
10. Wallace, *Close Encounters*, 83.
11. Wallace, *Close Encounters*, 84.
12. Ibid.
13. Mike Wallace, interview by Steve McClellan, "On Switching to Straight News Reporting [Interview, Part 2]."
14. Richard S. Salant, *Salant, CBS, and the Battle for the Soul of Broadcast Journalism: The Memoirs of Richard S. Salant*, Edited by Susan and Bill Buzenberg (Westview Press, 1999), 268.

Chapter Nine: Network News

1. Jeremy Gerard, "William S. Paley, Builder of C.B.S., Dies at 90," *The New York Times*, October 27, 1990, 1.
2. Don Hewitt, *Tell Me a Story* (New York: Public Affairs, 2001), 46.
3. Ibid.
4. Ibid.
5. Av Westin, *Newswatch: How TV Decides the News* (New York: Simon & Schuster, 1982), 40.
6. Wallace, *Close Encounters*, 473.
7. Westin, *Newswatch*, 38.
8. Ibid., 40.
9. Wallace, *Close Encounters*, 87.
10. Walter Cronkite, *A Reporter's Life* (New York: Ballantine, 1996), 343.
11. Wallace, *Close Encounters*, 87.
12. Wallace, *Close Encounters*, 89.
13. Westin, *Newswatch*, 41.
14. Wallace, *Close Encounters*, 89.
15. Conversation recalled by Av Westin, interview by author. Also reported in *Newswatch*, 41–42.
16. Ibid.
17. *TV Guide*.
18. Westin, *Newswatch*, 39.
19. Westin, interview by author.
20. Av Westin, interview by Terrence Smith, "Online NewsHour: Av Westin" Public Broadcasting Service Online, http://www.pbs.org/newshour/media/evening_news/westin.html (accessed July 21, 2011).
21. Leonard, *In the Storm of the Eye*, 90.
22. Ibid., 108.

23. Ibid., 110–111.
24. Ibid., 114–116.

Chapter Ten: Blood Looks Very Red on Color TV

1. Av Westin, interview by author.
2. David Blum, *Tick, Tick, Tick: The Long Life and Turbulent Times of 60 Minutes* (New York: HarperCollins, 2004), 21.
3. Wallace, *Close Encounters*, 108.
4. Ibid.
5. Mass Moments, "April 9, 1969: 'Harvard Students Occupy University Hall,'" Massachusetts Foundation for the Humanities, http://www.massmoments.org/moment.cfm?mid=108 (accessed July 28, 2011).
6. Ted Yates, quoted in Al Ramrus, interview.
7. Emily Saso, "'Blood Looks Very Red on the Colour Television Screen': The Evolution of Representing Modern War in America" The York Centre for International and Security Studies Working Paper No. 33 (March, 2005), http://www.yorku.ca/yciss/publish/documents/WP33 -Saso.pdf.
8. Wallace, *Close Encounters*, 222.
9. Unpublished memoir of Richard Norling, quoted in Dr. Tom Mascaro, "Overlooked: Ted Yates, Bob Rogers, and Vietnam: It's a Mad War" (research paper, Bowling Green State University).
10. *Personal Close-up*, June 7, 1967.

Chapter Eleven: Good Cop, Bad Cop

1. Quoted in Wallace, *Close Encounters*, 108–109.
2. Wallace, *Close Encounters*, 97–98.
3. Hewitt, *Tell Me a Story*, 110.
4. Hewitt, quoted in *Tick, Tick, Tick*, 6.
5. Hewitt, *Tell Me a Story*, 110.
6. Bill Leonard, *In the Storm of the Eye*, 142.
7. Blum, *Tick, Tick, Tick*, 28.
8. Salant, *Salant, CBS and the Battle*, 60.
9. Leonard, *In the Storm of the Eye*, 147.
10. *Salant, Salant, CBS, and the Battle*, 62.
11. Don Hewitt, quoted in Reasoner's *The New York Times* obituary, August 7, 1991.
12. Douglass K. Daniel, *Harry Reasoner: A Life in the News* (Austin, TX: University of Texas Press, 2007), 79.
13. Ibid.
14. Harry Reasoner, *Before the Colors Fade* (New York; Knopf, 1981), 145–146.
15. Salant, *Salant, CBS, and the Battle*, 62–63.
16. Harry Reasoner, quoted by Don Hewitt, *Minute by Minute: The Best Show on TV Becomes the Best Book on TV* (New York, Random House, 1985), 29.
17. Wallace, *Close Encounters*, 110–111.
18. Wallace, *Between You and Me*, 31.
19. Gates, *Airtime*, 294.

Chapter Twelve: Rough Beginnings

1. Wallace, *Close Encounters*, 112.
2. *The New York Times*, September 25, 1968.
3. Wallace, *Close Encounters*, 153.
4. Blum, *Tick, Tick, Tick*, 40–41.
5. Ibid.
6. Gates, *Close Encounters*, 157.
7. Reasoner, *Before the Colors Fade*, 162.
8. Ibid.
9. Hewitt, *Minute by Minute*, 63.
10. Leonard, *In the Storm of the Eye*, 148.
11. Wallace, *Close Encounters*, 154.
12. Leonard, *In the Storm of the Eye*, 148–149.
13. Reasoner, *Before the Colors Fade*, 173–175.
14. Daniel, *Harry Reasoner*, 126.
15. Ibid.

Chapter Thirteen: To Hell with Wallace

1. Hewitt, *Tell Me a Story*, 113.
2. Ibid., 120.
3. Hewitt, *Tell Me a Story*, 124.
4. Leonard, *In the Storm of the Eye*, 149–150.
5. Hewitt, *Minute by Minute*, 43.
6. Ibid.
7. Blum, *Tick, Tick, Tick*, 53.
8. Interview with Steve McClellan for the Academy of Achievement, Part 4.
9. Ibid.
10. Blum, *Tick, Tick, Tick*, 55.
11. Hewitt, *Tell Me a Story*, 109–110.
12. Wallace, McClellan Interview, Part 4.
13. Blum, *Tick, Tick, Tick*, 52–53.
14. Ibid., 143.
15. Frank Coffey, *60 Minutes: 25 Years of Television's Finest Hour* (Los Angeles: GPG, 1993), 34–35.
16. Wallace, McClellan Interview, Part 4.
17. Letter to Wallace from Publisher, Mike Wallace Papers, Box 149, University of Michigan Library.
18. Coffey, *60 Minutes*, 12.

Chapter Fourteen: Lacing Up the Gloves

1. Hewitt, *Minute by Minute*, 49.
2. Wallace, *Between You and Me*, 18–23; Hewitt, *Tell Me a Story*, 120–123.
3. Hewitt, *Tell Me a Story*, 124–125.
4. Wallace, *Between You and Me*, 18–19.

5. Hewitt, *Tell Me a Story*, 125.

6. Hewitt, *Minute by Minute*, 52–53.

7. Ibid.

8. Hewitt, *Minute by Minute*, 53.

9. Hewitt, *Tell Me a Story*, 126.

10. Ibid.

11. Hewitt, *Tell Me a Story*, 126.

12. Wallace, *Between You and Me*, 21.

13. Blum, *Tick, Tick, Tick*, 57.

14. Ibid., 58–59.

15. Ibid., 61.

Chapter Fifteen: Abuse of Power

1. Wallace, *Close Encounters*, 162.

2. Marion Goldin, interview with the author.

3. Ibid.

4. Ibid.

5. White House Press Conference, October 26, 1973.

6. Coffey, *60 Minutes: 25 Years*, 37.

7. Wallace, *Close Encounters*, 175.

8. Wallace, *Close Encounters*, 178.

9. Ibid., 188.

10. Ibid., 194.

11. Ibid., 252.

12. Coffey, *60 Minutes: 25 Years*, 59.

Chapter Sixteen: Nowhere to Hide

1. Hewitt, *Minute by Minute*, 111.

2. Mike Wallace, transcript of interview by Howard Kurtz, CNN.com, http://transcripts.cnn
.com/TRANSCRIPTS/0204/13/rs.00.html (accessed July 28, 2011).

3. Wallace, *Close Encounters*, 382.

4. Ibid., 378.

5. Lando, quoted in *Tick, Tick, Tick*, 101.

6. Ibid.

7. Wallace, *Close Encounters*, 387–397.

8. Mike Wallace, introduction to *Con Men: Fascinating Profiles of Swindlers and Rogues from the Files of the Most Successful Broadcast in Television History*, by Ian Jackman (New York: Simon & Schuster, 2003).

Chapter Seventeen: Sickeningly Happy?

1. *People*, January 10, 1977.

2. Neil Offen, interview by author.

3. Mike discussed Lorraine's use of tranquilizers with Peter Ross Range. *Playboy* interview: Mike Wallace, December 1, 1996. Lorraine's brother, James, mentioned her drinking in an interview with the author.

4. Quoted by an off-the-record source.

5. Mike Wallace, "Of Wives and Their Skills, Of Men and Their Dreams: A Fantasy Grows in Haiti," *The New York Times*, November 10, 1976, 53.

6. Wallace, *Close Encounters*, 367.

7. *People*, January 10, 1977.

8. Harry Stein, "How '60 Minutes' Makes the News," *The New York Times*, May 6, 1979, 235.

9. Ibid.

10. Steven Zito, "Inside 60 Minutes," *American Film*, December, 1977.

11. Leonard, *In the Storm of the Eye*, 153.

12. Wallace, quoted in *Miami Herald*, July 22–28, 1979 (TV Section).

13. Michael Ryan, *Us*, October 3, 1978.

14. Ibid.

Chapter Eighteen: A Life Beyond Reproach

1. Wallace, *Close Encounters*, 281–282.

2. Hewitt, *Tell Me a Story*, 162–163.

3. Barry Lando, interview with author.

4. Sally Quinn, *We're Going to Make You a Star* (New York: Simon & Schuster, 1975), 223.

5. Goldin, interview with author.

6. Barbara Dury, interview with author.

7. Goldin, interview with author.

8. Mark Hertsgaard, "The *60 Minutes* Man," *Rolling Stone*, May 30, 1991, 47.

9. Ibid.

10. Goldin, interview with author.

11. Wallace, *Close Encounters*, 398.

Chapter Nineteen: Mike Wallace Is Here

1. Mike Wallace, interview by Katie Couric, http://www.msnbc.msn.com/id/10397477/ns/dateline_nbc/.

2. Mike Wallace, interview by Jim Kelly, "10 Questions for Mike Wallace," *Time*, October 23, 2005.

3. Ibid.

4. Wallace, *Between You and Me*, 128–130.

5. Wallace, "Mike Wallace Interview," Academy of Achievement.

6. Coffey, *60 Minutes: 25 Years*, 139.

7. Lando, interview with the author.

8. Wallace, *Close Encounters*, 426.

9. Nancy Skelton, "Bank Catches Interviewer Mike Wallace Off Guard," *The Los Angeles Times*, January 10, 1982, SD1.

10. Ibid.

11. Ibid.
12. *Michigan Daily*, April 16, 1987.

Chapter Twenty: Three Strikes

1. Angus Yates, interview with the author.

Chapter Twenty-one: The Trial of His Life

1. Wallace, *Between You and Me*, 53.
2. Lowell Bergman, interview with the author.
3. Dan E. Moldea and Robert I. Friedman, "Networks Knuckle Under to Laxalt: The Story That Never Aired," *Village Voice*, March 5, 1985 and republished in 1999 at Moldea.com Web site: http://www.moldea.com/60Minutes.html.
4. Bergman, interview with the author.
5. Bob Brewin and Sydney Shaw, *Vietnam on Trial: Westmoreland vs. CBS* (New York: Atheneum, 1987), 89.
6. Ibid., 220.
7. Benjamin Burton, *Fair Play: CBS, General Westmoreland, and How a Television Documentary Went Wrong* (New York: Harper & Row, 1988), 115.
8. Angus Yates, interview with the author.
9. Hate mail to Wallace during Westmoreland trial. Mike Wallace Papers, University of Michigan Library.
10. Mike Wallace, transcript of interview by Larry King, "Interview with Mike Wallace," CNN.com, http://transcripts.cnn.com/TRANSCRIPTS/0510/31/lkl.01.html (accessed July 28, 2011).

Chapter Twenty-two: A Call for Help

1. Barry Lando, interview with the author.
2. Mike Wallace, "Mike Wallace: My Darkest Hour," re-printed at Grandparents.com from Guideposts.org, http://www.grandparents.com/gp/content/expert-advice/celebrity/article/mike-wallace-my-darkest-hour-with-depression.html.
3. Mike Wallace and Mary Wallace, interview by Dr. Jeffrey Borenstein, "Healthy Minds: Depression Featuring a Conversation with Mike and Mary Wallace," Brainline.org re-printing of transcript of interview held by WLIW 21 (New York) Public Broadcasting Service, http://www.brainline.org/multimedia/video/transcripts/healthy_minds_depression.pdf.
4. Mike Wallace, "Mike Wallace: My Darkest Hour."
5. Ibid.
6. Wallace, interview Academy of Achievement, http://www.achievement.org/autodoc/page/wal2int-7 (accessed August 16, 2011).
7. Ibid.
8. Ibid.
9. Ibid.
10. Mike Wallace, "Mike Wallace: My Darkest Hour."

11. Lando, interview with author.

12. Bob Brewin and Sidney Shaw, *Vietnam on Trial*, chapter 20, 344–361.

13. Wallace, *Between You and Me*, 202–204.

Chapter Twenty-three: Tabloid Satori

1. Wallace, "My Darkest Hour."

2. Ibid.

3. Mary Yates, quoted by Anne Sheffield, *Depressive Fallout: The Impact of Depression on Couples and What You Can Do* (New York, Harper Collins, 2003), xiii.

4. Angus Yates, interview with the author.

5. Ibid.

6. Burt Kearns, *Tabloid Baby* (Nashville, TN: Celebrity Books, 1999), vi.

7. Ibid., 81.

8. Ibid., 155.

9. Ibid., 268.

10. Peter J. Boyer, " '60 Minutes': A hit confronts the odds," *The New York Times*, September 13, 1987, A1.

11. Wallace, "CBS Cares: Mike Wallace Interview."

12. Wallace, "Mike Wallace Interview," Academy of Achievement.

Chapter Twenty-four: Oh, Shit. He's Dead!

1. Hewitt, *Tell Me a Story*, 227.

2. Blum, *Tick, Tick, Tick*, 192.

3. Peter Ross Range, "*Playboy* Interview: Mike Wallace," *Playboy*, December 1, 1996, 57.

4. Mike Wallace and Mary Wallace, interview by Dr. Jeffrey Borenstein, "Healthy Minds."

5. Lowell Bergman, interview by author.

6. Johnson, "What Mike Wallace was like in his younger days."

7. Wallace, "CBS Cares: Mike Wallace Interview."

8. Ibid.

9. Ibid.

10. Bergman, interview by author.

11. Wallace, *Between You and Me*, 212–213.

12. Ibid, 214.

13. Wallace, "Mike Wallace Interview," Academy of Achievement.

14. Daniel Schorr, "Smoke in the Eye," Frontline transcript dated April 2, 1996, Public Broadcasting Service re-printed by WGBH (PBS Boston), http://www.pbs.org/wgbh/pages/frontline/smoke/smokescript.html.

Chapter Twenty-five: Journalistic Malpractice

1. James Fallows, *Why We Hate the Media* (New York: Random House, 1996), Ch. 1 (summary of panel's discussion of journalist's duty to warn American soldiers of ambush), http://www.pbs.org/wgbh/pages/frontline/shows/press/vanities/fallows.html.

2. Howard Kurtz, "CBS Rebukes Wallace, Producer; '60 Minutes' Team Secretly Taped Writer," *The Washington Post*, November 17, 1994.

3. Ibid.

4. Ibid.

5. Ibid.

6. James Barron, "Wallace Is Rebuked for Taping on His Camera," *The New York Times*, November 17, 1994.

7. Range, "*Playboy* Interview: Mike Wallace."

8. Dan E. Moldea, *A Washington Tragedy: How the Death of Vincent Foster Ignited a Political Firestorm* (Washington, DC: Regnery Publishing, 1998), 323.

9. Ibid., 323–324.

10. Mike Wallace, telephonic interview by Reed Irvine (Accuracy in Media) on death of Vincent Foster, videotape including interview, "60 Minutes of Deception," [at 41:36] http://video .google.com/videoplay?docid=3273645970730386767#.

11. James Perigord (brother-in-law of Mike Wallace), interview by author.

12. Mike Wallace, transcript of interview by Terence Smith, "Death Watch," *NewsHour with Jim Lehrer*, Public Broadcasting Service, http://www.pbs.org/newshour/bb/media/july -dec98/suicide_11-24.html.

Chapter Twenty-six: Shifting Sands

1. Eames Yates (stepson of Mike Wallace), statement on his videotape, *Suicide*, HBO's *America Undercover* series (2001), http://www.ericbaxter.com/suicide/cmp/html/statement_yates .html (accessed July 24, 2011).

2. Ibid.

3. Angus Yates, interview by author.

4. Eames Yates, interview on his videotape for HBO's *America Undercover* series, Crank: Made in America—An Interview with Eames Yates," http://uritox.com/uriblog/?p=52xx (accessed July 24, 2011).

5. Mike Wallace and Mary Wallace, interview by Dr. Jeffrey Borenstein.

6. William Styron, "Darkness Visible," *Vanity Fair*, December 1989, http://www.vanityfair .com/magazine/archive/1989/12/styron198912.

7. Mike Wallace and Mary Wallace, interview by Dr. Jeffrey Borenstein.

8. Angus Yates, interview with the author.

9. Mike Wallace, *Guidepost: True Stories of Hope and Inspiration*, January 2002.

10. Martha's Vineyard, promotional film.

11. Michael Ryan, *US* magazine.

12. Martha's Vineyard, promotional film.

13. Mike Wallace, "A Haven on the Vineyard," Mike Wallace Papers, Box 160, University of Michigan Library.

14. Kelly, "10 Questions for Mike Wallace."

15. Mike Wallace, profile by Eve Berliner, "Mike Wallace: Probing the Inner Depths," *Eve's Magazine*, http://www.evesmag.com/wallace.htm.

16. Blum, *Tick, Tick, Tick*, 165.

17. Chris Wallace, quoted by John Carmody, *The Washington Post*, February. 27, 1996.

Chapter Twenty-seven: The Old Man Has Lost It

1. President Bill Clinton, interview by Chris Wallace, "Transcript: William Jefferson Clinton on 'FOX News Sunday,'" Foxnews.com, http://www.foxnews.com/on-air/fox-news-sunday/2006/09/26/transcript-william-jefferson-clinton-fox-news-sunday#ixzz1T5Qv7fWe (accessed July 26, 2011).

2. Wallace, *Between You and Me*, 60.

3. Chris Wallace, interview with Brian Lamb [on book], "Character: Profiles in Presidential Courage," C-Span's Booknotes, http://www.booknotes.org/Watch/183652-1/Chris+Wallace.aspx (accessed July 24, 2011).

4. Ibid.

5. Bob Somerby, "LION WITH LAMB! We chuckled darkly when Fox's Chris Wallace displayed his Millionaire Pundit Values," *The Daily Howler*, http://www.dailyhowler.com/dh120304.shtml (accessed July 24, 2011).

6. Michael A. Genovese, review of *Character: Profiles of Presidential Courage*, by Chris Wallace, *Library Journal* 130 (July–December 2005).

7. Mike Wallace, Internet Movie Database, Studio Briefing—Film News, "CBS's Mike Wallace to Promote Book on NBC," October 24, 2005, http://www.imdb.com/title/tt0103396/news?year=2005 (accessed August 17, 2011).

8. Tara McKelvey, "Close Encounters" [Review: Wallace, *Between You and Me*], *The New York Times*, January 22, 2006, http://www.nytimes.com/2006/01/22/books/review/22mckelvey.html (accessed July 24, 2011).

9. Mike Wallace, interview by Katie Couric, http://www.msnbc.msn.com/id/10397477/ns/dateline_nbc/ (accessed August 17, 2011).

10. Suzanne C. Ryan, "At 87, Wallace still tells it like it is," *The Boston Globe*, December 8, 2005, http://www.boston.com/ae/media/articles/2005/12/08/at_87_wallace_still_tells_it_like_it_is (accessed July 24, 2011).

11. Howie Carr, "Chris Wallace Says His Father, Mike, Has 'Lost It,'" Internet Movie Database, http://www.imdb.com/name/nm0139722/news.

12. Dalit Herdoon, "CBS' Mike Wallace cited for disorderly conduct," CNN.com, http://articles.cnn.com/2004-08-10/justice/wallace.arrest_1_inspectors-mike-wallace-tlc?_s=PM:LAW (Accessed July 25, 2011).

13. Daniel Schorn, "Mike Wallace Retires From '60 Minutes.'" CBSnews.com, http://www.cbsnews.com/stories/2006/03/14/60minutes/main1401600.shtml (accessed July 25, 2011).

Chapter Twenty-eight: Tough but Fair

1. C. K. Wolfson, "Mike Wallace: At this time of his life," *The Martha's Vineyard Times*, September 4, 2008, http://www.mvtimes.com/calendar/2008/09/04/mike-wallace.php (accessed July 25, 2011).

2. "Mike Wallace Says Iranian President an 'Impressive Fellow,'" Associated Press, August 9, 2006, reprinted by Fox News.Com, http://www.foxnews.com/story/0,2933,207664,00.html (accessed July 25, 2011).

3. C. K. Wolfson, "Mike Wallace: At this time of his life."

4. "Mike Wallace Says Iranian President an 'Impressive Fellow,'" Associated Press.

5. Richard Severo, "Art Buchwald, 81, Columnist and Humorist who Delighted in the Absurd,"

The New York Times, January 18, 2007 [Obituary], http://www.nytimes.com/2007/01/18/washington/17cnd-buchwald.html? (accessed July 25, 2011).

6. Ibid.

7. Mike Wallace, interview by Stephen Colbert, "*The Colbert Report*: Mike Wallace," Colbertnation.com, http://www.colbertnation.com/the-colbert-report-videos/81334/january-25-2007/mike-wallace (accessed July 25, 2011).

8. Richard Sandomere, "Steroids Spotlight for a Veteran Bulldog," *The New York Times*, Sports, January 4, 2008.

9. C. K. Wolfson, "Mike Wallace: At this time of his life."

10. *Vanity Fair*, "Proust Questionnaire: Mike Wallace."

11. Pauline Perigord, comments, "Man of the Year Induction [1989]," *Museum of Broadcast Communications*.

12. C. K. Wolfson, "Mike Wallace: At this time of his life."

13. *Vanity Fair*, "Proust Questionnaire: Mike Wallace."

Selected References

Adams, Val. "Man and Wife Team: 'Mike and Buff' Achieve a 'Different' Format." *The New York Times*, December 2, 1951, 133.

A&E HomeVideo, *Biography—Mike Wallace: TV's Grand Inquisitor*, DVD. A&E Home Video (1998; DVD release 2006).

Blum, David. *Tick, Tick, Tick: The Long Life and Turbulent Times of 60 Minutes*. New York: HarperCollins, 2004.

Boyer, Peter J. *Who Killed CBS?* New York, St. Martin's Press, 1988.

Brewin, Bob, and Sydney Shaw. *Vietnam on Trial: Westmoreland vs. CBS*. New York: Atheneum, 1987.

Burton, Benjamin. *Fair Play: CBS, General Westmoreland, and How a Television Documentary Went Wrong*. New York: Harper & Row, 1988.

Coffey, Frank. *60 Minutes: 25 Years of Television's Finest Hour*. Los Angeles: GPG, 1993.

Crichton, Robert. "Grand Inquisitor: The Mike Wallace Story." *Argosy*, May, 1957.

Cronkite, Walter. *A Reporter's Life*. New York: Alfred A. Knopf, 1996.

Daniel, Douglass K. *Harry Reasoner: A Life in the News*. Austin, TX: University of Texas Press, 2007.

Eigen, Jack. "Jack Eigen Speaking." *Chicago Tribune*, February 15, 1957.

Gates, Gary Paul. *Airtime: The Inside Story of CBS News*. New York: Harper & Row, 1978.

Hewitt, Don, *Minute by Minute: The Best Show on TV Becomes the Best Book on TV*, New York: Random House, 1985.

Hewitt, Don. *Tell Me a Story*. New York. PublicAffairs, 2001.

Jackman, Ian. *Con Men: Fascinating Profiles of Swindlers and Rogues From the Files of the Most Successful Broadcast in Television History*. New York: Simon & Schuster, 2003.

Johnson, Steve. "What Mike Wallace Was Like in His Younger Days." *Chicago Tribune*, November 25, 1996.

Kearns, Burt. *Tabloid Baby*. Nashville: Celebrity Books, 1999.

Kurtz, Howard. "CBS Rebukes Wallace, Producer; '60 Minutes' Team Secretly Taped Writer." *The Washington Post*, November 17, 1994.

Lardrer, James. "Up Against the Wallace; After Ten Years, The Hard Edge of '60 Minutes,' Is, If Anything, Harder. . . ." *The Washington Post*, September 18, 1977, Magazine.

Leonard, Bill. *In the Storm of the Eye: A Lifetime at CBS*. New York: G. P. Putnam's Sons, 1987.

Quinn, Sally. *We're Going to Make You a Star*. New York: Simon & Schuster, 1975.

Ramrus, Al. Written e-mail exchanges with the author, 2008.

Rather, Dan with Mickey Herskowitz. *The Camera Never Blinks: Adventures of a TV Journalist*. New York: William Morrow, 1977.

Reasoner, Harry. *Before the Colors Fade*. New York: Knopf, 1981.

Salant, Richard S. *Salant, CBS, and the Battle for the Soul of Broadcast Journalism: The Memoirs of Richard S. Salant*. Boulder, CO: Westview Press, 1999.

Saso, Emily. " 'Blood Looks Very Red on the Colour Television Screen': The Evolution of Representing Modern War in America." *The York Centre for International and Security Studies* Working Paper No. 33 (March, 2005).

Schorr, Daniel. "Smoke in the Eye," transcript of *Frontline* interview dated April 2, 1996, Public Broadcasting Service reprinted by WGBH (PBS Boston), http://www.pbs.org/wgbh/pages/frontline/smoke/smokescript.html.

Seely, Nancy. "Mike Wallace, Spotlight on the Nightbeat." *New York Post*, February 14, 1957, 4.

Sheffield, Anne. *Depressive Fallout: The Impact of Depression on Couples and What You Can Do*. New York: Harper Collins, 2003.

Stein, Harry. "How '60 Minutes' Makes the News," *The New York Times*, May 6, 1979, 235.

Styron, William. "Darkness Visible." *Vanity Fair*, December, 1989.

Swertlow, Frank. "Wallace Recalls Hectic Years Here." *Chicago Sun-Times*, May 11, 1978.

Unger, Craig. *Blue Blood: The Story of Rebekah Harkness and How One of the Richest Families in the World Descended into Drugs, Madness, Suicide, and Violence*. New York: William Morrow, Inc., 1988.

Wallace, Chris. Interview [on book] *Character: Profiles in Presidential Courage* with Brian Lamb for C-Span's Booknotes, http://www.booknotes.org/Watch/183652-1/Chris+Wallace.aspx.

Wallace, Mike:

- Interview, "CBS Cares: Mike Wallace Interview," CBS.com, http://www.cbs.com/cbs_cares/topics/depression.php.
- Interview by Academy of Achievement. "Mike Wallace Interview."
- Interview by John Callaway. Chicago Tonight (radio), reprinted in the *Chicago Sun-Times*, Mike Wallace Papers, University of Michigan Library.
- Interview by Katie Couric. "Mike Wallace, Man of the Hour." MSNBC.com, http://www.msnbc.msn.com/id/10397477/ns/dateline_nbc/.
- Interview by Larry King, transcript of "Interview with Mike Wallace." CNN.com, http://transcripts.cnn.com/TRANSCRIPTS/0510/31/lkl.01.html.
- Interviews by Steve McClellan. Archive Interview Collections (six interviews.) Emmy Legends.org, http://www.youtube.com/playlist?list=PL8C51EA7A7403AA2F.
- "Memorial Service: Leo Scharfman" (Speech) Mike Wallace Papers, University of Michigan Library.
- Mike Wallace Papers. University of Michigan Library. Ann Arbor, MI.

- Proust Questionnaire: Mike Wallace," *Vanity Fair*, November, 2005.
- Speech to CBS Radio Affiliates, 25 February 1979, Mike Wallace Papers, Box 78, University of Michigan Library.
- "University of Michigan Commencement Address" (Address, University of Michigan, May 2, 1987).

Wallace, Mike and Mary Wallace. Interview by Dr. Jeffrey Borenstein, "Healthy Minds: Depression Featuring a Conversation with Mike and Mary Wallace." Brainline.org reprinting of transcript of interview held by WLIW 21 (New York) Public Broadcasting Service, http://www.brainline.org/multimedia/video/transcripts/healthy_minds_depression.pdf.

Wallace, Mike and Gary Paul Gates. *Close Encounters*. New York: William Morrow, 1984.

Wallace, Mike with Gary Paul Gates. *Between You and Me: A Memoir*. New York: Hyperion, 2005.

Westin, Av. Interview by Terrence Smith, "Online NewsHour: Av Westin." *Public Broadcasting Service Online*, http://www.pbs.org/newshour/media/evening_news/westin.html.

Westin, Av. *Newswatch: How TV Decides the News*. New York: Simon & Schuster, 1982.

Wolfson, C.K. "Mike Wallace: At This Time of His Life." *The Martha's Vineyard Times*, September 4, 2008.

Wolters, Larry. "On Sunday: TV's Most Candid Mike." *Chicago Tribune*, April 27, 1957, F3.

Zurawik, David. "Premier Interviewer, Mike Wallace, Turns up in the Spotlight." *The Baltimore Sun*, September 26, 1990.

Index